Teaching Games and Sport for Understanding

This new book brings together leading and innovative thinkers in the field of teaching and sport coaching pedagogy to provide a range of perspectives on teaching games and sport for understanding. *Teaching Games and Sport for Understanding* engages undergraduate and postgraduate students in physical education and sport coaching, practicing teachers, practicing sport coaches, teacher educators and coach developers. The contributions, taken together or individually, provide insight, learning and opportunities to foster game-based teaching and coaching ideas, and provide conceptual and methodological clarity where a sense of pedagogical confusion may exist.

Each chapter raises issues that can resonate with the teacher and sport practitioner and researcher. In this way, the chapters can assist one to make sense of their own teaching or sport coaching, provide deeper insight into personal conceptualisations of the concept of game-based teaching and sport coaching or stimulate reflections on their own teaching or coaching or the contexts they are involved in.

Teaching games and sport for understanding in various guises and pedagogical models has been proposed as leading practice for session design and instructional delivery of sport teaching in PE and sport coaching since the late 1960s. At its core, it is a paradigm shift from what can be described as a behaviourist model of highly directive instruction for player replication of teacher/coach explanation and demonstration to instructional models that broadly are aimed at the development of players self-autonomy as self-regulated learners – 'thinking players'.

This innovative new volume both summarises current thinking, debates and practical considerations about the broad spectrum of what teaching games for understanding means as well as providing direction for further practical, pragmatic and research consideration of the concept and its precepts and, as such, is key reading for both undergraduate and postgraduate students of physical education and sport coaching as well as practicing teachers and sport coaches.

Shane Pill, PhD, is Associate Professor in Physical and Sport Education at Flinders University, Australia.

Ellen-Alyssa F. Gambles is an Academic Tutor in Exercise, Sport and Rehabilitative Therapies at the University of Sunderland, UK.

Linda L. Griffin, PhD, is a Professor in the College of Education at the University of Massachusetts Amherst, USA.

'There is a need for a text which (a) brings together the diverse game-based approaches for pre-service physical education teachers, and (b) provides detailed guidance on the nuanced application of a games-based approach within physical education. This text does both'.

Dr Phil Kearney, *Department of Physical Education and Sport Sciences, University of Limerick, Ireland*

'This book offers comprehensive and up-to-date information about Teaching Games for Understanding (TGfU) and other game-based approaches (GBAs) around the world. Both physical education teachers and sport coaches can gain a lot of practical information to improve their teaching/coaching and maximise students/players potential in an inclusive and learner-centred environment'.

Dr Kanae Haneishi, *Valley City State University, North Dakota, USA*

Teaching Games and Sport for Understanding

Edited by Shane Pill,
Ellen-Alyssa F. Gambles and
Linda L. Griffin

Routledge
Taylor & Francis Group

NEW YORK AND LONDON

Designed cover image: Peter Cade / Getty Images

First published 2023
by Routledge
605 Third Avenue, New York, NY 10158

and by Routledge
4 Park Square, Milton Park, Abingdon, Oxon, OX14 4RN

Routledge is an imprint of the Taylor & Francis Group, an informa business

ISBN: 978-1-032-28735-5 (hbk)
ISBN: 978-1-032-28729-4 (pbk)
ISBN: 978-1-003-29829-8 (ebk)

DOI: 10.4324/9781003298298

Typeset in Garamond
by MPS Limited, Dehradun

Access the Support Material: www.routledge.com/9781032287294

Contents

Figures

Tables

Contributors

Rick Baldock is the current Australian Council for Health Physical Education and Recreation (SA) (ACHPER) Branch Professional Learning Coordinator. After a distinguished career as a primary PE and class teacher and then Department of Education Health & Physical Education (HPE) Curriculum and Policy Officer, Policy and Program Officer, Physical Activity in the South Australian Department for Education and Child Development, Rick managed a primary school healthy weight project from 2009 to 2013. Rick also led a team in the development of a Physical Education curriculum in Qatar in 2008. Rick is a Life Member and Fellow of ACHPER.

Lars Borghouts (PhD) is a physical education teacher educator and researcher in the School of Sport Studies at Fontys University of Applied Sciences, in the Netherlands. His main area of teaching and research work is in assessment, student motivation, physical activity, teacher professional development and teacher education within the context of physical education.

Korey Boyd is an Assistant Professor in the School of Physical Education, Performance and Sport Leadership at Springfield College, Springfield, MA. He teaches Secondary method undergraduate and graduate courses in the Physical Education Teacher Education (PETE). His philosophy of PETE follows similar logic and produces the axiom: produce better thinkers, not better thinking. His research focuses on evidence-based teaching practices in PE that works towards achieving racial equity and cultural relevancy in PE pedagogy. He conducts and publishes research on the links between race and teaching physical education.

Jia Yi Chow (PhD) is currently the Associate Dean (Programme & Student Development) with the Office of Teacher Education (OTE) at the National Institute of Education, Nanyang Technological University, Singapore. His research interests include examining multi-articular coordination, visual perception in sports expertise and in a pedagogical approach (Nonlinear Pedagogy) where the focus is on exploring individualised movement solutions to support nonlinearity in learning. For his excellence in teaching, Jia Yi was inducted as a Fellow to the NTU Teaching Excellence Academy and was accorded the NTU Educator of the Year in 2018.

Christina Curry (PhD) is a Senior Lecturer and researcher in Health and Physical Education (HPE) in the School of Education at Western Sydney University. Her research interests are in learning and curriculum, with a focus on health and physical education pedagogy and game-based approaches, and she also continues to work with teachers and schools in this area. She was previously head of a HPE department and has taught in both Primary and Secondary Schools for 14 years.

Aspasia Dania (PhD) is an Assistant Professor of Physical Education and Sport Pedagogy working at the School of Physical Education and Sport Science, National and Kapodistrian University of Athens, Greece. She lectures at an undergraduate and postgraduate level, and she oversees preservice teachers' practicum in schools and sport clubs. She has an extensive record of research publications in the areas of physical education and school sport, teacher and coach education and continuing professional development, game-based learning, qualitative research and curriculum development, with a principal focus on equity, equality, diversity and inclusion.

Michael Davies (PhD) is an early career researcher. Michael's research experience includes outputs in the Spectrum of Teaching Styles and the Game-Sense Approach in Physical Education, Aboriginal sports pedagogy and Sport and Exercise Science. In practice, Michael brings nine years' experience of teacher and practitioner education and is a current teacher educator for the Bachelor of Primary and Secondary degrees in Health and Physical Education, where in 2021, he was an Australian Awards for University Teaching Team Citation recipient for Outstanding Contribution to Student Learning in Primary Health and Physical Education.

Frank de Kok is a physical education teacher educator in the School of Sport Studies at Fontys University of Applied Sciences, in the Netherlands. His main area of teaching is in game-based approaches and assessment in the context of physical education.

Sarah Doolittle (EdD) is a professor in the Department of Health and Sport Sciences at Adelphi University in New York. In 1982–1983, as a visiting graduate student at Loughborough University, she was involved (TGfU) with the development of Teaching Games for Understanding with Len Almond, Rod Thorpe, David Bunker, David Kirk and others. This group collaborated on re-thinking how sports and games were learned and taught in school physical education and produced the initial articles and books on TGfU. Since then, Dr Doolittle has published articles on TGfU, and on curriculum, teaching and assessment for secondary physical education.

John Evans (PhD) is Pro Vice-Chancellor Indigenous Engagement at Swinburne University of Technology. John was previously professor Indigenous Health Education at the University Technology Sydney (UTS). He has extensive academic and industry experience in Indigenous sport, physical activity and education and more recently in the area of building and infrastructure. John is an ARC Indigenous Research Fellow and holds several ARC competitive research grants. He has also been the lead academic from UTS's Faculty of Health in the establishment of The Indigenous Infrastructure and Sustainable Housing Alliance, which has had recent success in undertaking evaluation and monitoring research for Indigenous communities on the implementation of infrastructure and housing.

Ellen-Alyssa F. Gambles is an Academic Tutor in Exercise, Sport and Rehabilitative Therapies and Chair of the Enabled (disability) Staff Network at the University of Sunderland, in the UK. Ellen is also the Treasurer and Communications Coordinator for the AIESEP Teaching Games for Understanding Special Interest Group (TGfU SIG). For over 15 years she has been teaching and coaching sports, most notably swimming, to children, novice adults and triathletes. Her current teaching and researching interests are in game-based approaches, teacher education and equality, diversity and inclusion (EDI) within the context of physical education and sport.

Linda L. Griffin (PhD) is a professor at the University of Massachusetts Amherst. She has spent the past 30 years focused on a game-centred approach to teaching and learning sport. She has numerous publications and presentations on this topic. Linda has received several awards UMass Amherst Exceptional Merit Honor, Frostburg State University Wellner Scholar, AERA SIG: Research on Teaching and Learning in Physical Education, Exemplar Paper Award, and National Association of Sport and Physical Education, Physical Education Teacher Education Honor Award. She is Chair of the AIESEP Teaching Games for Understanding Special Interest Group.

David Gutierrez (PhD) is professor in the Faculty of Education at Universidad de Castilla-La Mancha (Spain). He has taught physical education at secondary-school and university levels since 1998. His main research focus is on pedagogical models, especially on TGfU and Sport Education Model, and more recently on the increase of movement time during the school day to enhance students' school wellness. Former TGfU Special Interest Group chair, David is currently chair of the international board of this association, whose mission is to promote and support game-based approaches to teaching and coaching.

Kanae Haneishi (EdD) is an Associate Professor at Western Colorado University and represents the US for the TGfU International Advisory Board. Her recent research focus is on pedagogical strategies to promote Justice, Equity, Diversity, and Inclusion in Physical Education and Sport Coaching. She was an accomplished soccer player winning the NCAA D2 National Championship with her university and the Silver Medal at the World University Games with the Japanese National team as well as serving as the team captain for New York Magic.

Stephen Harvey (PhD) is Professor of Coaching Education at Ohio University, USA. Stephen's research is focused on coaching behaviour and game-based pedagogies. He is author of over 100 peer-reviewed publications and book chapters and is the author/editor of several textbooks. In addition to his research, Stephen is a licensed physical education/geography teacher in the UK, has coached junior and master's level international field hockey teams, and currently coaches' youth soccer. Stephen is a qualified International Council for Coach Education Coach Developer through participation in the Nippon Sport Science University Coach Developer Academy and currently works as a coach educator for USA field hockey and is a trainee coach educator and coach educator developer for US Soccer.

Ruan Jones (PhD) is a senior lecturer in physical education within the Carnegie School of Sport at Leeds Beckett University. Ruan has a particular interest in phenomenological research perspectives on game-based approaches. He leads modules on the undergraduate PE degree specialising in models-based practice, social psychology and history. Prior to this he worked at Canterbury Christ Church University and University of Worcester. He also has over a decade of experience working in secondary PE departments where he coached girls' and boys' representative rugby union in Kent and North Yorkshire.

Jeroen Koekoek (PhD) is senior lecturer at the Physical Education Teacher Education faculty of Windesheim University of Applied Sciences, in the Netherlands. He teaches games. His research interests are in game-based approaches and teacher education related to game pedagogy. Jeroen is chair-elect of the executive board Teaching Games for Understanding special interest group (TGfU-SIG). Jeroen contributed to several books and papers on physical education and sport with a focus on teaching and learning. Jeroen co-edited a book on digital technology in PE. Jeroen has played Handball at national elite level.

Richard L. Light (PhD) is Professor Emeritus at the University of Canterbury, New Zealand and now works at The University of Sydney. He is a prominent international figure in the development of learner centred and inquiry-based teaching and coaching with a focus on Game Sense and Positive Pedagogy for Sport Coaching. He has held fulltime appointments in Australia, the UK and New Zealand and published 12 research books on sport, physical education and learning with the influence of culture on teaching or coaching and learning a prominent theme in his work.

Brendan Moy (PhD) is a senior lecturer in physical education teacher education at the Queensland University of Technology in Brisbane, Australia. His ongoing research have primarily focused on investigating the practical application of the constraints-led approach, an alternative physical education teaching approach informed by contemporary motor learning theory. This research combined with over 38 years of practical experience, and ongoing collaborations with expert colleagues and real-world partners has informed his own teaching. He recently received a national teaching award for developing university graduates as agents of change in physical education teaching practice.

Steve Mitchell (PhD) has been at Kent State University in Ohio since 1992. He is the Associate Dean for Administrative Affairs and Graduate Education in the College of Education, Health and Human Services, and a Professor in Physical Education Teacher Education. He has authored numerous articles and book chapters related to standards-based teaching in Physical Education, and has co-authored four textbooks, including two related to teaching games for understanding within public school physical education, with one now into its fourth edition. Steve has served in leadership roles at the state and national level organisations.

Bruce Nkala (PhD) is currently the Athletic Director at Sandy Spring Friends School in Maryland and is the former Physical Education & Pre-K to 12 Department Chair at the Shipley School. Previously he served as a Diversity, Equity and Inclusion coordinator at Shipley and mentor to Students and Staff. He specialises in teaching Invasion Games using TGfU in both Elementary school and Middle school. Bruce's previous research are on developing Pedagogical Content TGfU Knowledge for in-service training and developing student Content Knowledge using TGfU. His current interest is in developing pedagogy that intentionally embeds DEI concepts in PE lessons, while maintaining GBA PE lesson objectives.

David Piggott (PhD) is a senior lecturer in sport coaching at Leeds Beckett University, where he also leads the MSc programmes in Coaching and Coach Development. His main research interests are in coach development, model-based approaches to coaching and understanding peak experiences, such as flow. David is a basketball coach of 25 years and coach educator and has worked at every level of the sport in the UK.

Shane Pill (PhD) is an Associate Professor in Physical Education and Sport at Flinders University, Kaurna Yerta (Adelaide, South Australia). Shane teaches and researches in physical education and sport pedagogy and curriculum, sport coaching, sport development and educational leadership. Shane is a Life Member and Fellow of the Australian Council for Health, Physical Education and Recreation (ACHPER). He has been an active sport coach across several sports since 1988, and formerly taught physical education and science in schools for 18 years.

Ian Renshaw (PhD) is an Associate Professor at Queensland University of Technology, Brisbane, Australia. Previously he has worked as a PE teacher and then in the Higher Education Sectors in the UK and New Zealand. He currently teaches skill acquisition and coaching to trainee HPE teachers and Sport and Exercise scientists. Ian's research focus is in applying the ideas of Ecological Dynamics and specifically, the Constraints-Led Approach (CLA). Ian is working across a wide range of sports to support the uptake of CLA and bridge the gap between academia and practitioners.

Jean-François Richard is Professor and former Dean of Education at l'Université de Moncton in New Brunswick Canada. Specialising in sport pedagogy, Jean-François has contributed to the growing body of knowledge centred on TGfU during the past 25 years including the first two edited publications celebrating its evolution. His initial work in relation to TGfU were related to applications and adaptations of the Team-Sport Assessment Procedure (TSAP). Further collaborative work led to the 2005 publication *Teaching and Learning Team Sports and Games* (Routledge, 2023) co-authored with Jean-Francis Gréhaigne and Linda Griffin. Jean-François is a former Dr R. Tait Mckenzie Scholar (2007) awarded by Health and Physical Education Canada.

Karen Richardson (EdD) has been on the faculty at Bridgewater State University in Bridgewater, MA since 2003. She is the Chair of the Health and Kinesiology Department in the College of Education and Health Sciences and a Professor in Physical Education Teacher Education. Karen has published on game-based learning focused on modification through adaptation, lesson study; technology in physical education; and tactical decision-making competence in gameplay. Over her career, Karen has also been a leader in faculty development at Bridgewater State University and worked with colleagues to develop and then research the impact of student-faculty partnerships.

Teng Tse Sheng is a Master Teacher from the Physical Education and Sports Teacher Academy (PESTA), Ministry of Education, Singapore. Teng has a keen interest in game-based approach. Upon completing his Master of Education at the University of British Columbia, Teng has played an active role in deepening the understanding of GBA and promoting its use through conducting workshops, collaborating with teachers and presenting at local and overseas conferences. His current interest is in the use of Inventing Games Model to promote the learning of values and 21 century competencies in PE.

Brendan SueSee (PhD) is a Senior Lecturer at the University of Southern Queensland, Springfield, Australia. He was a high school teacher for 21 years and taught HPE, geography and history. He has coached from U7-to-adult in cricket, netball, Australian football, baseball, athletics, cross country, volleyball, touch football, softball and triathlon. Brendan has worked at the University of Southern Queensland (USQ) for 7 years. His research interests include teaching styles, alignment between HPE syllabus documents and reporting, and cognition. He is most recently the author and editor of *The Spectrum of Teaching Styles in Physical Education* (Routledge, 2020) and co-author of *The Spectrum of Sport Coaching Styles* (Routledge, 2021).

Naoki Suzuki (PhD) is currently Associate Professor of Tokyo Gakugei University in Tokyo. He completed his PhD in 2007 at Tokyo Gakugei University in Japan. He has an interest in teaching and researching about Physical Education and Teacher Training. He was a chair of the Executive Committee of the 6th International Game Sense Conference. At the conference, he made a platform for sharing information related to not only "Game Sense" but also a wide range of game-based approaches for researchers and practitioners. He contributed to the integration and development of a derivative teaching approach that was based on TGfU.

Adrian P. Turner (PhD) is an Associate Professor of Sport Pedagogy and Coaching at Bowling Green State University in Ohio, USA. Since the early 1990s his scholarship on TGfU has provided empirical support, as well as practical application of the model, to teaching and coaching practices in various sports. Adrian teaches a course on invasion sports, and another on educational games, to undergraduate students. He also teaches an instructional strategies class for pre-service physical education teachers, situated at a local secondary school. As the coaching facilitator, to a 150-player youth soccer club, he invokes a game-based approach to player development.

Wytse Walinga is senior lecturer at the Physical Education Teacher Education faculty of Windesheim University of Applied Sciences in the Netherlands. He teaches games. Wytse is chair of the games teaching staff. His research focuses on game-based approaches and the development of pedagogical tools for PE and youth sports. Wytse is co-author of the book *Discovery Learning in Youth Football* (daM uitgeverij, 2017). He worked as PE-teacher in secondary education. Wytse has played Volleyball at national elite level.

Gwen Weeldenburg is a physical education teacher educator, educational designer and researcher in the School of Sport Studies at Fontys University of Applied Sciences, and PhD candidate at the University of

Technology Eindhoven, in the Netherlands. Her teaching and research interests mainly focus on student motivation, game-based approaches, motivational learning climate, curriculum development, assessment and teacher education within the context of PE.

John Williams (PhD) is an Associate Professor in Physical Education in the Faculty of Education, University of Canberra, Australia, where he has taught for the last decade as a teacher educator for primary and secondary specialist Health and Physical Education (HPE) programmes. John is also an active researcher in the areas of quality physical education, transformative physical education and sport pedagogy, and the sociology of physical education. He is currently a National Board Director for the Australian Council for Health, Physical Education and Recreation (ACHPER), the national professional association for HPE teachers in Australia.

Enrico Zondag is a physical education teacher educator in the School of Sport Studies at Fontys University of Applied Sciences, in the Netherlands. His teaching interests mainly focus on creative and motivational learning climate, game-based approaches and practical teacher coaching and supervision within the context of PE.

Introduction

A History of Teaching Games and Sport for Understanding from Mauldon and Redfern to Bunker and Thorpe, Until Now

Ellen-Alyssa F. Gambles and Linda L. Griffin

This edited book marks the 40th anniversary of Bunker and Thorpe's seminal work published in the Bulletin of Physical Education special edition, which presented the Teaching Games for Understanding (TGfU) model as a concept for games teaching and learning. In the late 1960s, physical education (PE) practitioners were starting to explore game-based approach (GBA) concepts however, it was not until the 1982 Bulletin that there was an acceleration of interest amongst both academics, practising teachers and coaches.

Since the inception of the TGfU model, GBAs have been proposed as leading practice for the design and delivery of PE sports teaching and coaching. TGfU's influence has spread across the globe, and elaboration has given rise to the development of a variety of 'second generation' pedagogical models stemming from TGfU. There has been a considerable body of research to advance the model that has described both a sound pedagogical underpinning and detailed tools for practical application. Despite these efforts, there has been conceptual confusion at many levels and a sense of theory vs theory and model vs model within the field of teaching games for understanding.

The intention of this book is to provide a coherent, non-versus understanding of the rich diversity of the various 'second generation' models and inform their implementation in practice. In doing so we hope to engage our GBA community of practitioners and provide them with possibilities and perspectives on game-based teaching and sport coaching.

We recognise readers of this book will have differing levels of knowledge about GBAs. We hope that this edited book will support games teaching and learning for undergraduate and postgraduate students, practising teachers, sport coaches, teacher educators and coach developers to learn more about how GBAs can help your research and practice. Each chapter provides conceptual and methodological clarity of GBAs, which can assist readers to understand and stimulate reflections on their own teaching or coaching. This edited book summarises current global debates, knowledge and practical considerations about what teaching games for understanding means as well as providing direction for further practical, pragmatic and

DOI: 10.4324/9781003298298-1

research considerations of the concept and its pedagogical principles. In this chapter we will provide (a) a brief history of GBAs and TGfU, (b) a description of the growth and consolidation of GBAs, (c) an overview of each chapter and (d) some final thoughts.

A brief history of Game-Based Approaches (GBAs)

In the first half of the 20th century the recurring concerns of war led to a focus on military drills in the UK PE curriculum. Later, gymnastics and systematic exercises were widely adopted to promote health and fitness (Donovan et al., 2006). PE teaching in the 1950s and 1960s exhibited a paradigm shift towards emphasis on student proficiency (i.e., mastery approach) in sports techniques (Kirk, 2010). Games teaching in this approach focused on 'skills and drills' both prior to, and in isolation from, gameplay. Whilst the mastery approach was widely adopted, some educators had growing concerns about children not 'knowing' and understanding games (Bunker & Thorpe, 1982). In the late 1960s, some practitioners began to move away from skill-based mastery based on the behaviourist model – what is now referred to as the 'traditional approach' to games teaching – and embraced the ideas of researchers such as Bruner, Piaget and Vygotsky that focused on learner-centred learning.

   The rudiments of a GBA as applied to an English primary school setting described in 1969 by Mauldon and Redfern, presented a challenge to the prevailing skill-based mastery approach of games teaching. In place of teaching individual sports, they proposed a thematic curriculum of games with similar properties or game classifications to guide pupils' perceptions of the underlying principles of games in their wider sense. They based their four-stage approach upon the capabilities of the developing young child, progressing from exploratory play towards an emphasis on a fuller game that included competition and an understanding of rules and tactics (Mauldon & Redfern, 1969):

> to share ultimately in the process of making a new game or a variation of one already known, finding answers to problems arising and then playing it according to mutual consent, is surely of greater value than only learning prefabricated games with externally imposed rules.
>
> (Mauldon & Redfern, 1969, p. 17)

This quote embodies a vision of a learner-focused GBA for thinking players. The work of Mauldon and Redfern was a part of the changing tide towards more innovative sport pedagogy during this time, however, their ideas had a limited impact on transforming PE.

   Similarly, at Loughborough University in the 1960s, Allen Wade, Eric Worthington and Stan Wigmore had introduced their students to the possibilities of small-sided games and teaching through the principles of play. Although they were exploring the use of small-sided games, it is important to note their focus was primarily on teaching *'games skills'* (Thorpe & Bunker, 1986, p. 5). At the time one student, David Bunker, was employed as a school PE teacher and involved with National Governing Body coaching awards. He expressed a sense of dissatisfaction with the lack of progress he saw from his students when using a skills-based mastery approach in his teaching (Thorpe & Bunker, 1986). In 1968, Rod Thorpe moved to Loughborough and was later joined in 1972 by David Bunker, where they began to investigate a more conceptualised approach to teaching children incorporating modified equipment into modified games. This conceptualised approach led to the setting up of an undergraduate course with Rex Hazeldine and Stan Wigmore, which foregrounded the core elements of games and understanding what they were about (Thorpe & Bunker, 1986).

In the late 1970s, Loughborough University had become a focal point for researchers who shared the desire for educating students to understand the wider concepts of games and the problems that they raised. Len Almond, David Bunker and Rod Thorpe collaborated with a team of colleagues to refine their ideas into what would become known as the TGfU model (Ovens et al., 2021).

The 1982 publication of the Curriculum Model, commonly referred to as the TGfU model (Bunker & Thorpe, 1982), was the watershed event that launched GBAs, gaining national and global attention in the sporting community. Alongside it was numerous articles that focused on this different perspective in games with its editor, Len Almond, inviting a dialogue from readers into the potential of teaching games for understanding (Almond, 1982).

The Loughborough team sought to build upon the 1982 Curriculum Model, and throughout the 1980s they tested ideas at seminars and in practical sessions with teachers before sharing their ideas in several publications (Thorpe & Bunker, 1986). The impact of the 1982 articles was such that most English local education authorities set up working parties to investigate the practicalities of the ideas or ran courses for teachers (Thorpe et al., 1986a). In the following 1983 spring edition of the Bulletin of Physical Education, Rod Thorpe and David Bunker responded to this interest and request for specific examples, with further articles that discussed GBAs and detailed their practical application for teachers and coaches.

Len Almond was aware of the work of Terry Williamson, PE advisor for Suffolk, on raising questions around games, and together with the Loughborough team, introduced their ideas to PE teachers across the UK (Thorpe & Bunker, 1986). This collaboration led to a long-term action research project on understanding games by Len Almond, that consisted of Rod Thorpe presenting practical sessions to a group of teachers working in Coventry and culminating in a book publication of their findings entitled,

'Games: Case Studies in Teaching for Understanding' in 1985 with the Elm Bank Teachers Centre (Thorpe & Bunker, 1986).

The publication 'Rethinking Games Teaching' in 1986 collated a reprint of the 1982 Curriculum Model with key landmark articles aimed at the teacher and included practical details on an 'understanding approach' (Thorpe et al., 1986b) to aid transfer into practice. A number of the articles that had arisen from the 'Coventry project' detailed both researchers' and teachers' perspectives regarding TGfU.

As the team had sought to understand and demonstrate the theoretical application of the TGfU model, they became aware of a need for a system of classifying games and considered a number of approaches (Almond, 1986a). The earlier research of Mauldon and Redfern (1969), Brackenridge (1979 as cited in Almond, 1986b) and Ellis (1983 as cited in Thorpe et al., 1986a), helped to inform the TGfU games classification system (Almond, 1986a). Almond (1986a) highlighted the importance of creating a classification system to facilitate exposing children to a balanced spectrum of games, which demonstrate the similarities and differences among individual sports. The underpinning system for classifying games was based on similar tactical problems with four suggested classes namely, target games, net/wall games, fielding/run-scoring games and invasion games (Almond, 1986a).

The TGfU model was augmented further by the four fundamental pedagogical principles (Thorpe & Bunker, 1989; Thorpe et al., 1986a) described as game sampling, modification-representation, modification-exaggeration and tactical complexity. This allowed for the integration of the games classification system through the 'game sampling' pedagogical principle. These pedagogical principles will be discussed further in Chapter 1 alongside the TGfU model.

Growth and consolidation of GBAs

The initial publications created interest among pedagogical researchers and provided a unifying set of principles for a wide range of practitioners. The 1980s to 2000s was a period of rapid growth for TGfU as researchers sought to better understand the implementation and implications of the model. First, researchers have strengthened the research base for legitimacy using a range of theories, such as domain-specific knowledge schema theory, ecological psychology, constructivism and complexity theory (Ovens et al., 2021).

Second, different interpretations of the principles led to the creation of a number of second-generation variations around the globe including Game Sense (Thorpe, 1996), Tactical Games Model (Mitchell et al., 2021), Tactical Decision Learning Model (Grehaigne & Godbout, 1997), Invasion Games Competency Model (Tallir et al., 2005), Games Concept Approach (Rossi et al., 2006), Play with Purpose (Pill, 2007), Ball School (Roth & Kroger, 2015), Game Insight (Weeldenburg et al., 2016) and the Inventing

Games Model (Butler, 2016). Many of these variations will be explored in later chapters.

Third, has been the application of GBAs with other pedagogical models or ideas, such as the Sport Education Model (SEM) (Siedentop et al., 2020), producing a hybrid approach (e.g., Guijarro et al., 2021). In a GBA-SEM approach students play modified team games and serve in a variety of the roles present in authentic sports settings such as trainers, publicists, athlete, referee, etc. There has also been the emergence of the Digital Video Games Approach (Price & Pill, 2016) that creatively implements pedagogical principles from digital video games, such as missions, levelling up and game pausing/saving in modified games to develop meta-cognition skills in students.

Fourth, has been the development and exploration of authentic assessment instruments to assess performance for researchers and practitioners. For example, the Game Performance Assessment Instrument (GPAI) (Mitchell et al., 2021) and the Game Contribution Assessment Instrument (GCAI) (Suzuki et al., 2010) which were developed for both research and practice, and the Team Sport Assessment Procedure (TSAP) which is primarily a peer-assessment tool (Grehaigne et al., 2005).

Fifth, GBAs have expanded to a more holistic perspective. A recent development has been the application of the Spectrum of Teaching Styles with GBAs which details 11 distinct non-versus student-centred teaching styles, ranging from command to discovery, that teachers utilise as appropriate for the student (SueSee et al., 2020). Other holistic aspects include social emotional learning and topics such as equality, diversity and inclusion (EDI), using games as a vehicle for students to explore ethical issues, develop respect and feel a sense of belonging (e.g., Butler, 2016).

Formation of the TGfU Special Interest Group (TGfU SIG)

As an influential leader and researcher, Joy Butler had a significant impact on coalescing the early TGfU network into an international organisation. Butler convened the first TGfU conference, held in 2001 at Plymouth State University, New Hampshire, USA with over 150 delegates from 17 countries attending. Almost half of the delegates attended a town hall meeting that instigated the formation of the TGfU Task Force (Ovens et al., 2021). The membership of the Task Force encompassed 12 countries from 5 continents, with a commitment to coordinate and 'harness the groundswell of energy evident at the conference' (Butler & Griffin, 2010, p. 5). Ronald Feingold, then President of Association Internationale des Ecoles Superieures d'Education Physique (AIESEP), was present at the historical 2001 conference. His endorsement of the TGfU Task Force provided legitimacy for a partnership that would both assure the maintenance of quality research and help to sustain international interest (Ovens et al., 2021).

At the first official meeting of the Task Force (October 2002) the members drafted a mission statement, a list of objectives and committed to a series of biennial TGfU seminars. With the growth of the movement, a proposal was made at the 2006 AIESEP World Congress (Finland) that the Task Force transition into an AIESEP Special Interest Group (SIG) (Ovens et al., 2021). With the ratification of the SIG at the 2008 TGfU International Conference, an Executive Committee was elected with Joy Butler as the Chair, and later in 2010 the International Advisory Board (IAB) was formed to provide a networking process for the global community (Ovens et al., 2021).

About the chapters

This introductory chapter has described the genesis for this book. We have discussed a brief history of the formation and development of TGfU and outlined several second-generation pedagogical models situated in the field of GBAs. The contributors for this edited book number amongst the leading innovative researchers and practitioners engaged in teaching and sports coaching pedagogy. A range of perspectives has been brought together on teaching games and sport for understanding, focusing on developments in approaches, research perspectives and future directions.

In Chapter 1, Shane Pill introduces the six-step Curriculum Model and pedagogical principles that together with the classification of games inform Bunker and Thorpe's TGfU approach. Sarah Doolittle shares a personal commentary of her experiences as a graduate student at Loughborough University during the formation of TGfU in the early 1980s, and three key ideas which shaped her beliefs of PE teaching. Rick Baldock also shares his experiences of learning and teaching through GBAs, working with Rod Thorpe during the 1990s in Australia.

Section I of this book details key global developments influenced by TGfU. Linda Griffin and Steve Mitchell contributed Chapter 2, where they describe their thought processes in the development of the Tactical Games Model and the innovative GPAI that encompasses key tactical aspects with technical performance. Research and practice perspectives are offered alongside examples of the process and assessment tool.

In Chapter 3, the development of Games Sense is provided by Richard Light and Christina Curry. They identify the philosophical foundations and offer their suggestions of Games Sense through a bottom-up approach for teachers and coaches.

In Chapter 4, the application of Immersive Scenario-based Narratives (ISN) will be explained and illustrated in a youth coaching context by Ruan Jones and David Piggott. The chapter is composed of a four-scene dialogue to articulate the philosophical principles behind ISNs and their application in practice.

In Chapter 5 Gwen Weeldenburg, Lars Borghouts, Enrico Zondag and Frank de Kok introduce the Game Insight approach with the metaphor of green, blue, red and black ski slopes used in designing games of increasing complexity. The didactical components are explained and illustrated through practical invasion game examples.

Shane Pill and John Williams use the Games Sense approach to put forward an argument that the application of GBAs is far removed from simply 'let them play'. In Chapter 6, Pill and Williams emphasise that player learning requires explicit deliberate teaching to create play with purpose that is appropriate to their needs.

Section II of this book introduces research perspectives beginning with constructivist learning theory and its utilisation with the Tactical-Decision Learning Model explored in Chapter 7 by Linda Griffin and Jean-Francois Richard. An insightful discussion is provided of the pedagogical principles to be aware of when implementing the model.

In Chapter 8, Adrian Turner utilises the tactical versus technical paradigm to critically review the multifarious experimental research in sports pedagogy with reference to the impact on student learning.

Readers interested in The Spectrum of Teaching Styles will find Chapter 9 useful. Brendan SueSee and Shane Pill utilise The Spectrum to demonstrate that GBAs are a cluster of teaching styles not just the highly described 'guided discovery'.

In Chapter 10, Jia Yi Chow, Ian Renshaw and Brendan Moy explore how the teaching and learning mechanisms for TGfU may be underpinned by application of a Constraints-Led Approach (CLA). They provide practitioners with key theoretical ideas which aid the adoption and implementation of TGfU.

Readers with an interest in athlete-centred coaching (ACC) will find Chapters 11 and 12 informative. In Chapter 11, Richard Light and Stephen Harvey provide an outline of the development, features and application of Positive Pedagogy for sports coaching (PPed), a player-centred inquiry-based approach. PPed owes its origins to Games Sense augmented with Positive Psychology and was developed for application to skill-intensive individual sports but may also be utilised with team games. Additionally in Chapter 12, Shane Pill and Ellen-Alyssa Gambles explore the connection between GBAs and ACC. They spotlight the role of coach as facilitator co-constructing with players through inquiry-based teaching strategies and contextual game-based practice.

Teachers will find Naoki Suzuki and Karen Richardson's Chapter 13 discussion on Lesson Study and Aspasia Dania's Chapter 14 teacher reflective practice very helpful. Chapter 13 provides an overview of Lesson Study as a form of professional development with examples of its application in practice. Chapter 14 unpacks the complexities of teachers' reflective practice, drawing on critical pedagogy concepts and social justice perspectives towards its study within the field of GBA professional learning and development.

In Chapter 15, Wytse Walinga and Jeroen Koekoek introduce Game Balance Analysis, a practical procedure for teachers that explains how to exploit learning with experience-rich gameplay in a designed environment utilising structured interventions. Teaching examples are provided to demonstrate how game situations can be adapted to promote student thinking and learning processes.

Section III of this book explores future directions in teaching games for understanding. Readers interested in equality and diversity will find Kanae Haneishi, Teng Tse Sheng, Bruce Nkala and Korey Boyd's Chapter 16 and Michael Davies, Shane Pill and John Evans' Chapter 17 particularly useful. Chapter 16 discusses how GBAs can be used as a practical tool to foster an environment for addressing social issues by promoting justice, equality, diversity and inclusion. This can help all students to be respected and feel a sense of belonging within PE. Chapter 17 offers a cultural interface using a Games Sense Approach and Yunkaporta's (2009) 8 Ways, to 'close the gap' between Western and Aboriginal knowledge in the decolonisation of games teaching in PE.

Finally, in Chapter 18, leading members for the IAB of the TGfU SIG, David Gutierrez and Jeroen Koekoek, use their global perspective to describe the development of GBAs from specific approaches. They provide the recent consensus statement that aims to align the variety of GBAs and overcome segmentation. A contextual analysis of perspectives obtained from IAB members, relevant researchers and authors informs on the origins and future directions for the field of GBAs.

Final thoughts

We believe that games are a key component in the PE curriculum. GBAs have the game at the base of the teaching context, placing the learner firmly at the centre. Teaching and coaching through active problem-solving in the game leads to the development of movement and skill with an improved tactical awareness. GBAs have much to offer students with their intentional focus on both *about games* (i.e., rules, boundaries, etiquette, good sporting behaviour), and *in game* (skills, movements, tactics) knowledge. We hope that you enjoy the chapters and continue to grow our GBA knowledge and community.

References

Almond, L. (1982). Editorial. *Bulletin of Physical Education*, *18*(1), 3.

Almond, L. (1986a). Reflecting on themes: A games classification. In R. Thorpe, D. Bunker & L. Almond (Eds.), *Rethinking games teaching* (pp. 71–72). Loughborough University of Technology.

Almond, L. (1986b). Primary and secondary rules in games. In R. Thorpe, D. Bunker & L. Almond (Eds.), *Rethinking games teaching* (pp. 73–74). Loughborough University of Technology.

Bunker, D. & Thorpe, R. (1982). A model for the teaching of games in secondary schools. *Bulletin of Physical Education*, *18*(1), 5–8.

Butler, J. (2016). *Playing fair.* Human Kinetics.

Butler, J. & Griffin, L. L. (2010). *More teaching games for understanding: Moving globally.* Human Kinetics.

Donovan, M., Jones, G. & Hardman, K. (2006). Physical education and sport in England: Dualism, partnership and delivery provision. *Kinesiology, 38*(1), 16–27.

Grehaigne, J. & Godbout, P. (1997). Performance assessment in team sports. *Journal of Teaching in Physical Education, 16,* 500–516.

Grehaigne, J-F., Richard, J-F., Malhut, N. & Griffin, L. L. (2005). *Teaching and learning invasion sports and games.* Routledge.

Guijarro, E., MacPhail, A., Arias-Palencia, N. M. & González-Víllora, S. (2021). Exploring game performance and game involvement: Effects of a sport education season and a combined sport education—Teaching games for understanding unit. *Journal of Teaching in Physical Education, 1*(aop), 1–14.

Kirk, D. (2010). *Physical education futures.* Routledge.

Mauldon, E. & Redfern, H. (1969). *Games teaching: A new approach for the primary school.* MacDonald and Evans.

Mitchell, S. A., Oslin, J. L. & Griffin, L. L. (2021). *Teaching sport concepts and skills: A tactical games approach* (4th ed.). Human Kinetics.

Ovens, A., Gutierrez, D. & Butler, J. (2021). Teaching games for understanding: From conception to Special Interest Group. In S. Mitchell & L. Griffin (Eds.), *Lifetime contributions in physical education: Celebrating the lives & work of Len Almond (1938–2017) & Joy Butler (1957–2019)* (pp. 104–119). Scholary.

Pill, S. (2007). *Play with Purpose: A resource to support teachers in the implementation of the game-centred approach to physical education.* Australian Council For Health, Physical Education and Recreation.

Price, A. & Pill, S. (2016). Can Gee's good (digital) game design features inform game-based sport coaching? *Research Journal of Sports Science, 4*(8), 257–269.

Rossi, T., Fry, J. M., McNeill, M. & Tan, C. W. K. (2006). The Games concept approach (GCA) as a mandated practice: Views of Singaporean teachers. *Sport Education and Society, 12*(1), 93–111.

Roth, K. & Kroger, C. (2015). *Ballschule: Ein ABC fur spielanfanger.* Hofmann.

Siedentop, D., Hastie, P. A. & van der Mars, H. (2020). *Complete guide to sport education* (3rd ed.). Human Kinetics.

SueSee, B., Hewitt, M. & Pill, S. (2020). *The spectrum of teaching styles in physical education.* Routledge.

Suzuki, N., Matsumoto, D., Tsuchida, R., Suzuki, O., Hirose, K., Sakuma, N. & Isano, R., (2010, March 28). *New instrument for assessing performance in game observation settings-game contribution assessment instrument (GCAI).* Poster presented at the AAHPERD National Convention 2010, Indianapolis.

Tallir, I. B., Musch, E. & Valcke, M. (2005). Effects of two instructional approaches for basketball on decision making and recognition ability. *International Journal of Sport Psychology, 36,* 107–126.

Thorpe, R. (1996). Physical Education: Beyond the curriculum. In N. Armstrong (Ed.), *New directions in physical education: Change and innovation* (pp. 144–156). Cassell.

Thorpe, R. & Bunker, D. (1986). Landmarks on our way to 'Teaching for Understanding'. In R. Thorpe, D. Bunker & L. Almond (Eds.), *Rethinking games teaching* (pp. 5–6). Loughborough University of Technology.

Thorpe, R. & Bunker, D. (1989). A changing focus in games teaching. In L. Almond (Ed.), *The place of physical education in schools* (pp. 52–79). Kogan Page.

Thorpe, R., Bunker, D. & Almond, L. (1986a). A change in focus for the teaching of games. In M. Pieron & G. Graham (Eds.), *Sport pedagogy: The 1984 Olympic Scientific Congress Proceedings Vol. 6* (pp. 163–169). Human Kinetics.

Thorpe, R., Bunker, D. & Almond, L. (1986b). *Rethinking games teaching*. Loughborough University of Technology.

Weeldenburg, G., Zondag, E. & de Kok, F. (2016). *Spelinzicht: Een speler- en spelgecentreerde didactiek van spelsporten* [Game Insight: A learner-and-game-centred approach to teaching games]. Jan Luiting Fonds.

Yunkaporta, T. (2009). *Aboriginal pedagogies at the cultural interface*. Unpublished thesis. James Cook University.

1 TGfU: A Model for the Teaching of Games with a Changed Focus in Games Teaching – A Commentary

Shane Pill, Sarah Doolittle and Rick Baldock

The 1982 Spring Edition: 18(1) of the Bulletin of Physical Education contained a collection of articles with a different method to the common 'traditional' games and sport teaching approach, which Mosston (1966) described as *Demonstration-Explanation-Execution-Evaluation* and Tinning (2010) as *Demonstrate-Explain-Practice*. Len Almond (1982) as editor of the 1982 Spring Edition wrote that the collection of articles represented an "attempt to raise issues and questions about the role of 'teaching for understanding' in the games curriculum" (p. 3). The edition and the first paper particularly, 'A model for the teaching of games in secondary schools' (Bunker & Thorpe, 1982), were so popular that the issue sold out and Bunker and Thorpe's paper was re-printed a year later in a 1983 Spring special edition of the Bulletin of Physical Education: Games Teaching Revisited: 19(1), edited by David and Rod (Bunker & Thorpe, 1983). Forty years later, the 1982 paper has been cited nearly 2000 times (as of 1/02/22), and it has influenced the development of games teaching in physical education (PE) and sport coaching instructional models in the UK, United States, Australia, New Zealand and Singapore, as well as having been advocated in universities globally as a preferred model for games teaching in schools. There is a good argument that the 1982 paper and the concept of a 6-step model of teaching for understanding and progressing from game form to performance has been a significant idea in academic and scholarly literature. Therefore, at the start of this collection of work exploring perspectives on teaching games for understanding, we feel it appropriate to look again at the model, as it provides context for everything that follows in this book.

While the 6-step model that has come to be known as Teaching Games for Understanding (TGfU) is well known, perhaps less well known is the curriculum model for secondary school PE proposed by Thorpe and Bunker (1989). In the chapter 'A Changing Focus in Games Teaching' in Len's 1989 book, *The Place of Physical Education in Schools,* Thorpe and Bunker re-iterated the 1982 6-step model as it "is central to the way we plan lessons and/or units of work and indeed helps us to formulate an overall pro- gramme" (p. 53) and suggested the central theme of games education as building player understanding of how to play games. Thorpe and Bunker

DOI: 10.4324/9781003298298-2

extended the application of the model written initially for secondary school PE into primary school PE games curriculum as a 'foundation course' based on the pedagogy of sampling games in game categories and proposed a secondary PE games program based also on game categories.

The model

The 6-step model shifted the teaching emphasis in games teaching in PE, an emphasis described as sport-as-sport techniques (Kirk, 2010), which is "a technique dominated approach" (Bunker & Thorpe, 1986a, p. 11) with a very prescribed motor response taught before the reason for it had been experienced. The concentration on specific motor responses, labelled techniques, was seen to lack contextual application to the nature of the game being taught (Bunker & Thorpe, 1982). In contrast, Bunker and Thorpe proposed the learner start with "beginning to appreciate the tactical necessity for improving the specific technique required in a particular game situation" (1982, p. 5). Figure 1.1 illustrates the 6-step TGfU model which is to be coupled with four pedagogical elements: 1. Sampling; 2. Modification –

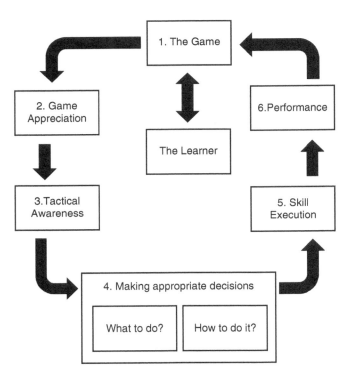

Figure 1.1 The TGfU 6-step model from game form to performance (see Bunker & Thorpe, 1982).

representation; 3. Modification – exaggeration; and 4. Tactical complexity (Thorpe & Bunker, 1989). "The sequential aspects of the model are critical. Unlike traditional teaching methods this approach starts with a game" (Bunker & Thorpe, 1982, p. 8). Briefly explaining the 6-steps, they are:

1   *Game form*: "While the full adult version of a game presents a long-term goal at which to aim and provides guidelines for teachers, it is necessary, in the early years of secondary school, to introduce children to a variety of game forms in accordance with their age and experience" (Bunker & Thorpe, 1982, p. 6);

2   *Game appreciation*: Understand the rules of the game to be played as rules give the game its shape and will determine the repertory of skills required. "It is axiomatic that alterations to the rules of a game will have implications for the tactics to be employed" (Bunker & Thorpe, 1982, p. 6);

3   *Tactical awareness*: "The principles of play, common to all games, form the basis of the tactical approach to the game" (Bunker & Thorpe, 1982, p. 7), and so it is necessary to consider now how tactics are used in the game;

4   *Decision making*: Attending to shortcomings in decision-making related to 'what to do?' and/or 'how to do it?' comes next. "The ability to recognise cues (involving processes of selective attention, cue redundancy, perception, etc.) and predict possible outcomes (involving anticipation of several kinds) is of paramount importance" (Bunker & Thorpe, 1982, p. 7). However, "there still remains the decision as to what is the best way to do it and selection of an appropriate response is critical" (Bunker & Thorpe, 1982, p. 7);

5   Skill execution is used to describe the production of the required movement, "and may include both the mechanical efficiency of the movement and its relevance to the particular game situation" (Bunker & Thorpe, 1982, p. 7); and

6   *Performance*: "This is the observed outcome of the previous process measured against criteria that are independent of the learner … and should be a measure of appropriateness of response as well as efficiency of technique" (Bunker & Thorpe, 1982, p. 8).

Acknowledging that games have been a means to develop players previously, Bunker and Thorpe proposed that in the new model "games are the lesson". That is not to say that games are all there is in the lesson – "we leave them occasionally to look at the technique of an individual or a group within the class" (Thorpe & Bunker, 1982, p. 10). The 6-step model didn't seem to be anti-teacher directed technique development as "teachers should ensure that techniques are taught as and when they are necessary" (Bunker & Thorpe, 1986a, p. 13), "our belief is that teachers will teach technique" (Bunker & Thorpe, 1986a, p. 14) but this is "subservient to increasing tactical awareness and helping children to make appropriate decisions" (Bunker & Thorpe, 1986a, p. 15). However, "the uniqueness of games is the 'decision-making' process which precedes the technique employed" (Bunker & Thorpe, 1986b, p. 28). While the pedagogical idea of progressing from a game to techniques, starting a lesson with a game or progressing from 'why' to 'how' with an emphasis on principles of play was not necessarily new (cf: Mauldon & Redfern, 1969; Williams & Willee, 1954, p.6) "its organisation and application has not previously been coherent" for secondary schools (Education Department of South Australia, 1984, p. 40).

The curriculum model: A framework for a games education from ages 5–16

Thorpe and Bunker (1989) proposed that:

> if one believes that the underlying central theme of games education is to build up an understanding of how to play games, it goes without saying that whatever games are selected they should be arranged in an order that allows the development of this understanding. (p. 56)

The TGfU curriculum model begins with the sampling of game forms arranged to build progressively an understanding of how to play games in game categories in primary school PE. The 'width' of experience associated with the pedagogical idea of sampling games formed the 'foundation course'. A curriculum structure still based on the game categories was maintained in the secondary PE program, however, depth was indicated by narrowing the number of games to allow those games to be developed over time (Table 1.1). While it was suggested that there be a specific focus on a game developed from Year 8 though to Year 10, the teacher was instructed to make parallels with related games, and the option to change the game from year to year was suggested. It was also suggested that the secondary PE

Table 1.1 An example games curriculum for secondary schools (Thorpe & Bunker, 1989, p. 79)

Year				
7	Foundation Course			
8	Invasion e.g., Basketball	Court e.g., Badminton	Game X	Fielding e.g., Cricket
9	Invasion continued	Court continued	Game X1	Fielding continued
10	Invasion continued	Court continued	Game X2	Fielding continued
11	New Game	Community linked course		Exam Term

games curriculum concludes with a game "investigated in the wider context of physical and psychological demands and its place in the community/ society" (Thorpe & Bunker, 1989, p. 78). The games curriculum was to be at least one hour a week (Thorpe & Bunker, 1989). The curriculum model was to provide "a coherent 'Games Education' leading to a 'Sport Education'" which "must be a major part of the *raison d'être* of the PE teacher" (Thorpe & Bunker, 1989, p. 80).

Commentary: Sarah Doolittle

I was at Loughborough University in 1982–83 for a year-long sabbatical from my American high school PE teaching job and had the distinct privilege of being a foreign MPhil graduate student involved with the original TGfU development with Len Rod Thorpe, David Bunker, David Kirk and others, who were together wrestling with the ideas, conducting teacher workshops, writing and revising the initial and follow-up articles that began the dissemination of this radical approach to teaching sports and games in schools.

TGfU has evolved and changed from the early 1980s. From the beginning I found the changes created by other scholars startling and incorrect, lacking fidelity. It took some time for me to recognise that TGfU, like other PE teaching models or curriculum approaches, should always be adapted to the specific circumstances of teachers' and researchers' workplaces, their biographies and value orientations, and most important, the interests and needs of their students. I have come to value the use of TGfU and other curriculum approaches as ideas or design models to create relevant pedagogy for students. In 1982–83 I experienced TGfU as one brilliant idea within a larger more complex mission at Loughborough, especially from Len's perspective. Three ideas, inextricably linked at the time to TGfU, changed my beliefs about PE teaching, curriculum and research, and may be relevant for teachers and researchers to consider now.

It's about the students

Student success, enthusiasm and motivation for learning, especially in mixed-ability secondary PE classes, were the primary reasons for developing TGfU. Rod Thorpe and David Bunker convey this rationale in their initial papers, saying that games teaching in early 1980's UK schools led many children to achieve little success due to the emphasis on technical or skill performance, and most school leavers failing to become knowledgeable about games as players or as spectators, at a time when games and sport were important forms of entertainment and leisure. They were also concerned as coaches that supposedly 'skillful' players in fact possess inflexible techniques and poor decision-making capacity and were dependent on their teachers and coaches to perform in games. In several articles, Thorpe and Bunker suggested that stressing the development of skill or technique before teaching why and how those actions was denying students the experience that games could be interesting and enjoyable for all students regardless of skill performance levels. Starting with the game and tactical awareness, instead of skill, allows "each and every child to participate in decision making, thereby retaining interest and involvement in the game" (Bunker & Thorpe, 1982, pp. 5–6). Teaching through questions in place of telling students what to do allowed students to think, experiment, voice their ideas and work at improving their performance. Using TGfU as a teaching approach, and emphasising student cognitive engagement, problem-solving, encouraging student ideas, taking responsibility in their lessons, are all what we might now consider constructivist teaching/learning. TGfU and other constructivist, student-centred and problem-solving approaches are now widely recognised solutions to improve secondary PE students' experiences.

Teacher/Curriculum development

In 1982–83 Len was engaged in, not only changing the way games were taught in secondary schools, but also in exploring the process of how PE teachers might develop curriculum and make changes in their own practice. While the TGfU model defined by Bunker and Thorpe in their several articles from 1982 to 1986 is deceptively simple, the classification of games, and related principles of play and tactics identified clearly by Williamson et al. (1982) was an elegant shift in teacher thinking suggesting in simple terms that invasion games, net games and striking/fielding games share several fundamental principles based on the tactics, rules or structure of the games. The sport-specific skills and techniques differ of course, but the goal of "helping children to understand principles of play and tactics in each of the three categories … supersedes the importance of isolated and repetitive teaching of specialized game techniques" (Williamson et al., 1982, pp. 25–26). This classification of games, which Len developed further in his 1986 volume, was suggested to help teachers decide WHICH games to teach. "Instead of a curriculum dominated by certain types of games, Len felt that young people should be exposed to a range of games which SAMPLED the whole spectrum and provided a BALANCE" (emphasis in the original, Almond, 1986b, pp. 71–72).

This game classification appeared to make an immediate change for teachers in the UK in the 1980s, and later became a powerful change for PE curriculum development worldwide. The TGfU classification of games not only broadened teachers' menu of activities for PE programs, but also likely deepened their content knowledge of each category of games and related principles of play. I believe the TGfU classification of sports and games pushes teachers towards content and pedagogical content knowledge development, making TGfU a continuing puzzle for teachers to question, consider and try in their work – an interesting idea to provoke teacher reflection and development.

In-service teachers and research

In TGfU workshops teachers learned to rethink their games teaching practice through:

- Actively participating in the TGfU process in invasion or net games;
- Group discussion about teachers' concerns and reactions;
- Some teachers left committed to trying this approach in their PE classes and returning after 8 weeks for a follow-up workshop.

Several of these teachers were challenged to experiment with this new teaching method, and to keep track of their teaching decisions, collect responses from their students and report back to an interested group of peer professionals. Teachers' notes and reports of experiences revealed advantages of TGfU from the teachers' perspectives: that students were initially dependent on traditional methods, but that a surprising number of them liked problem-solving activities, creating games and taking responsibility in their lessons.

Teachers reported that students showed real involvement and enthusiasm for lessons, and that 'low-ability' students showed a superior grasp of 'game sense'. These were all unexpected discoveries that the teachers had never seen before (Doolittle, 1983). This workshop process was drawn from Len's enthusiasm for 'Teacher as Researcher' (Stenhouse, 1975) and action research perspective (Almond, 1986a) as a way to re-engage teachers in their own learning, while also moving their curriculum forward.

Len Almond's decision to try Teacher-as-Researcher with TGfU re-cognised PE teachers' intelligence, creativity and expert pedagogical knowledge in their contexts, resulting in genuine contributions to theory development. This concept is similar perhaps to what is now described as a 'professional learning community' that also values parity among teachers and researchers. In addition to workshops like this, as BALPE editor, Len announced he had included articles by teachers about innovations and ideas they were implementing in their schools (Almond, 1982). In 1983, this teacher/researcher collaboration was a departure from the standard professional development model of the 'sage-on-the-stage' workshop. It embraced qualitative research methodology, contrasting sharply with research based in behaviourism and positivist quantitative research methods, conducted by university-based professionals, which was dominant at that time.

Forty years on I see that the TGfU classification of games, principles of play and TGfU lesson process have become essential constructs of TGfU. Teaching through questioning, games-making and other student-centred strategies appear sometimes. Other ideas I associate with TGfU, a focus on student success and engagement, teacher development through curriculum development, teachers as researchers, may not be critical to TGfU now, though seem relevant today. I am encouraged by the AIESEP SIG leadership for TGfU and the faithful devotees of this model. I am grateful for the efforts that keep TGfU going since it is a truly interesting model, which also can serve as a vehicle for keeping teachers and coaches intellectually engaged with their students in and through games and sport.

Commentary: Rick Baldock

In 1993, Rod Thorpe visited Australia on a Churchill Fellowship and I was working at the Australian Sports Commission (ASC). During this visit he spent a couple of weeks in Canberra working with staff from the ASC, the Australian Coaching Council (ACC) and the National AUSSIE SPORT Unit (NASU). Rod's visit was exploring how AUSSIE SPORT, established in 1986 as a nationally coordinated range of programs, included modification of children's sport as well as sports education targeting both primary and secondary school-age participants (Richards, 2020). During his visit he shared the TGfU approach while learning how sport in Australia provided opportunities for children to play sport. Thorpe remarked to me in a conversation one Saturday morning while being driven around Canberra, that this rarely occurred at that time in the United Kingdom and that he was most impressed by the participation of children in junior sport through clubs in Australia.

In the years preceding Thorpe's visit to Australia, the ASC had identified the six issues of widespread concern in junior sport across Australia:

- low participation rates in sports activities by children;
- poor levels of skill development among children;
- a limited range of sports available to children;
- an adult orientation in many sports;
- limited opportunities for girls to participate more fully; and,
- a lack of quality sports coaches.

(Richards, 2020)

The NASU and the ACC identified that common coaching/teaching approaches were contributing to the outcomes identified by the Children in Sport Committee and so were inappropriate for children and young people. Thorpe's TGfU approach to teaching and coaching pedagogy received a positive response from leaders at the ACC and the NASU as it was considered to provide a method which engaged players and addressed some of the concerns identified by the Children in Sport Committee. An invitation from the ACC was extended for him to return and lead a series of professional learning sessions around Australia for junior sport coaches and teachers of PE in 1994, which in Australia was the 'Year of the Coach'. Thorpe was also asked to contribute to the development of resources for sport coaches and PE teachers. I found his professional learning sessions provided both a theoretical and practical introduction to what was to become known as Game Sense, which was promoted by both the ACC and the NASU.

The professional learning sessions provided an impetus for coaches and teachers to begin experimenting with the Game Sense approach in their teaching and coaching in each Australian state, resulting in the ASC (ASC, 1996) *Game Sense: Perceptions and Actions Report*. Resources were developed by the ACC with the support of the NASU. This included an introductory video (ASC, 1997) and the *Game Sense Cards: 30 games to develop thinking players* (Barrett et al., 1999). Several articles on the Game Sense approach were also published in ASC publications AUSSIE SPORT Action and the Sport Coach journal to support teachers and coaches use of the Game Sense approach.

After spending a day with Rod Thorpe at one of these professional learning sessions in Adelaide in 1994, I returned to the school I was now working at wanting to experiment with this new Game Sense approach. I was pleasantly surprised by my students' response when compared to my usual 'skill and drill' approach. I remember the surprised looks and smiles on the faces of my students when I announced that we would begin with a game but what impressed me most were the conversations that students were having as they left the court at the conclusion of the lesson. They were discussing their plans and strategies they would be using in games at recess and lunchtime. My lessons had changed with students thinking more and taking greater responsibility for solving the problems that games and sports provide for players. In future lessons I observed some students who began to transfer and apply learning from other games and sports in the same game category. With this approach students were more engaged, and I no longer heard requests for 'When we were going to play the game?'. When it came to teaching techniques and applying them in a game, I no longer assumed that all players did not have the skills to play the game and needed to be drilled in them before playing. I now only taught the techniques to those who needed it and I remember that for the first time I had a student thank me for helping them to refine a technique before they returned to a game to apply this new learning.

The Game Sense approach worked for me and my students, but my biggest challenge as a teacher and coach was to sustain this approach across all four game categories and understand the progression for teaching strategies and tactics to my students. Over time I also found that I needed to:

• better design games to enable the game to focus questions and provide challenges for players to solve;
• get clearer about my learning intentions for players;
• allow for greater thinking time and discussion during lessons/sessions; and
• improve how I modified games across the four-game categories.

In 1994 it was an encouraging start but there was a lot more to be learnt before I could apply a game-based approach in all my lessons and when coaching.

Thorpe's work along with the active support of visionary leaders of the ACC such as Woodman, Schembri, den Duyen and MacCullum, and at the NASU Darcy, Oldenhove and Willis, continued and continue to influence games teaching in Australia. This includes the Game Sense approach being incorporated into the Playing for Life philosophy and Active After-School program (ASC, 2004), included in national sport coach accreditation courses, and now part of the Sport Australia Sporting Schools and Physical Literacy strategy (Sport Australia, 2022).

Conclusion

In 1986, Thorpe and Bunker concluded with, "we are left with one important question to answer: does it work?" (p. 79). Researchers have suggested that the evidence is yet to be conclusive that teaching for understanding is any better at achieving the player competence and confidence that underpin long-term participation for the focus area of games and sport teaching in PE that school curricula aspire to (Stolz & Pill, 2014). The chapters in this book, however, provide the sense that 'teaching for understanding' seems intuitively to make sense to many teachers, sport coaches, sport educators and PE teacher educators. TGfU, and in general game-based approaches for games and sport teaching in PE, with their central focus on developing thinking players using teacher-planned and player-centred critical thinking and inquiry strategies, sit comfortably with the constructivist 'student-centred' orientations of contemporary curriculum frameworks.

References

Almond, L. (1982). Editorial. *Bulletin of Physical Education, 18*(1), 3.

Almond, L. (1986a). Asking teachers to research. In R. Thorpe, D. Bunker & L. Almond (Eds.), *Rethinking games teaching* (pp. 35–44). University of Technology, Loughborough.

Almond, L. (1986b). Reflecting on themes: A games classification. In R. Thorpe, D. Bunker & L. Almond (Eds.), *Rethinking games teaching* (pp. 71–72). University of Technology, Loughborough.

Australian Sports Commission. (1996). *Game sense: Perceptions and actions research report.* Australian Sports Commission.

Australian Sports Commission. (1997). *Game Sense* (video). Australian Sports Commission.

Australian Sports Commission. (2004). *Playing for life: Active after-school communities program.* Australian Sports Commission.

Barrett, B., Den Duyn, N., Durham, D., Goodman, S., MacGraw, D., Murphy, G., Myers, J., Pappas, J., Thorpe, R. & Webb, P. (1999). *Game sense cards: 30 games to develop thinking players.* Australian Sports Commission.

Bunker, D. & Thorpe R. (1982). A model for the teaching of games in secondary schools. *Bulletin of Physical Education, 18*(1), 5–8.

Bunker, D. & Thorpe R. (1983). Editorial. *Bulletin of Physical Education, 19*(1), 1.

Bunker, D. & Thorpe, R. (1986a). From theory to practice. In R. Thorpe, D. Bunker & L. Almond (Eds.), *Rethinking games teaching* (pp. 11–16). University of Technology, Loughborough.

Bunker, D. & Thorpe, R. (1986b). Is there a need to reflect on our games teaching? In R. Thorpe, D. Bunker & L. Almond (Eds.), *Rethinking games teaching* (pp. 25–34). University of Technology, Loughborough.

Doolittle, S. (1983). Reflecting on an innovation. *Bulletin of Physical Education, 19*(1), 36–38.

Education Department of South Australia. (1984). *A model for the teaching of Games in secondary schools*. South Australian Physical Education Bulletin.

Kirk, D. (2010). *Physical education futures*. Routledge.

Mauldon, E. & Redfern, H. B. (1969). *Games teaching: a new approach for the primary school*. MacDonald & Evans.

Mosston, M. (1966). *Teaching physical education: From command to discovery*. Charles E. Merrill.

Richards, R. (2020). *AUSSIE SPORTS*. https://www.clearinghouseforsport.gov.au/kb/aussie-sports

Sport Australia. (2022). *Playing for life*. https://www.sportaus.gov.au/p4l/game_sense_approach

Stenhouse, L. (1975). *An introduction to curriculum research and development*. Heineman.

Stolz, S. & Pill, S. (2014). Teaching games and sport for understanding: Exploring and reconsidering its relevance in Physical Education. *European Physical Education Review, 20*(1), 36–71.

Thorpe, R. & Bunker, D. (1982). Issues that arise when preparing to 'teach for understanding'. *Bulletin of Physical Education, 18*(1), 9–11.

Thorpe, R. & Bunker, D. (1986). Where are we now? A games education. In R. Thorpe, D. Bunker & L. Almond (Eds.), *Rethinking games teaching* (pp. 79). Loughborough University.

Thorpe, R. & Bunker, D. (1989). A changing focus in games teaching. In L. Almond (Ed.), *The place of physical education in schools* (pp. 52–79). Kogan/Page.

Tinning, R. (2010). *Pedagogy and human movement: Theory, practice, research*. Routledge.

Williams, L. C. & Willee, A. W. (1954). *Playground games for secondary boys (technique of teaching)*. Blackie & Son Ltd.

Williamson, T., Jackson, S. & Jones, D. (1982). It's a different ball game! A critical look at the games curriculum. *Bulletin of Physical Education, 18*(1), 23–26.

Section I

Global Developments Influenced by Teaching Games for Understanding

2 The Tactical Games Model and Game Performance Assessment

Linda Griffin and Steve Mitchell

Games remain a large part of most physical education curriculums and, as noted elsewhere in this book, it is 40 years since Bunker and Thorpe (1982) first introduced the constructivist approach to games teaching known as Teaching Games for Understanding (TGfU). TGfU was the first Game-Based Approach (GBA), but several differing perspectives on the original approach emerged as TGfU was disseminated globally. One such perspective was our own work in developing what we called the Tactical Games Model (Mitchell et al., 2021). We have two aims in this chapter. First, we describe our thought processes as we sought to develop our own perspective on the original TGfU model. We proposed that 'tactical frameworks' could be developed for each game or game category (Almond, 1986). A tactical framework provides a process for breaking down the tactical components of gameplay so that scope and sequence (i.e., levels of tactical complexity) of instructional content can be planned. We describe and provide examples of this process. Our second aim is to outline our efforts to provide assessment tools for teachers. We recognised early in our work that instrumentation for measuring game performance was inadequate. Available instruments focused primarily on the observation and assessment of technical performance, while ignoring key tactical aspects of game performance such as decision-making and off-the-ball movement. Our goal was to develop a Game Performance Assessment Instrument (GPAI) that would yield data reflecting the entirety of game performance.

Tactical Games Model (TGM): Building the schema

The basis for our work came from the belief that sports and games can be fun, educative, and challenging and can enhance health and self-esteem. With respect to games and sport as content, for us it is not the matter (i.e., games and sport); it is the way games have traditionally been taught that we view as problematic. That is, skills taught in isolation, out of their tactical context. The TGM links tactics and skills by emphasising the appropriate timing of skill practice and application within the context of the game leading to the development of tactical awareness. Tactical awareness, critical

DOI: 10.4324/9781003298298-4

to game performance, is the ability to identify tactical problems that arise during a game and to respond appropriately. Responses might involve on-the-ball skills, such as passing and shooting, and off-the-ball movements, such as supporting and covering. For example, a tactical problem in soccer is for the team to maintain possession of the ball. Players maintain possession by selecting and executing passing, ball-control, and support skills. In a TGM, students are placed in a game situation that emphasises maintaining possession *before* they identify and practice solutions such as passing, ball control, and support. The link between skills and tactics enables students to learn about a game and improve their performance, especially because game tactics provide the opportunity for applying game-related skills and movements. In this section, we will present our organisation schema for a TGM: (a) rationale for the model; (b) tactical frameworks; (c) levels of tactical complexity; (d) a tactical model for teaching and the lesson format; and (e) TGM as games curriculum.

Rationale for a TGM

Our rationale is based on the idea that games teaching should be about games playing. A TGM promotes an interest in learning games, an understanding of gameplay, and the competence to play games.

Interest and excitement

First, a TGM provides an exciting alternative to a skill-based approach (i.e., mastery model) through which students can learn to play games with the game being the base of the lesson. Our research and the experience of others indicate that students find a tactical approach motivational and that teachers prefer it (Berkowitz, 1996; Burrows, 1986; Griffin et al., 1995; Gubacs-Collins, 2007; Hopper, 2003; Mitchell et al., 1994). Second, is the sequential nature of the model, which promotes a scope and sequence in games teaching. The scope and sequence eliminate redundancy (i.e., same drill; different year) for teachers and students.

Knowledge as empowerment

Although skill and movement execution are critical to game performance, deciding *what to do* in game situations is just as important. Common mistakes from students in sport may originate from a lack of knowledge about what to do in the context of a given sport situation (French & Thomas, 1987). Furthermore, Bunker and Thorpe (1986) proposed that the uniqueness of games lies in the decision-making processes that precede the use of appropriate techniques. Games have *in game* (i.e., skills, movements, situations) and *about game* (i.e., rules, rituals, ethics, etc.) knowledge. Not understanding the game impairs the student's ability to identify the correct technique for a situation.

Bunker and Thorpe (1986) also suggested that an increased understanding of games, achieved through teaching for tactical awareness, empowers students to more skillfully solve the problems each game situation poses. Enhanced decisions reflect greater knowledge of the game, an observation supported by the research of McPherson (1994, 1995).

Transfer of understanding and performance

A tactical focus may help your students carry understanding from one game to another. For example, tactical problems in soccer, field hockey, and basketball, all of which are invasion games, are similar. In our observations, the best novice soccer players are those with experience of other invasion games such as field and ice hockey, because they already understand the spatial aspects of soccer. These similarities enable the grouping of games according to their tactics.

Game frameworks

The foundation for the game frameworks is the games classification system. This classification system is based on similarities among primary rules that define the games (Almond, 1986; Ellis, 1986) (see Table 2.1).

For example, invasion games (e.g., soccer, team handball, and basketball) share the same tactical problems for scoring, preventing scoring, and re-starting play (see Table 2.2).

We developed game frameworks to help guide teachers in identifying and breaking down relevant tactical problems, a process originated by Spackman (1983). A specific game framework identifies tactical problems and the

Table 2.1 Games classification system

Invasion	Net and Wall	Striking and Fielding	Target
Basketball (FT)	Net	Baseball	Golf
Netball (FT)	Badminton (I)	Softball	Croquet
Team handball (FT)	Tennis (I)	Rounders	Bowling
Water polo (FT)	Table tennis (I)	Cricket	Lawn bowling
Soccer (FT)	Pickleball (I)	Kickball	Pool
Hockey (FT)	Volleyball (H)		Billiards
Lacrosse (FT)	Wall		Snooker
Speedball (FT/OET)	Racquetball (I)		
Rugby (OET)	Squash (I)		
Football (OET)	Handball (H)		
Ultimate (OET)			

FT = focused target; OET = open-ended target; I = implement; H = hand.
Adapted from Almond (1986). By permission of D.L. Bunker.

Table 2.2 Tactical problems in invasion games

Scoring	• Maintaining possession of the ball • Attacking the goal • Creating space in attack • Using space in attack
Preventing scoring	• Defending space • Defending the goal • Winning the ball
Restarting play	• Attacking and defending

off-the-ball movements and on-the-ball skills necessary for solving these problems. To develop our frameworks, we asked two questions:

1   What are the problems in scoring, preventing scoring, and restarting play?
2   What off-the-ball movements and on-the-ball skills are necessary to solve these problems?

Table 2.3 provides an example framework for soccer. The soccer framework identifies the major tactical problems in scoring, preventing scoring, and restarting play. To score, a team must solve the progressively complex problems of maintaining possession of the ball, attacking the goal, creating space while attacking, and using that space effectively. Each tactical problem includes relevant off-the-ball movements and on-the-ball skills. For example, to maintain possession of the ball, players must support teammates who have the ball and must pass and control the ball over various distances.

Levels of tactical complexity

To extend the game frameworks to ensure that tactical complexity of the game aligns with students' development, we identified levels of tactical complexity (i.e., tactical scope and sequence for games curriculum). Again, using soccer as the example, we identify levels of tactical complexity which help define how a game might be played at different stages (see Table 2.4). The table identifies at which level various skills should be introduced to students learning the game. For example, under Scoring in Table 2.4, the first row identifies what skills students must learn to be able to maintain possession of the ball. At Level I, students are introduced to dribbling and passing and controlling with their feet. Notice, these skills are not repeated in subsequent levels in this row because the students will already know them, having been introduced to them in Level I. Not all tactical problems are addressed at all levels because this would not be developmentally appropriate. As students improve their tactical understanding, games should

Table 2.3 Tactical problems, movements, and skills in soccer

Tactical Problems	Off-the-ball Movements	On-the-ball Skills
Scoring (offense)		

Maintaining possession of the ball	Dribbling for control
	    Supporting the ball carrier
		Passing—short and long
		    Control—feet, thigh, chest

Attacking the goal	Using a target player	Shooting, shielding, turning

Creating space in attack	Crossover play
	    Overlapping run
		First-time passing
		    Crossover play
		    Overlapping run

Using space in attack	Timing runs to goal, shielding	Width—dribbling, crossing, heading Depth—shielding
Preventing scoring (defense)		
Defending space	Marking, pressuring, preventing the turn, delaying, covering, making recovery runs	Clearing the ball
Defending the goal	Goalkeeping—positioning	Goalkeeping—receiving the ball, making saves, distributing (throwing and punting)
Winning the ball		Tackling—block, poke, slide
Restarting play		
Throw-in—attacking and defending	Defensive marking at throw-ins	Executing a quick throw

Corner kick—attacking and defending	Defensive marking at corners	Short corner kick
		    Near-post corner kick
		    Far-post corner kick

Free kick—attacking and defending	Defending—marking at free kicks Defending—setting a wall	Attacking—shooting from free kicks

involve problems of increasing complexity. The key question to ask is, *how tactically complex do I want the game to be?* In contrast, the question you address in a skill-based approach is, *what skills should I teach in my unit?* Identifying levels of tactical complexity and planning developmentally appropriate content becomes a process of designing versions of the game for students at varying stages of awareness.

Tactical model for games teaching and lesson format

A critical question that helped to guide us to implementing a TGM was, '*How do I teach for tactical awareness within the physical education lesson?*'.

Table 2.4 Levels of tactical complexity for soccer

Tactical Problems	Level I	Level II	Level III	Level IV	Level V
Scoring					
Maintaining possession of the ball	Dribbling for control Passing (short) Control (with the feet)	Supporting the ball carrier		Passing—long Control—thigh, chest	
Attacking the goal	Shooting	Shooting Turning Shielding	Using a target player		
Creating space in attack					Crossover play Depth—shielding Timing of runs to goal, shielding
Using space in attack			First-time passing	Overlapping run Width—dribbling, crossing, heading	
Preventing scoring					
Defending space		Marking, pressuring	Preventing the turn	Clearing the ball	Delaying, covering, making recovery runs
Defending the goal		Goalkeeper positioning and receiving the ball Distributing—throwing			Goalkeeping— making saves Distributing — punting
Winning the ball			Tackling—blocking, poking	Tackling—sliding	
Restarting play					
Throw-in—attacking and defending	Executing a quick throw	Defensive marking at throw-ins			
Corner kick—attacking and defending	Short corner kick	Defensive marking at corners	Near-post corner kick		Far-post corner kick
Free kick—attacking and defending			Attacking—shooting from free kicks		Defending—marking and setting a wall

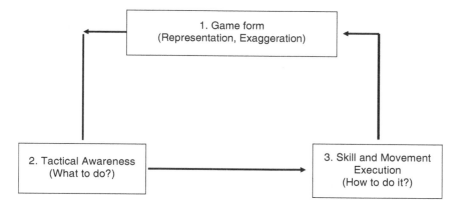

Figure 2.1 A TGM for teaching.

Bunker and Thorpe (1982) suggested a six-stage model for games teaching, TGfU, which has been very useful in guiding physical educators. We decided to consolidate the six-stage model into three stages (see Figure 2.1). The three-stage model provided a simplified visual and a more structured approach. The following provides our rationale for the increased structure:

1   Recognition that the teacher is an 'architect of task design'.
2   Game conditions present problems to solve and create predictable outcomes, which can be planned for and help guide the lesson.
3   Enables pre-planning of questions to ask, rather than waiting for students to ask questions.
4   Student thinking promoted because questions are planned.
5   Facilitates effective use of class time.
6   Pre-planning helpful for teachers who are not games 'specialists'.
7   Enables more effective longer-term curriculum planning:

    a   Tactical frameworks to help identify scope of content for instruction.
    b   Levels of Tactical/Game Complexity to help sequence of content.

8   Emphasis on transfer of understanding between games.

The outline in Figure 2.1 suggests that teaching for tactical awareness should start with a game, or more precisely, a game modified to represent its advanced form and exaggerated to present students with tactical problems (Thorpe et al., 1986).

    For example, a tactical problem in badminton is to set up the attack by creating space on the opponent's side of the net. The lesson would begin with a half-court singles game because it represents the full-court game but is played on a narrower court. The narrowness exaggerates the need to play shots to the back and front of the court to create space. The initial game form should relate to the level of student development. Consider the dimensions of playing areas, the number of students participating, and the equipment used when choosing a game form. If you establish a developmentally appropriate form, students' play can represent the advanced game. For example, small-sided volleyball games played in smaller areas with lighter balls and lower nets use the same principles, problems, and skills found in the full game.

Questions and critical conditions

After the initial game, questions are necessary, and the quality of your questions is the key to fostering students' critical thinking and problem-solving. First, ask about the goal of the activity, and then ask students what they must do to achieve that goal (i.e., what skills or movements they must use to be successful). Questioning why certain skills or movements are required might also be appropriate. Once students are aware of what they need to do and why, you can ask them how they should perform the necessary skills. Questions matter in this model because they place the students at the centre of solving the tactical problem and decision-making process. Questions help students identify skills, movements, and tactics to practice, which leads to the practice phase of the lesson. The quality of your questions is critical, and these questions should be an integral part of your planning. Literature on tactical games teaching, be it the original work of Bunker and Thorpe (1982), the Australian conception of *Game Sense* (den Duyn, 1997), or our own *Teaching Sport Concepts and Skills* (Griffin et al., 1997), and *Sport Foundations for Elementary Physical Education* (Mitchell et al., 2003), has consistently emphasised the importance of asking quality questions.

  Essential to the questions are game conditions. Games need conditions to encourage students to think tactically. Game conditions involve modifying the secondary rules. The essential question for students to consider during the initial game is, what must I do to succeed in this situation?

The following example illustrates the lesson flow

Establish an appropriate game form, such as two versus two (2v2) soccer in a restricted playing area with an objective of making a specific number of consecutive passes (such as four) before the ball is lost. This objective forces the student to confront what they must do to maintain possession. Appropriate teacher–student questioning might go as follows:

Teacher: What was the goal of that game?
Students: For each team to keep the ball for four passes.

Teacher: What does your team have to do to keep the ball for four consecutive passes?

Students: Pass the ball.

Teacher: Yes, and what else?

Students: We also have to receive passes.

Teacher: OK, you have to be able to pass and receive the ball, perhaps some practice with passing and receiving would be a good idea.

The teacher led students to identify the lesson focus through well-designed game conditions and through skilful questioning. At this point, formal practice of passing and receiving becomes appropriate through instruction and demonstration. The lesson concludes with gameplay that emphasises the skills and movements practised.

Your students' learning continues lesson by lesson, and you continue to modify the game so they can explore new aspects of tactical awareness. For example, you could introduce a 3v3 game, providing all players with an extra passing option so that they must effectively support the player with the ball. When students understand the need for good support, you can teach off-the-ball supporting movements before returning to the game. Thus, you progressively develop your students' game performance.

Planning format for tactical games lessons

Game _____ Lesson No. _____ Grade level _____

Major components of the plan are bolded, and points for you to consider are italicised.

Tactical problem: *What is the tactical problem addressed during the lesson?*

Lesson focus: *What is the focus in terms of how the tactical problem will be solved?*

Objectives: *What are the major cognitive and psychomotor learning objectives?*

Game: *What is the modified game being played?*

Goal: *What performance goal will you give to the students?*

Conditions: *What conditions will you put on the game to ensure that students address the tactical problem?*

Questions: *After initial game play, what questions might you ask (and what answers do you anticipate) to help students focus on the tactical problem and its solution?*

Practice task: *What skill practice will help students solve the tactical problem when they return to game play?*

Goal: *What performance goal will you give to the students for the skill practice?*

Cues: *What teaching cues will you use to assist skill acquisition?*

Extension: *How might you extend the skill practice to make it harder or easier to match the content with the varying abilities of students?*

Game: *What modified game may help students apply their newly learned skills to solve the tactical problem during play?*

Goal: *What performance goal will you give to the students for the game?*

Conditions: *What conditions will you put on the game to ensure that students use the skills they learned to address the tactical problem?*
Closure: *What would be an appropriate closure or ending discussion for the lesson?*

TGM as games curriculum

We developed a conceptual framework that outlines the major components of the curriculum (see Figure 2.2). Central to the model are the tactical problems that the various games present—problems that must be overcome to score, prevent scoring, and restart play. We believe that it is possible and desirable to develop a progressive and sequential tactical games curriculum across the compulsory education spectrum, beginning at second grade (about age 7). We offer two distinct pathways. First, a thematic approach as a means of building sport foundations in children by having students experience games across the classification system, for example a unit focused on net/wall games. Second, a more sport-specific approach to allow for greater specificity and greater development of performance competence.

In summary of this section on building the TGM schema, we wanted to emphasise the following:

1   Consider the tactical problems to address during your unit and decide on the complexity of the solutions to these problems;
2   Within each lesson, have students practice skills after they have experienced a game form that presents a tactical problem requiring that skill;
3   Link the initial modified game and the skill practice through your questions. The quality of these questions is critical; and
4   After your students have practised skills, give them the opportunity to apply their improved skills and tactical understanding in gameplay.

Authentic assessment: The game performance assessment instrument

The GPAI was developed as a comprehensive assessment tool for teachers to use and adapt for a variety of games. This flexibility means that teachers can use the GPAI for various games across the classification system (e.g., net and wall, invasion) or within a classification (e.g., basketball, soccer). We designed the GPAI to provide teachers and researchers with a means of observing and coding performance behaviours. The GPAI includes behaviours that demonstrate the ability to solve tactical problems by making decisions, moving appropriately, and executing skills. We initially developed

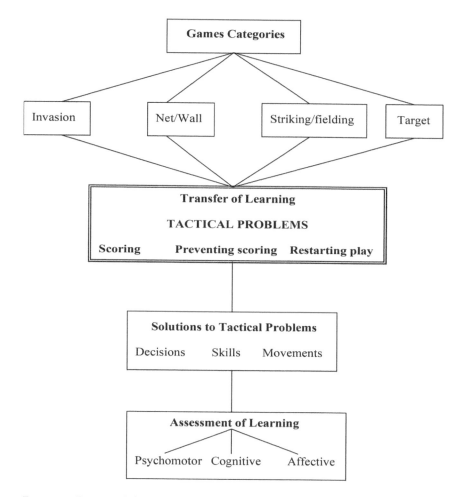

Figure 2.2 Conceptual framework.

performance components for the GPAI through consultation with five teacher-coaches who had expertise in each classification category. Our aim was to identify observable components of game performance that applied across game categories. The GPAI is composed of seven components of game performance, although not all components apply equally to all games. For example, in badminton, the base component is critical to court coverage, but players do not have to guard, or mark, opponents. The seven components listed next constitute a broad definition of game performance that entails much more than skill execution (Mitchell & Oslin, 1999). The main value of this broad definition lies in the ability to give credit to

Table 2.5 GPAI components and definitions

Component	Definition
Base	Appropriate return of performer to recover (base) position between skill attempts
Decision Making	Makes appropriate decisions about what to do with the ball during the game
Skill Execution	Efficient execution of selected skills
Support	Provides appropriate support for teammates with ball by being in position to receive a pass
Guard/Mark	Appropriate guard/mark of an opponent
Cover	Appropriate defensive cover, help
Adjust	Movement of performer offensively or defensively to help flow of game

students for all aspects of game performance, including the decisions they make and how hard they work both offensively and defensively, rather than just assessing only proficient skill execution.

Following are brief descriptions and examples of each component of game performance. Table 2.5 provides the definitions of each game component.

The appeal of the GPAI is that you can adapt and use the instrument according to the type and aspect of the game being played with students and in their playing context. The two basic scoring methods using the GPAI are the 1 to 5 system and the tally system. Mitchell and Oslin (1999) pointed out that the 1 to 5 scoring system is efficient for two reasons. First, observers (primarily the teacher) do not have to record each time a player is involved in the game. In invasion games and some net and wall games, this is impossible to do effectively because of the tempo, flow, and unpredictability of such games when players have a wide range of skill levels. Second, the 1 to 5 scoring system provides for a wide range of scoring but not so wide as to affect scoring consistency. Teachers can create criteria for the five indicators – that is, from very effective performance to very weak performance – or use a modified scale from always to never. The indicators should be based on the unit/lesson objectives, students' abilities, and the time available for physical education.

The tally system can be used with striking and fielding games and some net and wall games because they are played at a slower pace and have natural breaks (between pitches, bowls, or points), which gives the observer an opportunity to score or tally every event. The tally system also provides a more precise performance measure.

Using the tally system, teachers can also give students a bigger picture of their gameplay by calculating game involvement and overall game performance scores. Game involvement can be measured by adding all incidences of involvement in the game, including inappropriate decisions made

Table 2.6 GPAI performance measures

Performance measure	Calculation
Decision-making index (DMI)	Appropriate decision made/Appropriate decisions made + Inappropriate decisions made X 100
Skill execution index (SEI)	Efficient skill execution/Efficient skill execution + Inefficient skill execution X 100
Support Index (SI)	Appropriate support/Appropriate support + Inappropriate support X 100
Game Performance	$\frac{DMI + SEI + SI \times 100}{3}$
Game Involvement	Appropriate decisions + Inappropriate decisions + Inefficient skill execution + number of appropriate support movements

and inefficient skill execution attempts. Inappropriate guarding (or marking), supporting, adjusting, and covering are *not included* because an inappropriate response in these components indicates that the player was not involved in the game. Game involvement provides an inclusive measure as it can provide encouragement towards game participation whereas; a performance measure may not appeal to all students (Table 2.6).

There is no question that there are challenges in implementing the GPAI. First, time and large class size. We offer the following solutions: (a) limit the number of students and game performance components you assess at one time; (b) plan for assessment time in every lesson and assess on an ongoing basis; and (c) use peer assessment as formative assessment.

In summary, the GPAI is an authentic assessment tool and can be used for both formative and summative purposes (Oslin, 2005). The GPAI provides a more complete definition of game performance than traditional assessments in games. The instrument provides researchers and teachers with a flexible and authentic tool to measure player performance in game situations (Oslin et al., 1998). Assessment of performance should be based on what has been taught. The GPAI has the capacity to give credit to all facets of performance, which benefits the lower-skilled student.

Final thoughts

We are appreciative of the work of Bunker, Thorpe, Almond, and others before them for foregrounding the game in games teaching. Our contributions, which include the simplified three-stage teaching model, game frameworks and levels of tactical complexity, and the GPAI, are intended to make TGfU 'doable' and meaningful for teachers and students in physical education. We embrace the idea that what we learn from play, we learn about life, so let us keep learning from playing games. GBAs have much to offer as a holistic approach to teaching and learning for all students. We are grateful for our opportunities to contribute to the GBA movement as the TGfU global community celebrates the 40th anniversary of the model and initial publication (Bunker and Thorpe, 1982).

References

Almond, L. (1986). Reflecting on themes: A games classification. In R. Thorpe, D. Bunker & L. Almond (Eds.), *Rethinking games teaching* (pp. 71–72). Loughborough University of Technology.

Berkowitz, R. J. (1996). A practitioner's journey from skill to tactics. *Journal of Physical Education, Recreation and Dance, 67*(4), 44–45.

Bunker, D. & Thorpe, R. (1982). A model for the teaching of games in secondary schools. *Bulletin of Physical Education, 18*(1), 5–8.

Bunker, D. & Thorpe, R. (1986). Is there a need to reflect on our games teaching? In R. Thorpe, D. Bunker & L. Almond (Eds.), *Rethinking games teaching*, (pp. 25–34). Loughborough University of Technology.

Burrows, L. (1986). A teacher's reactions. In R. Thorpe, D. Bunker & L. Almond (Eds.), *Rethinking games teaching* (pp. 45–52). Loughborough University of Technology.

den Duyn, N. (1997). *Game sense: Developing thinking players*. Australian Sports Commission.

Ellis, M. (1986). Making and shaping games. In R. Thorpe, D. Bunker & L. Almond (Eds.), *Rethinking games teaching* (pp. 61–65). Loughborough University of Technology.

French, K. E. & Thomas, J. R. (1987). The relation of knowledge development to children's basketball performance. *Journal of Sport Psychology, 9*, 15–32.

Griffin, L. L., Mitchell, S. A. & Oslin, J. L. (1997). *Teaching sport concepts and skills: A tactical games approach* (1st ed.). Human Kinetics.

Griffin, L., Oslin, J. & Mitchell, S. (1995). Two instructional approaches to teaching net games. *Research Quarterly for Exercise and Sport Suppl, 66*(1), 65–66.

Gubacs-Collins, K. (2007). Reflective pedagogy through action research: Implementing a tactical approach to teaching games in PETE. *Physical Education and Sport Pedagogy, 12*(2), 105–126.

Hopper, T. (2003). Four R's for tactical awareness: Applying game performance assessment in net/wall games. *Journal of Teaching Elementary Physical Education, 4*(2), 16–21.

McPherson, S. L. (1994). The development of sport expertise: Mapping the tactical domain. *Quest, 46*, 223–240.

McPherson, S. L. (1995). Expertise in women's collegiate tennis: Development of knowledge and skill. Paper presented at the annual conference of the North American Society for the Psychology of Sport and Physical Activity, Monterey, CA.

Mitchell, S. A. & Oslin, J. L. (1999). *Assessment series K-12 physical education series: Assessment in games teaching*. National Association for Sport and Physical Education.

Mitchell, S. A., Griffin, L. L. & Oslin, J. L. (1994). Tactical awareness as a developmentally appropriate focus for the teaching of games in elementary and secondary physical education. *The Physical Educator, 51*(1), 21–28.

Mitchell, S. A., Oslin, J. L. & Griffin, L. L. (2003). *Sport foundations for elementary physical education: A tactical games approach*. Human Kinetics.

Mitchell, S. A., Oslin, J. L. & Griffin, L. L. (2021). *Teaching sport concepts and skills: A tactical games approach* (4th ed.). Human Kinetics.

Oslin, J. (2005). The role of assessment in teaching games for understanding. In L. Griffin & J. Butler (Eds.), *Teaching games for understanding: Theory, research and practice* (pp. 125–135). Human Kinetics.

Oslin, J. L., Mitchell, S. A. & Griffin, L. L. (1998). The Game Performance Assessment Instrument (GPAI): Development and preliminary validation. *Journal of Teaching in Physical Education, 17,* 231–243.

Spackman, L. (1983). Invasion games: An instructional strategy. *British Journal of Physical Education,* 14(4), 98–99.

Thorpe, R., Bunker, D. & Almond, L. (1986). A change in focus for the teaching of games. In M. Piéron & G. Graham (Eds.), *Sport pedagogy: The 1984 Olympic Scientific Congress proceedings* (pp. 163–169). vol. 6. Human Kinetics.

3 Learning to Teach Game Sense: A Bottom-Up Approach

Richard L. Light and Christina Curry

A range of strategies has been suggested to increase the uptake of Game-based Approaches (GBA) such as Game Sense which, like many other GBA, was developed from Teaching Games for Understanding (TGfU). As a models-based practice, the idea of providing a well-defined progression of steps for the implementation of TGfU by teachers or coaches enjoys significant support, but is not without its critics. Along with some others (see Landi et al., 2016) we have some reservation about what we suggest can be considered a prescriptive, top-down approach. Game Sense does not have a model for implementation and is generally accepted as a looser approach that is open to teacher or coach interpretation and adaptation (see Light & Curry, 2021). With this in mind, we follow Light and Light's (2021) suggestion for assisting coaches' and teachers' implementation of Game Sense by taking a bottom-up approach in which learning to implement Game Sense sits upon an understanding of the philosophical positions of holism and humanism as its foundation. Before expanding on this idea, we briefly outline the history of Game Sense to locate it in the virtual plethora of GBAs and outline the ideas that inform it.

The idea of game-based teaching and coaching

During the early development of TGfU, Thorpe, Bunker and Almond (see Thorpe et al., 1986) located learning to play games within practice games modified to suit the learners and the learning objectives to develop game-playing ability within game contexts. This included skill performed in context, awareness, tactical understanding, anticipation, decision-making and the range of other abilities needed to play games. The focus of TGfU on the game instead of on technique or skill separated from the game presented a radical challenge to the dominant, reductionist skill-drill approach but the basic idea was not completely new. It was similar to some previous ideas that emerged over the 1960s and early 1970s, such as those of Wade (see, 1967) in the teaching of football. He promoted the use of small-sided games while urging teachers to be imaginative and creative when teaching football and to 'guide a child toward appropriate answers' (Wade, 1967).

DOI: 10.4324/9781003298298-5

The 1960s was a period of new ideas that included constructivist-informed teaching and progressive education with new thinking about teaching games and team sport. Over this period, Mauldon and Redfern (1969) argued for the use of games to develop primary school students' skills instead of using drills, with similar ideas proposed in France by Mahlo (1973) who focused on tactics in play instead of skills. All these ideas and suggestions are manifested in different ways within Game Sense.

Game Sense is a holistic approach to teaching with its focus on the game as a whole entity rather than reducing it to the notion of fundamental skills or techniques that must be learned before playing the game or to enable students to play it. By locating learning in practice games designed and modified to suit the abilities and dispositions of learners, Game Sense makes learning and the activities used, relevant and meaningful for them (Light, 2021). It also addresses concerns with student boredom and disengagement in physical education by bringing back the fun that should always be associated with playing games and/or sport as a form of play. To this end, contending that play is of central importance for the generation of any culture, Dutch historian and cultural theorist, Huizinga (1938) suggested that one of the most significant human and cultural aspects of play is that it must be fun.

TGfU and game sense

Bunker and Thorpe's (1982) first publication on TGfU attracted attention as an innovative idea that challenged the accepted and unquestioned approach to teaching games focused on skill. It was not, however, until it gained the interest of scholars in the US a decade later, that it began to get the global exposure and interest that it, and similar approaches such as Game Sense (den Duyn, 1997), the Tactical Games Approach (Griffin et al., 1997) and the Games Concept Approach (see Rossi et al., 2007) have enjoyed. TGfU was originally a relatively loose approach that placed learning within game contexts and promoted thinking through questioning by the teacher to encourage dialogue and reflection (Light, 2013) but has since developed more structure to guide teachers more efficiently towards implementing it as an approach that challenged traditional games teaching. This shift was confirmed in an address by Thorpe and Bunker at the 2008 International TGfU conference in Vancouver (Thorpe & Bunker, 2008) where they asked whether TGfU still met its original intentions. It was also recognised by Thorpe at the 2003 International TGfU Conference chaired by the first author and where Thorpe suggested that Game Sense was effectively the original TGfU.

The development of game sense

During 1994–1996, Thorpe made several trips to Australia where he collaborated with Australian coaches and the Australian Sports Commission (ASC) in the development of a similar approach to TGfU for sport coaching.

He noted how many Australian coaches were already using games in their coaching but without it being a systematic part of their approach (Light, 2004). One of the features of Game Sense and other GBA is the use of questioning to generate thinking, as reflected in den Duyn's (1997) publication, *Game Sense: Developing Thinking Players*. In a study that inquired into the use of Game Sense by Australian coaches, some participants suggested that the main thing Thorpe brought to the table in the development of Game Sense was the systematic questioning (Light, 2004).

Game Sense is a flexible approach that emphasises developing thinking players with an understanding of the game. It employs the basic pedagogical features such as emphasising questioning over instruction and learning through dialogue and reflection on experience, that are common to most GBA. This flexibility and adaptability across different cultures and institutions was evident at the 2019 *Game Sense for the International Coaching and Teaching Conference* held in Tokyo and the book arising from it that we both edited (Light & Curry, 2021). Up to 2019, these conferences had only been held in Australia and New Zealand but the shift to Tokyo illuminated the extent to which it has been adapted to the very different contexts outside Australia and New Zealand such as in Asia, Europe, South America and the USA (see Light & Curry, 2021). There has not been a model suggested for Game Sense with the name chosen as an accurate description of what it aims to achieve (game sense), and to distance it from schools and physical education as a way of giving it more appeal for sport coaches (Light, 2013; Pill, 2018).

The looseness, flexibility and adaptability of Game Sense can be highlighted when compared to contemporary TGfU and other structured approaches such as Tactical Games from the USA (see Griffin et al., 1997). Despite their similarities during the development of Game Sense in Australia over the 1990s there is now significant difference between TGfU and Game Sense. TGfU can now be seen as a prescriptive, education-focused model and Game Sense as a performance-focused approach that is open to interpretation by coaches and teachers.

A bottom-up approach

As a models-based teaching approach, TGfU now provides step-by-step guidance for teachers interested in implementing it, that as we have suggested can be seen as a top-down approach. Given the challenges teachers and coaches face in implementing authentic GBA in schools and community-based clubs, this approach is well justified but here, we explore an alternative, bottom-up approach.

Our use of the term bottom-up refers to learning how to teach and/or coach Game Sense from first developing a deep foundational understanding of the philosophical positions it sits upon. This understanding can then inform the range of decisions teachers and coaches make when using Game Sense during lessons/sessions or terms/seasons. In our eyes, this parallels the decision-making of students and athletes when learning through a Game Sense approach. When teaching pre-service teachers in physical education, we both focus on facilitating a conceptual understanding of the game. For example, in invasion games the core concepts are the manipulation of space and time, with us advising pre-service teachers or coaches to focus dialogue and questioning on the use of space and time when teaching invasion games. When this is understood, issues around skill execution, technique, decision-making and particularly, tactical understanding, have more meaning for learners.

It is not uncommon to see references to a teaching or coaching philosophy in the pedagogy literature as a common-sense use of the term, philosophy. It typically refers to a set of basic principles that underpin practice more than to any philosophical positions, which is our focus. Here, we dive deep into the core philosophical positions that we argue underpin the practice of Game Sense and which teachers and coaches should have a good understanding of to make the range of decisions that they have to make about teaching or coaching. Drawing on Light and Light (2021), the two positions of holism and humanism are the core foundations of Game Sense.

Game Sense focuses on the whole game instead of on separate parts of it such as technique or skill. It is very difficult, if not impossible, to focus on just tactical understanding, decision-making or anticipation without using a practice game or replicating some aspects of the game. Netball is an excellent sport to use when helping players or students learn to work off the ball, but how could you possibly enhance learning without some sort of game, or game-like activity? There are frequent references in the literature to GBAs to teaching and coaching being holistic and/or humanistic, but with ambivalence about the meaning of the terms. The number of references to holism and humanism were noted by Cassidy (2010) over a decade ago with her questioning understanding of them. In response, Light and Light (2021) provide a recent and detailed explanation of holism and humanism that we have drawn on here to suggest how they form the philosophical foundations of Game Sense for a bottom-up approach.

A holistic approach

Greek philosopher, Aristotle argued that the whole is greater than the sum of its parts but the first reference to holism was by Jan Smuts in 1926 as an approach that is commonly used in philosophy. Holism sits in contrast to reductionism which seeks to understand systems by reducing them to simpler, independent component parts (Light & Light, 2021) and which provides for a useful philosophical comparison between Game Sense and the traditional skill-drill approach to teaching and coaching.

Humanistic psychologist, Maslow's (1968) approach to education considered the entire physical, emotional, social and intellectual qualities of the learner as a whole person. In contemporary sport coaching Lombardo (1987) was one of the first to promote holistic coaching as a focus on the development of the whole athlete that encouraged athlete reflection on the subjective experience of participation. Game Sense focuses on the player as a whole person and on the game as-a-whole, which stands in contrast to the reductionist and objectivist skill-drill approach. Holistic teaching and coaching treat the learner as a living, thinking and feeling being that is reflected in the importance of relationships and social interaction in Game Sense, other GBA and Positive Pedagogy for sport coaching (see Light, 2017).

The holistic emphasis of Game Sense on the whole person and on the game as a whole is diametrically opposed to the reductionism of breaking the game into independent techniques and skills. Our use of the term 'whole person' includes recognition of the complexity of the individual learner and their inseparability from the social and cultural contexts that they live and play in. This is not to say that teachers cannot focus on a particular physical, mental or even spiritual aspect of play and experience but instead, that they cannot be completely separated from the learner's make up and experience. This is evident in how students are empowered to think, engage in dialogue and contribute to decisions about practice and the game in Game Sense. Our reference to the whole person includes the emotional, political, social, spiritual and cultural aspects of play, and of being (Light & Light, 2021).

With the aim of Game Sense teaching being to engage learners in reflection, the expression of ideas, being creative and thinking, social interaction and positive relationships are of central importance. Building positive relationships between the teacher and the students, and between the students, purposeful and productive dialogue, individual and collective reflection, having a sense or worth and belonging and caring about each other are all (or should be) common aspects of learner's experiences in a Game Sense environment.

A humanistic approach

Humanism is a philosophical system of thought and a progressive societal shift that took place over the 19th and 20th centuries as a holistic and human-centred perspective emphasising human development, self-actualisation, human values and free will (Light & Light, 2021). The humanistic movement of the 1950s and 1960s was manifested in humanistic psychology (from 1954 to 1973) as a sub-field of psychology. Maslow (see 1968) saw humanistic psychology as a progressive stance underpinned by individualism and self-actualisation (Buss, 1979) that stands in opposition to the determinism of behaviourism.

Humanistic coaching emerged in the 1980s in response to concern over reductionist coaching that dehumanised and objectified athletes with humanistic coaching emphasising the subjective nature of participation in sport (see Lombardo, 1987). This approach was very much influenced by the humanistic psychology of Maslow (1968) and Rogers (1951) that resonates with what we suggest are the underpinning pedagogical features of

Game Sense and other GBAs. For example, Rogers (1951) argued that one person cannot directly teach an individual or class directly but can effectively *facilitate* their learning. Later, Maslow (1968) argued that experience should be the focus of studying human learning and emphasised choice, creativity, values and self-realisation as important human qualities.

Although we have discussed humanism and holism separately, they are interrelated with the holistic features of Game Sense that we have suggested requiring a humanistic approach. For example, monitoring the team talks used in small-sided games and the larger team or class discussions all require a humanistic perspective on the part of the teacher or coach. Managing team talks to involve as many students as possible require empathy and sensitivity to the students in the team or group as does stopping a game with a call of 'freeze' to focus on an aspect such as awareness and the use of space with a question like 'where is the space?' The same feel for what is going on is necessary when adjusting the level of challenge for the practice games used and understanding individual engagement, or non-engagement. Teachers know full well how every student is different, and the sensitivity required to motivate and engage them all.

We encourage our pre-service teachers to develop energy and flow in the modified games used to promote enjoyment and optimise learning. This requires them tuning into the level of challenge involved in the small-sided and larger games used, with Csikszentmihalyi (1997) suggesting that achieving flow requires the learners being tested and taken to the point where they can only just meet the demands of the game and are lost in the flow. He saw this state of flow as providing optimal experience and learning and, from our experiences of teaching, it typically generates high levels of joy and fun. This is high-quality teaching that requires a humanistic approach to establish and maintain what Csikszentmihalyi (1997) called the challenge-skill balance. Teaching or coaching for flow requires a humanistic understanding of learner experience. The teacher or coach must be able to have a subjective understanding of how they are feeling, their levels of en-gagement, emotions, confidence and so on, to adjust the level of challenge and maximise both enjoyment and learning.

Conclusion

The loose and flexible nature of Game Sense encouraged us to propose the bottom-up approach that we suggest teachers, coaches and academics working in physical education and sport pedagogy can draw on for its implementation. We were also motivated by our preference for ways of learning to use Game Sense that empower teachers and coaches to develop and tailor their teaching and coaching to their dispositions and institutional and cultural environments as well as to learners and educational objectives. We want to equip them to advance and develop their ideas, creativity and ability to tune into student/athlete experiences of learning and adapt to them. As we have argued, a sound understanding of the foundational philosophic positions that Game Sense sits upon empowers teachers and coaches to make the wide range of decisions needed during each lesson or training session and/or over the term or season. For us, this is a logical suggestion that not only makes sense but is also compelling. It is, however, not without its challenges.

A prescriptive approach such as that suggested in models-based practice would be more easily implemented than what we suggest in this chapter. It can achieve its aims of guiding teachers in learning how to use Game Sense in their teaching, but through doing so, disempowers them due to its top-down approach that is results-driven and prescriptive. Too much prescription and not enough thinking can develop a shallow understanding of the pedagogical approach which, in our opinion, should be the focus.

We suggest a teaching approach that helps teachers and coaches get on top of using Game Sense by having a sound understanding of the philosophical positions it sits on and which inform its pedagogical features. Our view is that by learning from the bottom-up, teachers and coaches would be empowered by deep understanding of what Game Sense is about when making the range of decisions they must make when adopting and sometimes adapting the Game Sense approach.

References

Bunker, D. & Thorpe, R. (1982). A model for teaching games in secondary school. *Bulletin of Physical Education*, *10*, 9–16.

Buss, A. R. (1979). *A dialectical psychology*. Ardent Media.

Cassidy, T. (2010). Holism in sport coaching: beyond humanistic psychology. *International Journal of Sport Science and Coaching*, *5*(4), 439–501.

Csikszentmihalyi, M. (1997). *Finding flow: The psychology of engagement with everyday life*. Basic Books.

den Duyn, N. (1997). *Game Sense: Developing thinking player*. Australian Sports Commission.

Griffin, L. L., Mitchell, S. A. & Oslin, J. L. (1997). *Teachings sport concepts & skills: A tactical games approach for ages 7–18* (1st edition). Human Kinetics.

Huizinga, J. (1938). *Homo Ludens*. Random House.

Landi, D., Fitzpatrick, K. & McGlashan, H. (2016). Models based practices in physical education: A sociocritical reflection. *Journal of Teaching in Physical Education*, *35*(4), 400–411.

Light, R. (2004). Australian coaches' experiences of Game Sense: Opportunities and challenges. *Physical Education and Sport Pedagogy*, *9*(2), 115–132.

Light, R. (2013). *Game Sense: Pedagogy for performance, participation and enjoyment*. Routledge.

Light, R. L. (2017). *Positive pedagogy for sport coaching: Athlete centred coaching for individual sports*. Routledge.

Light, R. L. (2021). Game Sense: Its history, development and future. In R. L. Light & C. Curry (Eds.), *Game Sense for coaching and teaching* (pp. 4–12). Routledge.

Light, R. L., & Curry, C. (Eds.) (2021). *Game Sense for coaching and teaching.* Routledge.

Light, R. L., & Light, A. L. (2021). Holism and humanism: The philosophical foundation of Game Sense. In R. L. Light & C. Curry (Eds.), *Game Sense for coaching and teaching* (pp. 15–35). Routledge.

Lombardo, B. (1987). *The humanistic coach: From theory to practice.* Charles Thomas Publisher.

Mahlo, F. (1973). *Act tactique en jeu* [Tactical action in play]. Vigot.

Maslow, A. H. (1968). *Toward a psychology of being.* D Van Nostrand Company.

Mauldon, E. & Redfern, H. D. (1969). *Games teaching: A new approach for the primary school.* McDonald and Evans Ltd.

Pill, S. (2018). *Perspectives on athlete-centred coaching.* Routledge.

Rogers, C. R. (1951). *Client centred therapy: Its current practice, implications and theory.* Haughton Miffin.

Rossi, T., Fry, J. M., McNeill, M. & Tan, C. W. K. (2007). The Games concept approach (GCA) as mandated practice, Views of Singaporean teacher. *Sport, Education & Society, 12*(1), 93–111.

Smuts, J. C. (1926). *Holism and evolution.* Macmillan.

Thorpe, R. & Bunker, D. (2008). Teaching Games for Understanding – Do current developments reflect original intentions? paper presented at the fourth Teaching Games for Understanding conference, Vancouver, BC, Canada, 14-17 May.

Thorpe, R., Bunker, D. & Almond, L. (Eds.) (1986). *Rethinking game teaching.* Loughborough University of Technology.

Wade, A. (1967). *The FA guide to training and coaching.* Heinemann.

4 Immersive Scenario-Based Coaching Narratives: A Philosophical Dialogue

Ruan Jones and David Piggott

In this chapter we aim to deepen our ideas about Immersive Scenario-based Coaching Narratives (ISNs). ISNs are rooted in existential philosophical thinking (Jones & Piggott, 2020) and reflect an attempt to 'layer' existential principles over TGfU principles to create more authentic and meaningful experiences for participants (Piggott & Jones, 2020). Specifically, we aim to clarify the main principles of ISNs by illustrating how they can be applied in a youth coaching context. We have chosen to write this chapter in the form of a dialogue between the authors for two reasons. First, in common with Jones (2007), we believe more experimental writing of this nature can yield more 'interesting, believable and meaningful' material, the aim of which is to assist reflection and to support the consideration of different viewpoints. Second, we believe that the dialogue helps us to articulate more clearly and simply both the philosophical principles behind ISNs and the struggle a coach might have in attempting to apply them.

The dialogue is composed of four 'scenes' and features two main characters: Ruan (a philosopher) and Dave (a U12 basketball coach). It is constructed as a 'creative non-fiction' (Sparkes, 2002) insofar as the characters are based on our real roles, ideas and experiences and the dialogue based on our real conversations, with some exaggerations and simplifications due to space (and the need to maintain some anonymity in the examples). The scenes unfold in a way that represents the general shape of conversations we have had together over the last two years.

Scene 1: Something's missing

Dave enters the coffee shop craning his head. He spots Ruan sitting in the far corner; they exchange knowing nods. Dave then collects two cups of tea before dropping down into the chair opposite Ruan, apparently exhausted.

RJ: So, what's up? You look knackered!
DP: I'm OK. Just had a long night.
RJ: Go on.

DOI: 10.4324/9781003298298-6

DP: Well, you know Wednesday is my long coaching night. I had the U12s for three hours. The session was OK, but I couldn't sleep after. I don't think it's working how I want it to, and I just kept turning it over.

RJ: What's not working?

DP: It's the games-based stuff. I mean, it *is* working at one level: the kids seem to be having fun most of the time, they're playing a lot of basketball. Nobody asks me: "when can we play a game?" anymore. That's all fine. I've used the game form model and the curriculum model[1] – I'm happy with that. It's just ... (scratching his head and screwing up his face)

RJ: (quizzically) Just what?

DP: (looking into space) There's something missing. So, we play the games, but the intensity isn't there. The joy isn't there. Some of them – like the better lads, the talented ones – it seems it's becoming like a job to them. They're good players, they know how to play; they answer the questions, and they can apply the skills. All the stuff I write in my learning outcomes. But there's still a big difference between what they're like in practice and how they are in tournaments.

RJ: Hmm… So the lads play, but don't *play* – "it's becoming like a job". Let's break that down. What are the reasons that you think the lads play basketball, or games more generally?

DP: (smiling) So, I reckon kids play for three main reasons: first, to get better or improve, to feel competent; second, for social reasons, to be with their mates or to feel related to a team; and third, for the pure enjoyment, for the sense of freedom they get from expressing themselves through a game![2]

RJ: Sure, those are our 'classic' participation motives. I bet if you sat them all down and asked formally using a pen and paper, or a questionnaire, they'd come back with those. But, what about why *your* players play?

DP: I don't get you.

RJ: Have you ever caught an unguarded conversation among them, perhaps when they thought you weren't listening?

DP: (thinks for a moment) You know what … I have heard some say that they wish they could do the "real thing", that the games we play are just "muck-abouts". They don't muck-about – don't misunderstand me – but it's just that our games are always simplified and 'constrained' in some way or another. I just overlooked those comments to be honest, because how could game forms, in which I've given strict attention to benchmarks, be "muck abouts"?[3]

RJ: What do you think they mean by that?

DP: If I was to hazard a guess, I'd say the "real thing" is the full-adult version that they see on TV and social media: the NBA, the razzamatazz, the sounds, the kit the players wear, the buzzers beaters, the high-stakes, the drama, etc.

RJ: Do your game forms include any of these?

DP: (thinking again) … Not really. No. But those things aren't part of games-based approaches as far as I've read about it. Full-sided adult games would be chaos with these boys; there's no evidence that would work with kids.

RJ: As you point out, to my knowledge, these elements aren't 'enshrined in text', but does that mean you can't play about with them a bit?[4] Besides, you pointed out that there are other elements *associated* with the "real thing".

DP: Do you mean introduce something that is characteristic of the 'real' game? The buzzer-beaters, the high-stakes, the kit and things like that?

RJ: Yes, exactly, something that gives them the feeling or the impression of 'being there'.[5] Is that something you could introduce next time, just to take them a little closer to the real thing, even if it isn't 5v5 full court games?

DP: Well, I have a Nicola Jokic shirt at home. Whoever wears that, perhaps, is provided with some sort of super-power[6] … maybe they score double, or an assist increases the value of the shot or something?

RJ: (nodding). Why don't you try it out and tell me how you get on?

Scene 2: Being there

Dave enters the cafe, this time with a spring in his step. He walks straight past the counter and starts opening his bag as he approaches Ruan, starting the conversation before Ruan can even say 'hello' …

DP: (excitedly, pulling out a tactics board) So that thing we talked about really worked! Let me show you what we did … Okay, so look at this (showing tactics board, see Figure 4.1). I ran this last night. We worked in the 'create the attack' moment, specifically on cutting to get open away from the ball. We did a lot of 3v3 games, like normal, but I gave the Jokic shirt to the player at the top of the key. The reward system was that a basket was worth 2 points if a pass was made to a player cutting from outside to inside the key; and if the pass was made by 'Jokic' it was worth 3 points (all other baskets were worth 1 point). We've done similar games before, but this really got them super excited. I could see them really trying to get the ball back to the Jokic player and then cutting hard to get it back. The Jokic player was always trying to stay in the middle, too, just like the big man does in a game; he becomes the fulcrum of the offence.[7] The best thing, though, was the absolute joy when they got the Jokic assist. They were celebrating like crazy! Then, of course, they all wanted to wear the Jokic shirt.

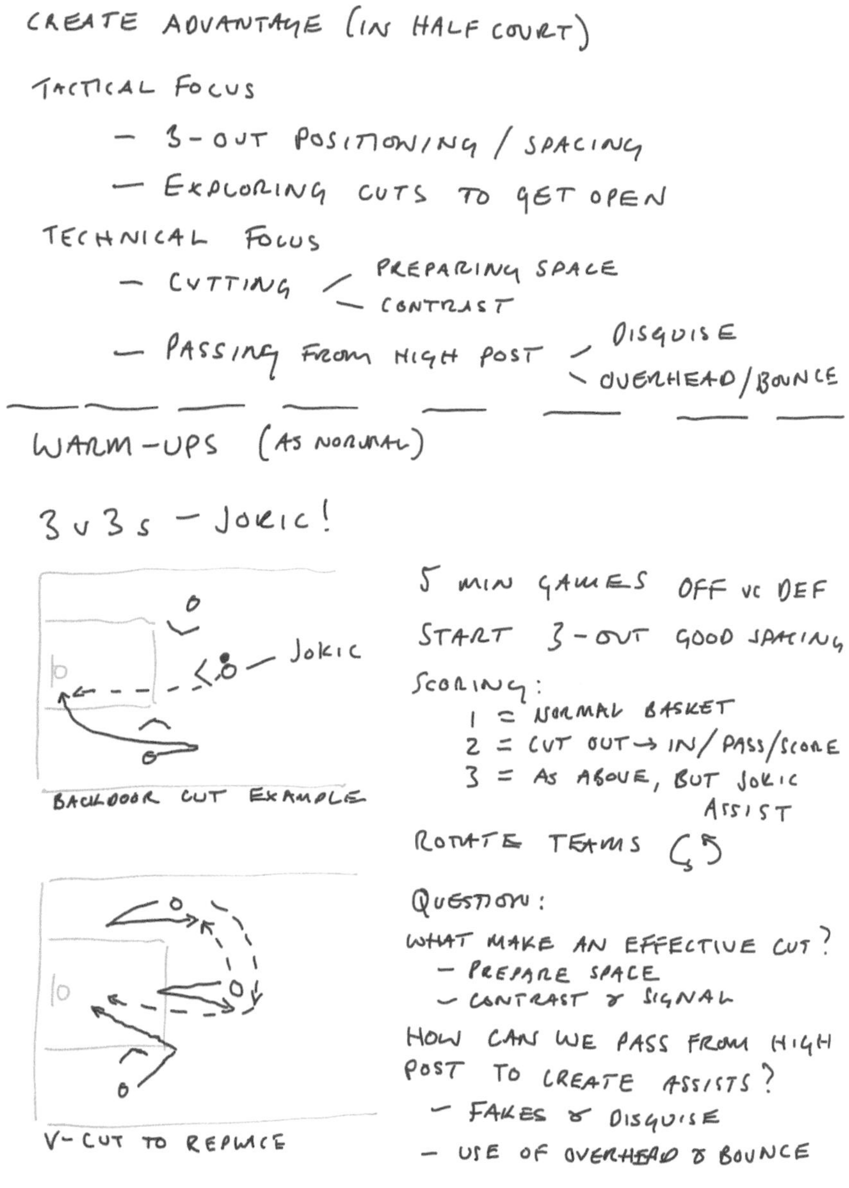

CREATE ADVANTAGE (IN HALF COURT)

TACTICAL FOCUS

 — 3-OUT POSITIONING / SPACING

 — EXPLORING CUTS TO GET OPEN

TECHNICAL FOCUS

 — CUTTING ⟋ PREPARING SPACE

  ⟍ CONTRAST

 — PASSING FROM HIGH POST ⟋ DISGUISE

  ⟍ OVERHEAD / BOUNCE

———————————————————

WARM-UPS (AS NORMAL)

3 v 3 s — JOKIC !

BACKDOOR CUT EXAMPLE

V-CUT TO REPLACE

5 MIN GAMES OFF vc DEF

START 3-OUT GOOD SPACING

SCORING :

  1 = NORMAL BASKET

  2 = CUT OUT → IN / PASS / SCORE

  3 = AS ABOVE, BUT JOKIC

  ASSIST

ROTATE TEAMS (5)

QUESTION :

WHAT MAKE AN EFFECTIVE CUT ?

 — PREPARE SPACE

 ⌣ CONTRAST & SIGNAL

HOW CAN WE PASS FROM HIGH

POST TO CREATE ASSISTS ?

 — FAKES & DISGUISE

 — USE OF OVERHEAD & BOUNCE

Figure 4.1 The Jokic shirt session plan.

RJ: You are so enthused – your body language, tone of voice, what you have to say. It would appear the 'Jokic' player has transformed the experience for them. I want to come back to this notion of 'being there', that we chatted about at the end of our last catch-up. Specifically, I want to explore how you are beginning to build this … (pausing, appearing lost in thought, then snaps back) 'world'! For want of a better word – world.

DP: If I recall, it was the world of NBA – the "real thing" – players, buzzers, sounds, spectators, tension, drama …

RJ: … and the first aspect of this world you have introduced is the Jokic shirt. When you explained the session, and showed them the Jokic shirt, what was the exact response?

DP: (quizzically) 'I want to be Jokic', yeah, quite a few said that. Why does that matter?

RJ: Quite a lot really. Did anyone say: I want to pretend to be him; I want to play him.

DP: No, but what's the big deal with what they said?

RJ: If someone is pretending, what does that immediately bring into your mind?

DP: That they are putting on a front or act, a fantasy, something is made up. Not real even?

RJ: The moment those players put on the Jokic shirt, they are not pretending to be Jokic. They are Jokic – there is nothing fantastical or make believe about it.

DP: So, the player and the game are inseparable – one creates the other?

RJ: Consider how carefully you curated the session with Jokic. In my understanding you took great care and attention placing him at the top of the key, and conditioning play through this avenue. Is that correct?

DP: Absolutely.

RJ: You didn't just throw Jokic randomly into the game?

DP: No, because it wouldn't reflect the authentic nature of what he does, the possibilities he brings into being within the game. That's who he is.

RJ: We have established, therefore, that merely wearing the shirt is not enough; the game form must reflect with precise detail the role that Jokic fulfils within the context of the game to *become* him.

DP: That was crucial. Look, I want to keep going with building this 'world' as you called it. How can I continue with this?

RJ: You tell me – you have mentioned plenty.

DP: I have a tournament this week, and I could give greater attention to all those things that provide the drama, anxiety or joy within the tournament.

RJ: Why is that?

DP: Because these are what makes everything so real – just like the Jokic shirt.

RJ: (raises an eyebrow, nodding) excellent I look forward to our next conversation already.

Scene 3: The buzzer beater

Ruan walks into the cafe and notices that Dave is already there with a tactics board at the ready and what looks like a little book full of notes. He eagerly beckons Ruan over.

DP: (buzzing with excitement) I need to tell you about the weekend: we had a great tournament! I've had loads of emails from parents since. It was the first one since Covid where we were allowed to have spectators again, so it was super loud in the gym. To top it all off, one of the lads – Isaac – hit an amazing 3-point buzzer beater to win in the final game. We were down 2 and he launched the shot as the buzzer sounded. It was like the ball was in the air for what felt like a minute. Then it rattled and went down. The place exploded! You should have seen the look on his face.

RJ: Sounds fantastic. And you had games with referees and shot clocks and scoreboards and so on?

DP: Yes, we wanted to try to make it as real as possible, like we discussed, to help the lads learn what it will feel like when they go into national league basketball next year.

RJ: Hmmm ... 'Feel' is an interesting choice of word there ...

DP: Yes, well the game *feels* very different when you can see the score and the time, and the 24-second shot clock is ticking down on every possession. Different to practice, that is.

RJ: So, the buzzers and the shot clock that counts down to that dreaded sound are an indelible part of the real game then?

DP: Yep, it all leads to that. There is no way out, no escape. You must face it.

RJ: That's very profound. Philosophical even.

DP: It's true though. The players will find themselves in all sorts of situations, and to add to that there is a clock counting down to the buzzer that will ultimately end their turn on attack, or the game.

RJ: Put it like that, and I feel a little anxious!

DP: Yes, but that's necessary, isn't it? I experienced that delirium of the buzzer beater, and the panic of getting a shot in. I was reflecting on what you said last time and realised that we hardly ever do this in practice.

RJ: Hardly ever do what?

DP: Well, in most practices, most of those features – the score, the time, the consequences – aren't present. But in the game, all those things will impact your decision-making.[8] So that's something I wanted to bounce off you. In the spirit of our discussion about the 'real thing', I assume these are things that we should layer into practice, too? Maybe by 'throwing' them into a situation – like the one Isaac was in, with the score and the time counting down – and saying: "Now get out of that!"[9]

RJ: Go on ...

DP: Umm, well I could re-present similar scenarios that they would have faced during tournament play, "under the lights" so to speak, in which they face a specific problem – not abstract but lived or very real – and the team navigate their way out by resolving the problem.[10] Along the way I want to build some level of discomfort or tension, culminating in resolution, relief, joy and elation.

RJ: (smiling wryly) You are making U12 basketball sound like a fight for survival.

DP: It does a bit, is that OK for under-12s to experience do you think?

RJ: Well, it sounds to me like what you're proposing is very sensible. Isn't it just exposing them more frequently to situations that are 'real' in how they *feel*, tapping into powerful emotional experiences, like hitting 'buzzer beaters', to connect them to the game and to help them learn the game, in all its glory?

DP: Yes, but … there are some who might say we're putting them under too much pressure, too early. And if we always play with a score and a time there are therefore winners and losers, which can be a problem if someone is always on the losing side. I guess it's back to what we discussed last week about 'feeling competent' and motivation.

RJ: Ah, but I'm sure a coach of your experience is well capable of avoiding that. Wasn't it the great basketball coach, John Wooden, who redefined success as nothing to do with winning?

DP: Yes, you're right. Wooden always taught that success was 'peace of mind achieved in knowing you gave your best effort', or something to that effect. I just have to be really clear that success and failure are not related to winning and losing.[11] Success, for us, is individual improvement, because we're a talent development programme.

RJ: (looking at his watch) Yes, that sounds sensible. Look, I'd love to talk more but I must go. Same time next week maybe?

DP: Sure!

Scene 4: Facing into it

Dave and Ruan meet the following week, in the usual place, with Dave once again animated and eager to share his thinking with Ruan.

RJ: (smiling) Ah, I see you're ready for me again …

DP: (pulling out tactics board) Well because we were cut a bit short last week, I went straight home and tried to write out a plan, based on what we'd discussed, then delivered it last night. I had this idea of 'layering' up the principles, adding to my usual TGfU repertoire, as it were (showing the plan to RJ – see Figure 4.2).

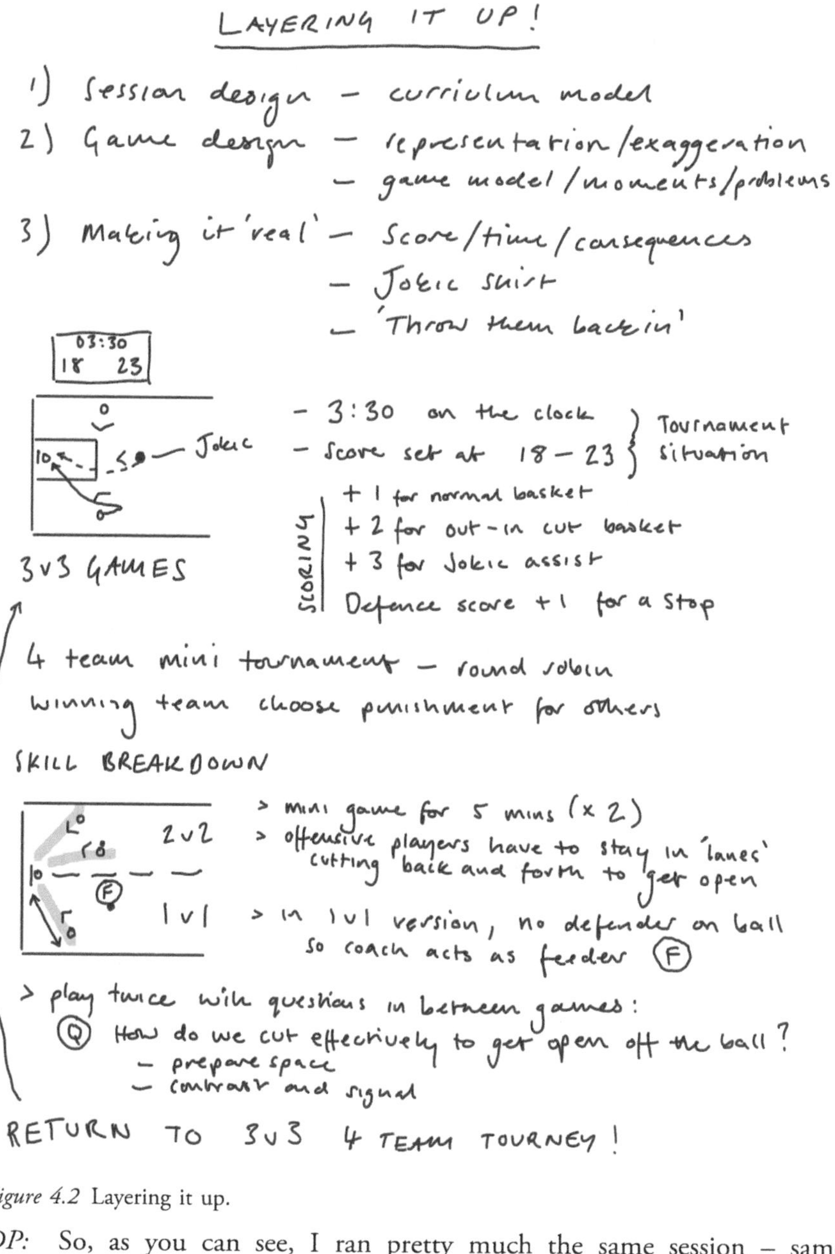

LAYERING IT UP!

1) Session design — curriculum model
2) Game design — representation/exaggeration
   — game model/moments/problems
3) Making it 'real' — score/time/consequences
   — Jokic shirt
   — 'Throw them back in'

03:30
18 23

3v3 GAMES

- 3:30 on the clock ⎫ Tournament
- Score set at 18 – 23 ⎬ situation

SCORING
+ 1 for normal basket
+ 2 for out-in cut basket
+ 3 for Jokic assist
Defence score +1 for a stop

4 team mini tournament — round robin
winning team choose punishment for others

SKILL BREAKDOWN

2v2 > mini game for 5 mins (x 2)
     > offensive players have to stay in 'lanes'
       cutting back and forth to 'get open'
1v1 > in 1v1 version, no defender on ball
       so coach acts as feeder (F)

> play twice with questions in between games:
   (Q) How do we cut effectively to get open off the ball?
   — prepare space
   — contrast and signal

RETURN TO 3v3 4 TEAM TOURNEY!

Figure 4.2 Layering it up.

DP: So, as you can see, I ran pretty much the same session – same
objectives, same structure, same basic games with the Jokic shirt again –
but this time I layered on the tournament experience stuff (tapping
point 3 on the plan). Instead of just playing games, we ran a four team

round robin; we got out the scoreboard and set the exact time and score when we started our big comeback in last week's tournament: down 18–23 with 3:30 left. This was the basis of each game: we were 'throwing them back in' to that situation. Then, finally, I added consequences, or the option for the winning team to choose a punishment for the others.

RJ: Fantastic! And tell me: how did the boys respond?

DP: It took a little while to get used to, and of the first three games of the round robin nobody got close to winning. But in the fourth game we got a buzzer-beater situation and they just missed, so that brought back all the excitement. The final two games were won in the final seconds and full of all the things we spoke about: the dread and panic as they scrambled plays in the final seconds; the desperate glances at the clock, all shouting and pointing; the elation of the winning shot going in. It was incredible!

RJ: And it seems to me it has had an invigorating effect of you, too! I remember when we first started discussing this and you were rather down. Now you're alive with enthusiasm. You seem much more like your authentic self; like you're truly following your values as a coach.

DP: You're right. It was a genuine pleasure to be there last night. There was real emotion in the gym, and, with that, *real* decisions, and *real* skill development.[12] I managed to keep the focus on getting better – by having two rounds of games, with the goal of beating your previous score – which is what the programme is all about. But more than that, I just felt *alive*: like 'this is why I'm here', if you know what I mean?

RJ: (smiling knowingly) Indeed I do, my friend.

Notes

1 In our experience, young coaches value and, with effort, can apply the broad session design process identified in the TGfU curriculum model (Thorpe et al., 1986). For many this can be a revolutionary or 'threshold' concept (Meyer & Land, 2006) leading to a transformation in practice. We have also found TGfU principles to be useful in the identification of the core tactical problems of game forms, supporting the development of comprehensive medium- to long-term plans or curricula (Cf. Mitchell et al., 2013).

2 Basic psychological needs theory predicts that players will become motivated if their basic psychological needs – for competence, autonomy and relatedness – are met through participation in an activity. The role TGfU can play in meeting these needs has been well explored in recent years (Gil-Arias et al., 2021).

3 Authoritative texts have offered guidelines or 'benchmarks' explaining how to faithfully apply (with a high degree of 'validity') a TGfU approach (Metzler, 2011). In this example, we would argue that DP is already applying the 'full version' of TGfU (O'Leary, 2016), insofar as all benchmarks are being met.

4 Casey et al. (2021) advocate for a move from practice (something fixed and essential) to practising (something temporal, in development) in the application of pedagogical models.

5 Drawing on the fundamental concept of Martin Heidegger's (1927/1962) existential philosophy – *Dasein*. Literally translated as 'there being'. This phrase encapsulates the experience of human being that is situated in a particular time and place.

6 Amy Price has previously articulated fruitful connections between TGfU principles and digital video game concepts like power-ups, pauses and levelling (Price, 2021). Nicola Jokic is currently the NBA's most valuable player (in 2020/21 and 2021/22) and is known for his pinpoint passing and flashy assists.

7 The major pedagogical principles of representation and tactical complexity inform this design, with a 3v3 half court simplifying the game for U12s, and with the scoring condition supporting the emergence of desirable representative behaviour, in this case cutting from wing to basket (the 'backdoor' cut) with a pass from the 'high post' position.

8 Clive Pope (2005) was one of the first scholars to notice that there is an important *affective* dimension to decision-making in games, a consideration that was absent from the original TGfU curriculum model.

9 Being thrown into the middle of a game situation in this respect can be viewed as a real or factual decision by the coach or teacher. However, Heidegger (1927/1962) used the phrase *geworfenheit* – 'thrownness' – to characterise the struggles of existence that we must face daily. Does one put things off, 'follow the crowd' and prevaricate or face uncomfortable choices with resoluteness and determination. We contend that games too can provide opportunities for these moments of existential meaning (see Arnold, 1979; Jones et al., 2014).

10 There is a distinction here between a general game problem, such as 'how do we create an advantage?', which we might use to create a modified game, and a specific experiential problem that might arise in a given context, with a specific score, time, opposition, and so on.

11 These principles are borrowed from John Wooden's *Pyramid of Success* (Wooden & Carty, 2010) and Ronald Smith and Frank Smoll's seminal work on motivation in youth sport (e.g., Smoll & Smith, 2003).

12 Headrick and colleagues (2015) note that emotions are an important *perceptual* component in the perception-action cycle when acquiring expertise, and therefore need to be *represented* through practice environments.

References

Arnold, P. (1979). *Meaning in movement, sport and physical education.* Heinemann.

Casey, A., MacPhail, A., Larsson, H. & Quennerstedt, M. (2021). Between hope and happening: Problematizing the M and the P in models-based practice. *Physical Education and Sport Pedagogy, 26*(2), 111–122.

Gil-Arias, A., Harvey, S., Garcia-Herreros, F., Gonzalez-Villora, S., Praxades, A. & Moreno, A. (2021). Effect of a hybrid TGfU/Sport Education unit on elementary students' self-determined motivation in physical education. *European Physical Education Review, 27*(2), 366–383.

Headrick, J., Renshaw, I., Davids, K., Pinder, R. & Araujo, D. (2015). The dynamics of expertise acquisition in sport: the role of affective learning design. *Psychology of Sport and Exercise, 16,* 83–90.

Heidegger, M. (1927/1962). *Being and time* (trans. Macquarrie and Robinson). SCM Press.

Jones, R. (2007). Coaching redefined: an everyday pedagogical endeavour. *Sport, Education and Society, 12*(2), 159–173.

Jones, R., Harvey, S. & Kirk, D. (2014). Everything is at stake; yet nothing is at stake: exploring meaning making in game-centred approaches. *Sport, Education and Society, 21,* 888–906.

Jones R. & Piggott, D. (2020). Because we're here lad, and nobody else. Just us. In S. Pill, (Ed.), *Perspectives on games-based coaching* (pp. 35–44). Routledge.

Metzler, M. (2011). *Instructional models for physical education*. Holcomb Hathaway.

Meyer, J. & Land, R. (2006). *Overcoming barriers to student understanding: threshold concepts and troublesome knowledge*. Routledge.

Mitchell, S., Oslin, J. & Griffin, L. (2013). *Teaching sports concepts and skills: a tactical games approach* (3rd ed). Human Kinetics.

O'Leary, N. (2016). Learning informally to use the 'full version' of teaching games for understanding. *European Physical Education Review, 22*(1), 3–22.

Piggott, D. & Jones, R. (2020). The practical application of immersive game-based narratives. In S. Pill (Ed.), *Perspectives on games-based coaching* (pp. 45–56). Routledge.

Pope, C. (2005). Once more with feeling: affect and playing with the TGfU model. *Physical Education and Sport Pedagogy, 10*(3), 271–286.

Price, A. (2021). Digital video games as a games-based coaching tool. In S. Pill (Ed.), *Perspectives on games-based coaching* (pp. 11–22). Routledge.

Smoll, F. & Smith, R. (2003). Athletes first, winning second. *Soccer Journal, 48*, 19–23.

Sparkes, A. (2002). *Telling tales in sport and physical activity*. Human Kinetics.

Thorpe, R., Bunker, D. & Almond, L. (1986). *Rethinking games teaching*. Loughborough University.

Wooden, J., & Carty, J. (2010). *Coach Wooden's pyramid of success: Building blocks for a better life*. Gospel Light.

5 Game Insight: A Game-Based Approach with Emphasis on Acknowledging and Addressing Differences between Players' Abilities

Gwen Weeldenburg, Lars Borghouts,
Enrico Zondag and Frank de Kok

Creating a learning environment in which all players can gain positive experiences, improve their game skills, and deepen their understanding of game tactics and strategies, is a complex task (Lebed, 2022). Especially given the considerable heterogeneity in the psychomotor, cognitive, and affective skills of students within physical education (PE) classes, there is a constant need for differentiation and modification of games to meet the abilities of individual players. Therefore, based on the philosophy and principles of the Teaching Games for Understanding concept (Bunker & Thorpe, 1982) and other game-based approaches (e.g., Tactical Games model and Game Sense approach), the Game Insight (GI) approach (Weeldenburg et al., 2016, 2020) and the corresponding curriculum model (see Figure 5.1) were developed with an emphasis on acknowledging and addressing differences between players. To enhance players' motivation and learning, it is crucial to confront them with challenging, yet achievable learning tasks in which they perceive a sense of effectiveness (Ryan & Deci, 2017). Therefore, the GI approach uses the metaphor of the green, blue, red, and black ski slopes to provide PE teachers with a framework that supports them in designing and teaching meaningful game activities in which the players' differing abilities and needs are met. The green game slope represents the least complex game context within this framework, whereas the black game slope represents the most complex game context for players to apply specific game skills. To design meaningful and effective green, blue, red, or black game slope activities, the insights and principles of the constraints-led approach (Newell, 1986) are used, which is underpinned by the theoretical framework of ecological dynamics (Chow et al., 2021). This nonlinear pedagogical approach articulates that movement skill acquisition occurs through the constantly interacting individual, environmental, and task constraints (Renshaw & Chow, 2018). By modifying the learning environment and playing conditions the PE teacher can implicitly shape and enforce specific player behaviour. Moreover, the modification of the

DOI: 10.4324/9781003298298-7

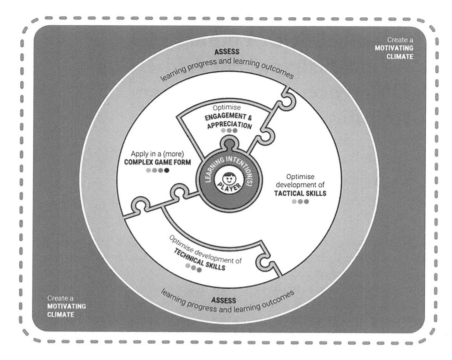

Figure 5.1 The didactical components within the Game Insight curriculum model. (With permission from Weeldenburg et al., 2020.)

constraints enables the teacher to design more complex or less complex game activities (i.e., green, blue, red, or black game slope activities) and thus address the variety in players' abilities and needs.

In the following paragraphs, the didactical components of the GI curriculum model (see Figure 5.1) will be explained and illustrated through practical examples of small-sided game activities of different complexity levels, using the game slope concept. The examples will focus on invasion games, particularly rugby. Additional information and examples regarding other game categories (i.e., net/wall games, striking/fielding games, and target games) can be accessed on the website www.routledge.com/9781032287294.

Determine learning intentions and success criteria

A teacher can only make meaningful and purposeful decisions and modifications when they are guided by clearly defined learning intentions. For this reason, the didactical component 'learning intentions', together with 'player', is positioned in the centre of the GI curriculum model (see Figure 5.1). To enable intentional learning and apply relevant and effective modifications, it is vital to make the learning intentions explicit at the outset of the learning process and to translate them into success criteria. The importance of clarifying intentions and goals for students learning and motivation has been acknowledged by several scholars (e.g., Hattie & Timperley, 2007; Shute, 2008). At the same time, these learning intentions and success criteria guide the decision-making of the teacher within the teaching process and form the basis for providing players with relevant information and suggestions during the learning process on how to improve and close the gap between current and intended game behaviour.

To ensure inclusivity within PE, the learning intentions and success criteria need to be defined broadly enough. In the GI approach, the learning intentions are defined based on holistic 'game challenges' that players face, which are particular to playing an invasion, net/wall, striking/fielding, or target game. Each game challenge is operationalised into success criteria and into game principles defined as 'if-then rules' (see Table 5.1). These 'if-then rules' are principles in which specific game situations are combined with optimal decisions. This information provides teachers with a framework through which they can intentionally design and teach games that facilitate the development of players' tactical knowledge and understanding. It has been suggested that this form of explicit learning is effective, especially in high-complexity game situations (Raab, 2003; Votsis et al., 2009).

For the operationalisation of the game challenges within other game categories see the website www.routledge.com/9781032287294.

Optimise engagement and appreciation

To foster engagement, it is suggested to provide players with meaningful, fun, and exciting learning activities in which their initiative-taking is supported (Reeve, 2006). In line with the game-based approach philosophy, the learning process of players should, therefore, begin with active gameplay rather than with practising techniques that have no meaning for players at that moment. Through participation in challenging and fun game forms where players are frequently confronted with the game challenge that was defined as the learning intention, they gain positive experiences that nurture their appreciation for the (complexity of the) game and understanding of the game intentions and rules. Thus, it is important to provide players with game activities within players' individual 'zone of proximal development' (Vygotsky, 1978). To nurture individual players' feelings of competence, it is imperative to differentiate by providing players with multi-level (i.e., green, blue, red, or black) game forms (Sproule et al., 2011). Games that involve competition and decision-making, and are modified to suit the level of experience and abilities of the players concerning the defined learning intention. For example (see Table 5.2), keeping possession of the ball and passing a volleyball in a 2 plus 1 versus 2 game form (i.e., 'colour ball green') is easier and therefore more appropriate for less skilful players, than in a 3 versus

Table 5.1 Operationalisation of learning intentions into game challenges for invasion games

INVASION GAMES

Players' Role	Game Challenge	Success Criteria	Game Principles	
			If ...	Then ...
Offender	**Keeping ball possession and passing the ball**	Shielding the ball	*If your opponent has a chance to take the ball from you ...*	*... then shield the ball by placing your body between the ball and the opponent.*
		Scanning the field	*If you are in possession of the ball ...*	*... then constantly look over the ball to determine the position of your teammates and opponents.*
		Playing a receivable pass	*If ball loss is imminent or your teammate is in a better position ...*	*... then pass the ball, tailoring the speed and direction of the ball to the space and skills of your teammate.*
	Moving and positioning to receive the ball	Creating a triangular position	*If your teammate has possession of the ball ...*	*... then create together with a teammate two passing lines for your teammate in ball possession.*
		Moving from the defender	*If your teammate is ready to play the ball ...*	*... then move quickly from the defender and 'ask for the ball'.*
		Catching the ball	*If the ball is passed to you by your teammate ...*	*... then get in the line of the ball and make 'soft' contact by moving (your body parts) in the direction of the ball's trajectory.*
	Attempting to score	Moving into a promising field position	*If your teammate in ball possession is (almost) ready to pass and there is an open space near the goal ...*	*... then effectively move away from your direct opponent and 'ask' the ball in a promising position near the goal.*
		'Attacking' the goal	*If you have ball possession and the line to the goal is open ...*	*... then approach the goal as quickly as possible into a promising scoring position and make a goal attempt.*

		Shooting	If you can't get closer to the goal and a clear shot can be taken ...	... then aim and shoot the ball in a dynamic balance to the goal.
Defender	**Preventing passing**	Supporting	If a teammate of your direct opponent is in ball possession ...	... then move to the (help) side where the ball is located, without losing sight of your direct opponent.
		Covering	If the player in ball possession is more threatening towards the goal than your direct opponent ...	... then take a central position in the space between the goal, your direct opponent, and the player in ball possession
		Intercepting the ball	If the ball is passed between opponents and the ball is within your reach ...	... then quickly get into the ball's trajectory and intercept the ball.
	Preventing scoring	Guarding	If your direct opponent has ball possession and is (almost) in a promising scoring position ...	... then reduce the distance to your opponent with the ball and increase the pressure.
		Determining movement direction	If your direct opponent in ball possession does not try to dribble past you ...	... then keep your opponent in front of you and force the player further from the goal or to pass the ball.
		Capturing the ball	If the ball of your direct opponent is within reach and passing is made impossible ...	... then suddenly but in a controlled manner, step in and capture the ball.

Note: 'ball' can also refer to any other playing object.

Table 5.2 Example of small-sided game activities of different complexity levels focusing on optimising engagement and appreciation

OPTIMISE ENGAGEMENT & APPRECIATION

Through participation in meaningful, challenging and fun game forms where players are frequently confronted with the game challenge defined as learning intention, the players gain positive experiences that nurture their engagement and appreciation for the (complexity of the) game and understanding of the game intentions and rules.

● **Colour Ball Green (2 + 1 v 2)**

Playing rules

- The offending team needs 3 successful passes to gain 'the right to score'. The defending players try to intercept the ball.
- At the third successful pass of the offending team, the coach calls a side-line colour (i.e., yellow, green, blue, or red) where all offending players must position themselves as quickly as possible.
- The offending players now try to score by grounding the ball behind the opposite line in max. 5 passes.
- The defending players try to prevent scoring by interception of the ball and stopping the offensive player in ball possession from moving by a 'touch' on the hips with both hands.
- When 'touched' the offensive player has to pass the ball.

Organisational guidelines

- Dimension playing field: 10 × 10 metres.
- Mark the sidelines with four different coloured cones.
- Play with a volleyball or soccer ball.
- Switch roles after a score or 5 attempts to score.

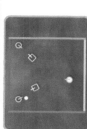

● **Colour Ball Blue (2 + 1 v 2)**

Playing rules

- Same rules as 'colour ball green' with the addition:
- Once the 'right to score' is gained, forward passing is no longer permitted for the offending team.

Organisational guidelines

- Same guidelines as 'colour ball green' with the addition:
- Switch roles also when the ball has been passed forward.

● **Colour Ball Red (3 v 3)**

Playing rules

- Same rules as 'colour ball blue'.

Organisational guidelines

- Same guidelines as 'colour ball blue' with the addition:
- Play with a rugby ball.

3 game form using a rugby ball and forward passing prohibited (i.e., 'colour ball red').

For the complete example see the website www.routledge.com/97810 32287294.

Optimise the development of tactical skills

Once the players are actively involved in the learning activities and have gained meaningful experiences and game appreciation within a range of authentic game forms, the focus in the curriculum model will shift toward optimising the development of tactical skills (see Figure 5.1). These skills can be defined as knowledge about in-game adaptions and decision-making activities within the game (Elferink-Gemser et al., 2010). Players become tactically aware by knowing *what, when,* and *why* to do in certain complex game situations, empowering them to make better decisions and actions in the game to gain an advantage over the opponents (Martens, 2012). When playing games, the tactical skills will continuously interact with the technical skills of the player, and therefore they will affect, restrict, or strengthen each other. However, if players have no idea of the intention of the game and lack basic tactical skills (e.g., understanding of favourable field positions and promising actions), it is not particularly meaningful for players to provide them with rules and extensive verbal instructions on how to execute a particular technical skill. After all, explicit knowledge about the technical skill execution of catching and throwing a playing object within an invasion game, for example, only becomes meaningful for players when they first succeed in getting in position in time to receive the playing object at all. Players will develop their technical skills implicitly, through playing games. To promote and support tactical learning, however, the technical skill level of players mustn't impede successful participation in the game activity. Therefore, the game form should be modified to suit players' technical skill ability. The application of the pedagogical principles of 'representation' and 'exaggeration' (Stolz & Pill, 2014) and the 'if-then rules' (see Table 5.1) allow the teacher to design authentic game activities of variable complexity, with specific tactical elements of the game highlighted, and where the prerequisite technical skills are reduced. In the following example (see Table 5.3), the environment is adjusted so that the tactical challenge of 'keeping possession of the ball' by the offensive player is highlighted and is less difficult (i.e., 'hot and cold potato green') or more difficult (i.e., 'hot and cold potato red') to address.

For the complete example see the website www.routledge.com/978103 2287294.

Optimise the development of technical skills

Technical skills refer to actions involving a specific task or goal that require the coordination of multiple motor competencies relative to context and time

Table 5.3 Example of small-sided game activities of different complexity levels focusing on optimising the development of tactical skills

OPTIMISE THE DEVELOPMENT OF TACTICAL SKILLS

Through participation in meaningful game forms where players are frequently confronted with the tactical elements of the game challenge defined as learning intention, the players gain learning experiences that strengthen their tactical skills.

● Hot & Cold Potato Green (2 + 1 v 2)

Playing rules

- Each time the offending team completes 5 successful passes in a row, without dropping the ball on the floor, they score 1 point.
- The defending players try to intercept the passes or grab the ball from the hands of an offending player.
- Ball possession of an offending player is restricted to 3 seconds maximum (quick passing and count out loud).
- As soon as the coach calls 'cold potato' the player in ball possession must hold and protect the ball for a minimum of 5 seconds before being allowed to pass the ball to a teammate and the 'potato' becomes 'hot' again.

Organisational guidelines

- Dimension playing field: 8 × 8 metres.
- Play with a volleyball or soccer ball.
- Switch roles after 5 points, an interception or when the ball is dropped on the floor.

● Hot & Cold Potato Blue (2 + 1 v 2)

Playing rules

- Same rules as 'hot & cold potato green' with the addition:
- Passing *over* defending players is no longer permitted
- The defending team can score bonus points by pushing the player in ball possession (guided) beyond one of the sidelines in the 'cold phase'.

Organisational guidelines

- Same guidelines as 'hot & cold potato green' with the addition:
- Play with a rugby ball
- Switch roles when the ball is passed *over a* defending player or the offensive player in ball possession is pushed beyond a sideline.

● Hot & Cold Potato Red (3 v 3)

Playing rules

- Same rules as 'hot & cold potato blue'.

Organisational guidelines

- Same guidelines as 'hot & cold potato blue' with the addition:
- Play with a rugby ball XXL.

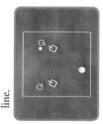

(Breivik, 2016). In the domain of games, unlike for example the domain of gymnastics, these skills are not an end in themselves, but a means to the execution of appropriate tactics within certain game situations. Therefore, these technical skills only become meaningful for players within game contexts in which they are related to tactical skills (i.e., decision-making activities) rather than in isolated technical drill exercises. They become even more meaningful and relevant for players when they experience within the game that their technical skills limit their tactical solutions and decisions. At that moment, the improvement of technical skills can be explicitly emphasised. To design appropriate learning activities and environments for the improvement of technical skills, one needs to acknowledge that movement skill acquisition occurs based on the interplay of numerous interacting individual, environmental, and task constraints (Renshaw & Chow, 2018). Moreover, given the differences in players' body structures, fitness levels, motor skill abilities, motivation, and anxiety (i.e., individual constraints) each player will use distinct strategies to address movement problems while playing games, leading to specific adaptations and variability in movement patterns (Davids et al., 2006). Consequently, movement patterns could differ between players and these differences should be considered functional as each player seeks to achieve a task in their own way. The teacher's role is to identify and manipulate the key constraints within the learning context in order to optimise players' technical skill development and facilitate the emergence of functional movement patterns in different game situations.

Games can be seen as open-skill sports and complex dynamic systems in which multiple sources of information constantly influence the players' actions and decisions. Technical skills are mostly performed in unpredictable environments and involve ongoing adaptability (Duarte et al., 2012; Wang et al., 2013). Therefore, it is suggested to situate technical skill practice also in unpredictable and complex contexts, rather than in isolated skill drill situations which lack decision-making actions (Machado et al., 2018). To maintain skill performance in these complex game situations, prevent a heavy load on working memory resources, and make technical motor skills more robust and less reliant on declarative knowledge, it is suggested to use implicit rather than explicit instruction-based learning methods (Farrow et al., 2013; Raab et al., 2016). Accordingly, the teacher should minimise the use of explicit rules and verbal instruction on how to execute a particular technical skill or movement and instead distract players' attention by using secondary stimuli to have them develop procedural knowledge without depending on working memory processes (Lola & Tzetzis, 2020; Votsis et al., 2009).

Based on the learning intention 'keeping possession of the ball and passing the ball', in the following example, players are provided with meaningful, game-like, and dual-task situations. Explicit technical instruction on how to pass the ball is reduced to a minimum, and the context implicitly provide players with relevant information and procedural knowledge. Some players will already be challenged by having to pass the

Table 5.4 Example of small-sided game activities of different complexity levels focusing on optimising the development of technical skills

OPTIMISE THE DEVELOPMENT OF TECHNICAL SKILLS

Through participation in meaningful learning activities where players are frequently confronted with the technical elements of the game challenge defined as learning intention, the players gain learning experiences that strengthen their technical skills.

● Zone Ball Green (2 & 2)

Playing rules

- Each time the two offending players can get across to the other side without dropping the ball on the ground, they score 1 point.
- In each zone, they must pass the ball at least once. Only backward passing is permitted.
- When the players get across to the other side or dropped the ball, they walk back through the centre of the playing field as 'distractors'. Two new players start crossing to the other side.

Organisational guidelines

- Dimension playing field: 12 × 5 metres.
- Play with a rugby ball.

● Zone Ball Blue (2 & 2)

Playing rules

- Same rules as 'zone ball green' with the addition:
- The two players who walk back through the centre of the playing field from now on try to intercept or tip the ball away from the offensive players while moving forward in a straight line.

Organisational guidelines

- Same guidelines as 'zone ball green'.

● Zone Ball Red (2 v 2)

Playing rules

- Same rules as 'zone ball blue with the addition:
- Two defending players are now positioned in two different zones and try to intercept the ball within their own zone.

Organisational guidelines

- Same guidelines as 'zone ball blue' with the addition:
- After 5 interceptions the defending players become offending players again, and two other offending players become defending players.

ball successfully within the 'Zone Ball Green' activity (see Table 5.4), whereas others, more skilful players, need more complexity (e.g., 'Zone Ball Red') for meaningful learning.

For the complete example see the website www.routledge.com/9781032287294.

Apply skills in a (more) complex game form

By applying the strategy of part practice in which the emphasis is placed on a particular (technical or tactical) element of the more advanced game, the cognitive and motor demands placed on players can be reduced (Magill & Anderson, 2013; Schmidt & Wrisberg, 2000). For optimal learning, the practice must be aligned with the characteristics of the skill and environment, and the abilities of the players (Newell, 1991). The skill of passing the ball in basketball, for example, cannot be functionally learned by isolating the skill from its intention (i.e., placing the ball in the hands of a teammate) and game-like elements such as time and the position of the direct opponent. Neither helpful is practising different components of the technical skill (e.g., aiming, ball release, and foot placement) separately (Fontana et al., 2009; Schmidt & Lee, 2014). Additionally, a potential threat of this so-called part practice is that players may lose sight of the need, intention, and ultimate goal of the practice, thereby decreasing their engagement. To maintain and optimise active involvement, appreciation, enjoyment, and understanding during the learning process, the players, therefore, should be regularly confronted with authentic games that progressively become more complex. This explains the emergence of the black game slope in this particular didactical component of the GI curriculum model (see Figure 5.1). Players who started their learning process within the game from 'colour ball green', 'colour ball blue', or 'colour ball red', can respectively be confronted with the 'colour ball blue', 'colour ball red', or 'colour ball black' game form in this phase (see Table 5.5).

For the complete example see the website www.routledge.com/9781032287294.

Assess learning progress and learning outcomes

Assessment is an integral part of the teaching and learning process. For an effective (games) curriculum, it is imperative that learning intentions, learning activities, and assessment activities are aligned. This constructive alignment (Biggs, 1996) may seem obvious, but research has shown that in PE it is often suboptimal (Borghouts et al., 2017). As we have seen, the game challenge 'keeping possession of the ball and passing the ball' can be translated into success criteria such as 'shielding the ball by placing the body between the ball and the opponent'. If the focus of the learning activities has been to optimise the development of these skills, it would be illogical (and

Table 5.5 Example of small-sided game activities of different complexity levels focusing on applying skills in a (more) complex game form

APPLY IN A (MORE) COMPLEX GAME FORM

Confront players regularly with meaningful game activities that progressively become more complex to maintain and optimise their active involvement, appreciation, enjoyment, and game understanding during the learning process.

● **Colour Ball Green (2 + 1 v 2)**

See 'optimise engagement & appreciation' for playing rules and organisational guidelines.

● **Colour Ball Blue (2 + 1 v 2)**

See 'optimise engagement & appreciation' for playing rules and organisational guidelines.

● **Colour Ball Red (3 v 3)**

See 'optimise engagement & appreciation' for playing rules and organisational guidelines.

● **Colour Ball Black (4 v 4)**

Playing rules

- The offending team needs 3 successful passes to gain 'the right to score'. The defending players try to intercept the ball.
- At the third successful pass of the offending team, the coach calls a side-line colour (i.e., yellow, green, blue or red) where all offending players must position themselves as quickly as possible.
- The offending players now try to score by grounding the ball behind the opposite line in max. 5 passes.
- Only backward passing is permitted.
- The defending players try to prevent scoring by interception of the ball and stopping the offensive player in ball possession from moving by a 'touch' on the hips with both hands.
- When 'touched' the offensive player has to pass the ball.

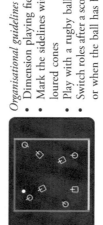

Organisational guidelines

- Dimension playing field: 10 × 10 metres
- Mark the sidelines with four different coloured cones
- Play with a rugby ball
- Switch roles after a score, 5 attempts to score, or when the ball has been passed forward.

unfair) to place the emphasis on the technical skills of catching during assessment activities. In that case, the curriculum would be 'misaligned'. Moreover, assessment should not only serve the purpose of end-of-process evaluation (assessment *of* learning) but also be used to evaluate and support the ongoing learning process (assessment *for* learning) (Griffith, 2008). Assessment for learning (Black & Wiliam, 1998) is considered one of the most powerful didactical tools available to teachers (Hattie & Timperley, 2007). The emphasis the GI approach places on differentiation and modification of the learning environment to suit the needs and abilities of all players should therefore also extend to the assessment process. Just as students will have been able to develop their skills in situations of variable complexity, so will they be allowed to show their level of proficiency on different game slopes. This 'adaptive assessment' leaves a choice to students enabling them to attain the learning intentions and accompanying success criteria. Supporting feelings of competence and autonomy, this approach to assessment is believed to foster desirable, autonomous forms of motivation (Slingerland et al., 2017).

Create a motivating learning climate

The GI approach is rooted in motivational theory since PE (in the Netherlands) is expected to motivate students for lifelong participation in sport and physical activity. Two motivational theories that have proven useful for providing practical guidance for PE are Achievement Goal Theory (AGT) (Elliot & McGregor, 2001; Nicholls, 1984, 1989) and Self-Determination Theory (SDT) (Deci & Ryan, 2000). The AGT discerns two types of learning environments, namely an ego-oriented climate (i.e., performance climate) and a task-oriented climate (i.e., mastery climate) (Ames, 1992; Duda et al., 2014). In an ego-oriented climate, players are made to feel that it is important to outperform others. Mistakes are not tolerated, and the emphasis lies on winning. In a task-oriented climate, the focus is on improving oneself, learning new skills, cooperation, and personal learning progress. Generally, students have a higher quality of motivation in a task-oriented climate (Harwood et al., 2015). The GI approach, with its game slope concept to catering students of all ability levels, helps students to focus on their individual learning process, instead of having to perform according to pre-set norms that are identical for all students.

According to SDT, such an approach supports the need for feeling competent, one of three basic psychological needs, together with autonomy and relatedness (Deci & Ryan, 2000). *Competence* refers to the need of experiencing a level of effectiveness and confidence. *Autonomy* refers to regulation by the self, the experience of volition and having a choice. The concept of *relatedness* refers to the need to feel connected with others, to feel included and cared for by others. When these needs are satisfied students are more likely to be driven by favourable, self-determined forms of motivation. SDT states that it is crucial for players' engagement, enjoyment, and interest (i.e., intrinsic motivation) that they perceive the ability to carry out a learning task successfully and experience a sense of effectiveness (Ryan & Deci, 2017). By adapting the learning context to the ability of the students, all students can feel *competent*. By involving players in solving game challenges (for example by asking open questions), and giving them voice and choice (e.g., which playing materials to use, which game slope to practice on, what playing rules to apply), the need for *autonomy* is supported. And finally, by applying a non-directive, non-controlling teaching style, listening to and observing players, being open to discussion and sensitive to students' emotions, the need for *relatedness* can be supported. The resulting autonomous forms of motivation have been shown to result in students being more physically active and to yield better learning outcomes (Van den Berghe et al., 2012).

Conclusion

We believe that given the considerable heterogeneity in students' skills within PE classes, there is a constant need for differentiated instruction and modification of games. In this chapter, we presented the game-based approach and curriculum model GI and proposed the 'game slope' concept. By embedding this concept in the didactical components of the GI curriculum model we hope to support PE teachers in designing and teaching meaningful game activities, in which players' differing abilities and needs are met.

References

Ames, C. (1992). Achievement goals, motivational climate, and motivational processes. In G. C. Roberts (Ed.), *Motivation in sport and exercise* (pp. 161–176). Human Kinetics.

Biggs, J. (1996). Enhancing teaching through constructive alignment. *Higher Education*, *32*(3), 347–364.

Black, P. & Wiliam, D. (1998). Assessment and classroom learning. *Assessment in Education: Principles, Policy & Practice*, *5*(1), 7–74.

Borghouts, L. B., Slingerland, M. & Haerens, L. (2017). Assessment quality and practices in secondary PE in the Netherlands. *Physical Education and Sport Pedagogy*, *22*(5), 473–489.

Breivik, G. (2016). The role of skill in sport. *Sport, Ethics and Philosophy*, *10*(3), 1–15.

Bunker, D. & Thorpe, R. (1982). A model for teaching games in secondary schools. *Bulletin of Physical Education*, *18*, 5–8.

Chow, J. Y., Davids, K., Button, C. & Renshaw, I. (2021). *Nonlinear pedagogy in skill acquisition: An introduction* (2nd ed.). Routledge.

Davids, K., Bennett, S. & Newell, K. M. (2006). *Movement system variability*. Human Kinetics.

Deci, E. L. & Ryan, R. M. (2000). The "what" and "why" of goal pursuits: Human needs and the self-determination of behavior. *Psychological Inquiry*, *11*(4), 227–268.

Duarte, R., Araújo, D., Correia, V. & Davids, K. (2012). Sports teams as superorganisms. *Sports Medicine*, *42*(8), 633–642.

Duda, J. L., Papaioannou, A. G., Appleton, P. R., Quested, E. & Krommidas, C. (2014). Creating adaptive motivational climates in sport and physical education. In A. G. Papaioannou & D. Hackfort (Eds.), *Routledge companion to sport and exercise psychology: Global perspectives and fundamental concepts* (pp. 544–558). Routledge.

Elferink-Gemser, M. T., Kannekens, R., Lyons, J., Tromp, Y. & Visscher, C. (2010). Knowing what to do and doing it: Differences in self-assessed tactical skills of regional, sub-elite, and elite youth field hockey players. *Journal of Sports Sciences*, 28(5), 521–528.

Elliot, A. J. & McGregor, H. A. (2001). A 2 × 2 achievement goal framework. *Journal of Personality and Social Psychology*, 80(3), 501–519.

Farrow, D., Baker, J. & MacMahon C. (2013). *Developing sports expertise* (2nd ed.). Routledge.

Fontana, F. E., Furtado, O., Mazzardo, O. & Gallagher, J. D. (2009). Whole and part practice: A meta-analysis. *Perceptual and Motor Skills*, 109(2), 517–530.

Griffith, S. A. (2008). A proposed model for assessing quality of education. *International Review Education*, 54(1), 99–112.

Harwood C. G., Keegan R. J., Smith J. M. J. & Raine A. S. (2015). A systematic review of the intrapersonal correlates of motivational climate perceptions in sport and physical activity. *Psychology of Sports and Exercise*, 18, 9–25.

Hattie, J. & Timperley, H. (2007). The power of feedback. *Review of Educational Research*, 77(1), 81–112.

Lebed, F. (2022). *Complexity in games teaching and coaching: A multi-disciplinary perspective* (1st ed.). Routledge.

Lola, A. C. & Tzetzis, G. (2020). Analogy versus explicit and implicit learning of a volleyball skill for novices: the effect on motor performance and self-efficacy. *Journal of Physical Education and Sport*, 20(5), 2478–2486.

Machado, J. C., Barreira, D., Galatti, L., Chow, J. Y., Garganta, J. & Scaglia, A. J. (2018). Enhancing learning in the context of Street football: a case for Nonlinear Pedagogy. *Physical Education and Sport Pedagogy*, 24(2), 1–14.

Magill, R. A. & Anderson, D. (2013). *Motor learning and control: Concepts and applications* (10th ed.). McGraw-Hill.

Martens, R. (2012). *Successful coaching: The most authoritative guide on coaching principles*. Human Kinetics.

Newell, K. M. (1986). Constraints on the development of coordination. In M. G. Wade & H. T. A. Whiting (Eds.), *Motor development in children: Aspects of coordination and control* (pp. 341–361). Martinus Nijhoff Publishers.

Newell, K. M. (1991). Motor skill acquisition. *Annual Review of Psychology*, 42, 213–237.

Nicholls, J. G. (1984). Achievement motivation: Conceptions of ability, subjective experience, task choice, and performance. *Psychological Review*, 91(3), 328–346.

Nicholls, J. G. (1989). *The competitive ethos and democratic education*. Harvard University Press.

Raab, M. (2003). Decision making in sports: Influence of complexity on implicit and explicit learning. *International Journal of Sport and Exercise Psychology*, 1(4), 406–433.

Raab. M., Wylleman, P., Seiler. R., Elbe, A. & Hatzigeorgiadis, A. (2016). *Sports and exercise psychology research: From theory to practice* (1st ed.). Academic Press.

Reeve, J. (2006). Teachers as facilitators: What autonomy supportive teachers do and why their students benefit. *The Elementary School Journal*, 106, 225–236.

Renshaw, I. & Chow, J. Y. (2018). A constraint-led approach to sport and physical education pedagogy. *Physical Education and Sport Pedagogy*, 24(2), 1–14.

Ryan, R. M. & Deci, E. L. (2017). *Self-determination theory: Basic psychological needs in motivation, development, and wellness.* Guilford Press.

Schmidt, R. A. & Lee, T. D. (2014). *Motor learning and performance: From principles to application.* Human Kinetics.

Schmidt, R. A. & Wrisberg, C. A. (2000). *Motor learning and performance: A problem-based learning approach* (2nd ed.). Human Kinetics.

Shute, V. (2008). Focus on formative feedback. *Review of Educational Research, 78*(*1*), 153–189.

Slingerland, M., Borghouts, L., Jans, L., Weeldenburg, G., Van Dokkum, G., Vos, S. & Haerens, L. (2017). Development and optimisation of an in-service teacher training programme on motivational assessment in physical education. *European Physical Education Review, 23*(1), 91–109.

Sproule, J., Ollis, S., Gray, S., Thorburn, M., Allison, P. & Horton, P. (2011). Promoting perseverance and challenge in physical education: The missing ingredient for improved games teaching. *Sport, Education and Society, 16*(5), 665–684.

Stolz, S. & Pill, S. (2014). Teaching games and sport for understanding. *European Physical Education Review, 20*(1), 36–71.

Van den Berghe, L., Vansteenkiste, M., Cardon, G., Kirk, D. & Haerens, L. (2012). Research on self-determination in physical education: key findings and proposals for future research. *Physical Education and Sport Pedagogy, 19*(1), 97–121.

Votsis, E., Tzetzis, G., Hatzitaki, V. & Grouios, G. (2009). The effect of implicit and explicit methods in acquisition of anticipation still in low and high complexity situations. *International Journal of Sport Psychology, 40*(3), 374–391.

Vygotsky, L. S. (1978). *Mind in society: Development of higher psychological processes.* Harvard University Press.

Wang, C. H., Chang, C. C., Liang, Y. M., Shih, C. M., Chiu, W. S., Tseng, P., Hung, D. L., Tzeng, O. J. L., Muggleton, N. G. & Juan, C. H. (2013). Open vs. closed skill sports and the modulation of inhibitory control. *PLoS ONE, 8*(2), e55773.

Weeldenburg, G., Zondag, E. & De Kok, F. (2016; 2020). *Spelinzicht: Een speler- en spelgecentreerde didactiek van spelsporten [Game Insight: A learner- and game-centred approach to teaching games].* Jan Luiting Fonds.

6 Play with Purpose: Teaching Games and Sport for Understanding as Explicit Teaching

Shane Pill and John Williams

Play with Purpose derives from the Game Sense approach (GSA) (Australian Sports Commission [ASC], 1996). The GSA is a game-based teaching/ coaching approach founded on athlete-centred inquiry teaching styles, such as guided discovery where well-considered questioning is a characteristic. It was intended as an alternative to the traditionally dominant transmission pedagogy of directive and practice style instruction of games teaching (ASC, 1996). The athlete-centred narrative of player responsibility for learning associated with the GSA (Pill, 2018) challenges traditional directive teaching of 'sport-as-sport-techniques' (Kirk, 2010) taught through demonstrate-explain-practice (DEP: Tinning, 2010). This historical popular approach to teaching generally divides the session into an introductory activity or warm-up, a technique skill practice section, then a game or game play, finishing with a warm-down (Pearson & Webb, 2009). Typically, attainment of technical competency is viewed as necessary before game play (Light, 2013; Pill, 2017), occurs after a series of closed and open drills, at the end of the session. Alternatively, the more reality congruent approach, meaning' ... the knowledge of it that is possible' (Giovannini, 2015) to sport teaching and coaching provided by *play with purpose* (Pill, 2007), seeks to enhance sport participation and facilitate retention through practice sessions more aligned with the reasons people participate in sport – to be able to play the game. Game play is therefore indicated as the central element and focus of practice sessions of the GSA (ASC, 1996). The GSA continues to inform sport-related games teaching and coaching as the pedagogical basis of the Sport Australia *Playing for Life Philosophy* and programs like Sporting Schools (Sport Australia, 2021). However, it is our experience PE teachers and sport coaches often misunderstand teaching games for understanding as 'let them play' as 'the game will be the teacher'.

We propose that to be effective as a context for game learning aimed at developing 'thinking players' (den Duyn, 1997a), a game-based approach must retain its fidelity as explicit and deliberate teaching through strong teacher (or coach) guided participation, which we call *play with purpose* (Pill, 2007). The teacher/coach needs to clearly articulate learning intentions and the associated forms of '*doing*', promoting purposeful shaping and focusing of players' game play as a form of 'practice'. In other words, the play is

DOI: 10.4324/9781003298298-8

always intentional as the teaching is focused on an explicit learning outcome and is therefore deliberate. It is strongly guided preferentially through questions to shape player behaviour and focus player cognition.

Play with purpose: A shift in thinking about learning

In technique-based sport teaching and coaching, deviations from a prescribed common (or optimum) idea of a movement model are typically considered 'incorrect' requiring a teacher/coach intervention to 'fix'. Commonly, there is an emphasis on movement cues focusing on players attaining specific body movements. In this technique-based teaching scenario, the emphasis is on the player, who through practice and replication attains specific body movements provided by the teacher/coach. The pedagogical emphasis tends to be learning by command and practice, with the teacher/coach privileging directive instruction. Alternatively, play with purpose centres on using games to develop tactical-strategic thinking with movement responses as complementary pairs (den Duyn, 1996; Smith, 2016). The realistic context of a game or a game-form "becomes the focus and starting point of practical sessions" (ASC, 1996, p. 1), developing more reality-congruent understanding of the game than 'drill-based' movement experiences. In suggesting *play with p*urpose as a game-based approach, we put forward an alternative to traditionally common sport teaching/coaching that more closely meets learning intentions. We recognise the emphasis on game play characterises most game-based models (e.g., ASC, 1996; den Duyn, 1997b). In this chapter, we use the term model to mean the functional representation of a specific arrangement of teaching styles serving to guide instructional and content planning for sessions (Pill, 2017).

The idea of *play with purpose* stems from the GSA. The skill equation for the GSA, originally described as "technique + game context = Skill" (den Duyn, 1997b, p. 6), was subsequently modified by Pill (2013) to highlight the role of perception-action coupling in player decision-making and the emergence of movement responses to the in-the-moment demands of play (Figure 6.1). The context specific notion of skill attached to a GSA is both the movement response or technique, and player knowledge of how to enact that reaction. The latter in meeting the demands of the moment of play to achieve a purposeful outcome is equally as important and complementary in skill development (Pill, 2017). This focus on skill attainment being a long-held position in human motor learning literature (McMorris, 1998).

Decision Making +	Movement Knowledge =	Skill
[What to do -	[How to do it -	[Movement Capability
Game context]	Technique]	- Able to do it]

Figure 6.1 The Game Sense equation (see Pill, 2013, 2017).

Nonetheless, the actualisation of skilled performance in the moment of play is complex (Pill, 2014), and from constructivist epistemology, where:

> learners can only make sense of new situations in terms of their existing understanding. Learning involves an active process in which learners construct meaning by linking new ideas with their existing knowledge.
> (Naylor & Keogh, 1999, p. 93)

Within a game and sport context, the complexity we refer to in the moment of play is explained as a process of continual adaptation and responsiveness to a constantly changing environment (Pill, 2014). What one observes as a player movement response in the dynamics of the moment of play is therefore in effect a tactical action (Grehaigne et al., 2005).

Extending the above representation, Figure 6.2 illustrates a skill acquisition model for the GSA recognising the complementarity of cognition, action/tactical, and technical/movement response game behaviour (Pill, 2017). It incorporates Hopper's (2003) explanation of game behaviour and Mahlo's (1974 in Grehaigne et al., 2005) explanation of skilled behaviour. In the model, skill is a construction in the moment of play (Pill, 2017). Explained from a constructivist epistemology, the skilled action of the player has occurred as the player has: (1) Effectively perceived and analysed the moment; (2) Resolved a solution to the problem of the moment; and

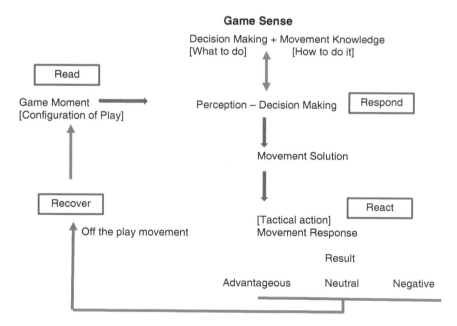

Figure 6.2 Expanded game sense modelling of skill performance in play. (Adapted from Pill, 2017, incorporating Mahlo, 1974, and Hopper, 2003.)

(3) Produced a motor skill response (Grehaigne et al., 2005). Incorporating Hopper's (2003) heuristic paradigm, where the player has to: *read* the game, *responded* to their reading of the game with a decision, *react* with a movement corresponding to their perception-action decision-making response, and then *recovers* to begin the process again in the next moment of play.

A key feature of developing game sense through *play with purpose* is the use of carefully considered questions and the weighed use of inquiry strategies to focus and shape player engagement, by influencing behaviour via education of player attention and thinking in preference to a reliance on directive instruction, such as 'telling' (ASC, 1996; den Duyn, 1996; Light, 2013). Some have described this preference on use of questions and inquiry strategies as guiding player discovery of understanding and developing thinking players (den Duyn, 1997a; Light, 2013; Pill, 2012). We suggest, however, that guided inquiry is possibly more accurate than guided discovery, as guided inquiry captures the teaching objective to retrieve, or consolidate, extend or elaborate understanding. Guided inquiry encourages extended reasoning, helping refine and consolidate existing understanding or enable critical and creative thinking, and complex problem-solving. Further, questioning has been shown in control group studies to be more effective at developing decision-making and skill execution (cf: Garcia-Gonzalez et al., 2014; Praxedes et al., 2016).

Play with purpose

So far, we have suggested *Play with Purpose* extends on the GSA thinking of practice situations where players learn through play (Hopper & Sanford, 2010; Kidman & Lombardo, 2010; Storey & Butler, 2010). We have suggested explicit instruction using teacher/coach-directed inquiry based on evidence to question the presumptions of learning through play and self-discovery without active guidance (MacNamara et al., 2015). Accumulation of time spent on physical activity is not enough to ensure learning, where learning is a positive change in movement skill competency (Fischer et al., 2005). From the perspective of education theory, the suggestion that learning occurs with greater understanding from personal discovery rather than thoughtful processing is not substantiated (Hattie & Yates, 2014).

Kirschner et al. (2006) contended evidence is "overwhelming and unambiguous" and that guidance is required that is "specifically designed to support the cognitive processing necessary for learning" (p. 76). Our argument is therefore developing 'thinking players' as outlined in Figure 6.2 is not distinguished by using the 'game as teacher', rather, using the game as context for learning. Using the GSA with the assumption 'the game is teacher' is likely to result in limited or fantastical understandings of the actual benefits and outcomes that can be achieved. In other words, using a GSA as the 'game as teacher' has limited reality congruence. Kirschner et al. (2006) concept of 'specifically designed' is what we now turn to in explaining Play with Purpose (Pill, 2017).

Our propositions moving forward, in summary, are:

- accumulation of physical activity will not of itself result in movement skill
- learning and the development of 'thinking players';
- the game is a context for learning and the game is not the teacher;
- deliberate effort in the form of inquiry must be made for movement learning

Developing players understanding by design – play with purpose

The critical elements that can enable our perspective broadly under teacher/ coach control are planning, pedagogy, goal or learning intention setting, and feedback (Hattie & Yates, 2014). Guided inquiry may encourage players' extended reasoning, a goal consistent with current calls in education frameworks such as the *Australian Curriculum for Health and Physical Education* (AC: HPE) (Australian Curriculum Assessment and Reporting Authority [ACARA], 2016), for students to develop critical and creative thinking, and the skill of complex problem-solving. Play with Purpose (Pill, 2007) was proposed on the concepts of explicit teaching through understanding by design (Pill, 2017; Wiggins & McTighe, 2005) to help teachers facilitate the above critical elements by foregrounding the education design aspect attached to the use of games as a context for player learning.

Understanding by design

Whatever framework or theory guides PE teacher/coach planning, objectives or outcomes for player learning can be organised into what the player should understand (transferable concepts), know (factual information) and be able to do (skills and processes) (Wiggins & McTighe, 2011). Undertaking this planning assists the design of games as reality congruent practice directed to player learning as the teacher/coach has planned with foresight the use of player knowledge organisation, knowledge application, meaning-making, and knowledge transfer (Erickson & Lanning, 2014). Clarity of expectations for learning and task presentation coherence are factors shown to relate to skill learning (Rink, 2013), while intelligibility about what is to be learnt and what constitutes learning attainment are considered the most influential factors in progressing educational outcomes (Hattie & Yates, 2014; Marzano, 1998). Planning learning objectives or intentions from session content expectations aligned with elaborations of success criteria is recognised as a high-impact action for achievement (Hattie & Yates, 2013).

Play with purpose – explicit teaching and deliberate practice

Sport coaching, like PE teaching of the games and sport focus area, is an education endeavour (Jones, 2006; Pill et al., 2021) towards a context-specific version of reality congruence. In education literature, deliberate practice is suggested to be the "essential prerequisite for skill learning" (Hattie & Yates, 2014, p. 96). It is a pattern of teacher-learner interaction purposefully directed to changing the quality of mental representations of performance (Ericsson & Pool, 2016). Over time, in a games/sport environment players develop faster and more accurate performance decisions. Towards the development of 'thinking players' from play with purpose, we highlight the importance of assisting players to understand their attention, what they 'concentrate' on. By attention, we refer to players consciously or unconsciously selecting information for cognitive processing (Oliver et al., 2020). To direct attention, Oliver and colleagues (2020) suggested players require knowledge and control of their 'attention system', which from a cognitive perspective relies on knowing they are focusing on what is most important (expert players are better at selecting visual information because they 'know' when and where to look or what information to attend to), and the player is able to implement control routines to attend to the most relevant information for performance. Ericsson and Pool (2016) suggested the reality congruent task design typical of deliberate practice requires purposefully informed activity through an environment designed for learning, not just *doing*.

Practising deliberately in the ways we have suggested influences the neural circuit (Coyle, 2009; Ericsson & Pool, 2016). *Play with purpose* can therefore be thought of as seeking to influence player habits. The 'mechanism' targeted to develop player habits of 'thinking and doing' is neuroplasticity. It is the quality of player attention that initiates and drives neuroplasticity. Neuroplasticity is greatest when one pays voluntary attention. In making sense of what neuroscience is telling about brain development, we understand skills which are at the autonomous stage of development might be considered habits prompted by context-triggering neural pathways enabling action to proceed without the perception of thought, with the mechanism for this being the absence of the prefrontal cortex in the decision making. The prefrontal cortex can be bypassed as habits come from strengthened neural connections negating the need for choice. To learn or change a habit, it appears to be that the prefrontal cortex is activated, as now the player is in a process requiring voluntary attention in order to make choices, and this engages neuroplasticity to create new ways of thinking, or new 'mental models' (Chang, 2014; Coyle, 2009; Dayan & Cohen, 2011; Floyer-Lea & Matthews, 2005; McKenzie et al., 2014; Sampaio-Baptista et al., 2013).

Teacher/coach instructions, whether directive or inquiry-oriented, need to influence neuroplasticity and this is accomplished by priming players thinking using information. This preparation is achieved by a type of availability bias, called anchoring: that is, teacher/coach decisions about what information is made available to players (from an ecological perspective, this would be considered constraining information). Understanding priming has implications for the way teachers/coaches frame questions to players. Closed questions always prime the answer. For example, "the ball is either in or out when it touches the line, which one is it?". Closed questions are not open to challenge. They require what Kahneman (2011) called System 1 'fast thinking'. If as a teacher/coach we desire conscious, analytical, reflective, abstract, deliberate, decontextualised, or re-contextualised (as when seeking transfer from the known/familiar to an unknown/unfamiliar context) – what Kahneman (2011) called System 2 'slow thinking', we need to prime player thinking by wording questions differently:

> "tell me more ..."
> "give me an example ..."
> "describe the situation ..."
> "what led up to this ..."
> "what made it work ..."
> "how did it happen ..."

From a constructivist perspective, priming is an advanced cognitive organiser, as the information availability orientates player thinking in advance of playing. This is what is being referred to when shaping player behaviour and focusing player thinking using questioning.

Play with purpose then can be described as deliberate practice with systematic attention to player learning (Pill, 2017). Observation of player performance in game play provides the teacher/coach with data that assists in planning games as progressively structured challenges that aim for player learning development (Lemov et al., 2012). For teachers/coaches, how the player practices is a primary concern (Patterson & Lee, 2013), although how much they do this deliberately is a factor in competence development, with many studies suggesting game play volume is influential (see for example, Berry et al., 2008).

Nonetheless, we acknowledge there is definitional controversy about deliberate practice related to concept misunderstanding (Ericsson & Pool, 2016), particularly with the idea of a '10,000-hour rule' as the accumulated practice volume needed to attain expertise. The notion of deliberate practice is that skill develops and improves over time with effort. The indication for teacher/sport coach pedagogy, is accumulation of practice and experience of themselves do not inevitably lead to learning (Ericsson et al., 1993).

Conclusion

In this chapter, we have suggested the recommendation for teachers/coaches that practice contexts designated for player learning, should be organised through principles of purposeful and explicit pedagogical intention. We have explained how the application of *play with purpose* can develop 'thinking players'. Play with Purpose (2007) is intended to direct

PE teachers and sport coaches to game-based approaches as deliberate practice and explicit teaching, and away from ideological or fantastical notions of 'the game as the teacher'.

References

Australian Curriculum, Assessment and Reporting Authority. (2016). *The Australian curriculum: Health and physical education.* Version 8.3. Australian Curriculum, Assessment and Reporting Authority.

Australian Sports Commission. (1996). *Game sense: Perceptions and actions research report.* Australian Sports Commission.

Berry, J., Abernethy, B. & Côté, J. (2008). The contribution of structured activity and deliberate play to the development of expert perceptual and decision-making skill. *Journal of Sport and Exercise Psychology, 30*(6), 685–708.

Chang, Y. (2014). Reorganization and plastic changes of the human brain associated with skill learning and expertise. *Frontiers in Human Neuroscience, 8*(35). 10.3389/fnhum.2014.00035

Coyle, D. (2009). *The talent code: Greatness isn't born. It's grown. Here's how.* Bantam.

Dayan, E. & Cohen, L. G. (2011). Neuroplasticity subserving motor skill learning. *Neuron, 72*(3), 443–454.

den Duyn, N. (1996). Why it makes sense to play games. *Sports Coach, 19*(3), 6–9.

den Duyn, N. (1997a). Game sense: Developing thinking players. A presenters guide and workbook. Australian Sports Commission.

den Duyn, N. (1997b). Game sense: It's time to play! *Sports Coach, 19*(4), 9–11.

Erickson, H. L. & Lanning, L. A. (2014). *Transitioning to concept-based curriculum and instruction: How to bring content and process together.* Corwin Press.

Ericsson, A. & Pool, R. (2016). *Peak: Secrets from the new science of expertise.* Houghton Mifflin Harcourt.

Ericsson, K. A., Krampe, R. & Tesch-Romer, C. (1993). The role of deliberate practice in the acquisition of expert performance. *Psychological Review, 100*(3), 363–406.

Fischer, A., Reilly, J., Kelly, L., Montgomery, C., Williamson, A., Paton, J. & Grant, S. (2005). Fundamental movement skills and habitual physical activity in young children. *Medicine and Science in Sports and Exercise, 37*(4), 684–688.

Floyer-Lea, A. & Matthews, P. M. (2005). Distinguishable brain activation networks for short-and long-term motor skill learning. *Journal of Neurophysiology, 94*(1), 512–518.

García-González, L., Moreno, A., Gil, A., Moreno, M. P. & Del Villar, F. (2014). Effects of decision training on decision making and performance in young tennis players: An applied research. *Journal of Applied Sport Psychology, 26*(4), 426–440.

Giovannini, P. (2015). Using fantasy: Notes on Elias's sociology. *Human Figurations, 4*(3). https://quod.lib.umich.edu/h/humfig/11217607.0004.306/–using-fantasy-notes-on-eliass-sociology?rgn=main;view=fulltext

Grehaigne, J. F., Richard, J. F. & Griffin, L. (2005). *Teaching and learning team sports and games.* Routledge.

Hattie, J. & Yates, G. (2013). Plenary 4-Understanding learning: Lessons for learning, teaching and research. *ACER Research Conference.* http://research.acer.edu.au/cgi/viewcontent.cgi?article=1207&context=research_conference

Hattie, J. & Yates, G. (2014). *Visible learning and the science of how we learn.* Routledge.

Hopper, T. (2003). Four Rs for tactical awareness: Applying game performance assessment in net/wall games. *Teaching Elementary Physical Education, 14*(2), 16–21.

Hopper, T. & Sanford, K. (2010). Occasioning moments in the game-as-teacher concept: Complexity thinking applied to TGfU and video gaming. In J. Butler & L. Griffin (Eds.), *More teaching games for understanding: Moving globally* (pp. 121–138). Human Kinetics.

Jones, R. (2006). *The sport coach as educator: Re-conceptualising sports coaching.* Routledge.

Kahneman, D. (2011). *Thinking fast, thinking slow.* Farrar, Straus and Giroux.

Kidman, L. & Lombardo, B. J. (2010). TGfU and humanistic coaching. In J. Butler & L. Griffin (Eds.), *More teaching games for understanding: Moving globally* (pp. 171–186). Human Kinetics.

Kirk, D. (2010). *Physical education futures.* Routledge.

Kirschner, P. A., Sweller, J. & Clark, R. E. (2006). Why minimal guidance during instruction does not work: An analysis of the failure of constructivist, discovery, problem-based, experiential, and inquiry-based teaching. *Educational Psychologist, 4*(2), 75–86.

Lemov, D., Woolway, E. & Yezzi, K. (2012). *Practice perfect: 42 rules for getting better at getting better.* John Wiley & Sons.

Light, R. (2013). *Game sense: Pedagogy for performance, participation and enjoyment.* Routledge.

MacNamara, A., Collins, D. & Giblin, S. (2015). Just let them play? Deliberate preparation as the most appropriate foundation for lifelong physical activity. *Frontiers Psychology, 6,* 1548.

Mahlo, F. (1974). *Acte tactique enjeu [Tactical action in play].* Vigot.

Marzano, R. J. (1998). *A theory-based meta-analysis of research on instruction.* Mid-Continental Regional Educational Laboratory.

McMorris, T. (1998). Teaching games for understanding: Its contribution to the knowledge of skill acquisition from a motor learning perspective. *European Journal of Physical Education, 3*(1), 65–74.

Naylor, S. & Keogh, B. (1999). Constructivism in classroom: Theory into practice. *Journal of Science Teacher Education, 10*(2), 93–106.

McKenzie, I. A., Ohayon, D., Li, H., De Faria, J. P., Emery, B., Tohyama, K. & Richardson, W. D. (2014). Motor skill learning requires active central myelination. *Science, 346*(6207), 318–322.

Oliver, A., McCarthy, P. J. & Burns, L. (2020). Teaching athletes to understand their attention is teaching them to concentrate. *Journal of Sport Psychology in Action, 12*(3), 1–15.

Patterson, J. E. & Lee, T. D. (2013). Organizing practice: Effective practice is more than just reps. In D. Farrow, J. Baker & C. McMahon (Eds.), *Developing sport expertise: Researchers and coaches put theory into practice* (pp. 132–153). Routledge.

Pearson, R. J. & Webb, P. (2009). Improving the quality of games teaching to promote physical activity. In T. Cuddihy & E. Brymer (Eds.), *Creating Active Futures: Proceedings of the 26th ACHPER International Conference 2009* (pp. 405–414).

Pill, S. (2007). *Play with purpose.* ACHPER Publications.

Pill, S. (2012). *Rethinking sport teaching on physical education.* PhD thesis, University of Tasmania.

Pill, S. (2013). *Play with Purpose: Game sense to sport literacy.* ACHPER Publications.

Pill, S. (2014). Informing Game Sense pedagogy with constraints led theory for coaching in Australian football. *Sports Coaching Review, 3*(1), 46–62.

Pill, S. (2017). The Game Sense approach as explicit teaching and deliberate practice. In J. Williams (Ed.), *Participation in an Active and Healthy Lifestyle: Valuing the Participant Voice: Proceedings of the 30th ACHPER International Conference, 2017* (pp. 133–145).

Pill, S. (2018). *Perspectives on athlete-centred coaching*. Routledge.

Pill, S., SueSee, B., Rankin, J. & Hewitt, M. (2021). *The spectrum of coaching styles*. Routledge.

Praxedes, A., Moreno, A., Sevil, J., Garcia-Gonzalez, L. & Del Villar, F. (2016). A preliminary study of the effects of a comprehensive teaching program, based on questioning, to improve tactical actions in young footballers. *Perceptual and Motor Skills, 122*(3), 742–756.

Rink, J. E. (2013). Measuring teacher effectiveness in physical education. *Research Quarterly for Exercise and Sport, 84*, 407–418.

Sampaio-Baptista, C., Khrapitchev, A. A., Foxley, S., Schlagheck, T., Scholz, J., Jbabdi, S … & Johansen-Berg, H. (2013). Motor skill learning induces changes in white matter microstructure and myelination. *The Journal of Neuroscience, 33*(50), 19499–19503.

Smith, W. (2016) Fundamental movement skills and fundamental game skills are complimentary pairs and should be taught in complimentary ways at all stages of skill development. *Sport, Education and Society, 21*(3), 431–442.

Sport Australia. (2021). *Playing for life*. https://www.sportaus.gov.au/p4l

Storey, B. & Butler, J. (2010). Ecological thinking and TGfU: Understanding games as complex adaptive systems. In J. Butler & L. Griffin (Eds.), *More teaching games for understanding: Moving globally* (pp. 139–154). Human Kinetics.

Tinning, R. (2010). *Pedagogy and human movement: Theory, practice, research*. Routledge.

Wiggins, G. & McTighe, J. (2005). *Understanding by design* (2nd ed.). Association for Supervision and Curriculum Development.

Wiggins, G. & McTighe, J. (2011). *The Understanding by design guide to creating high-quality units*. Association for Supervision and Curriculum Development.

Section II
Research Perspectives

7 Games Based Approach as a Constructivist Model of Games Teaching

Linda L. Griffin and Jean-Francois Richard

Many scholars have supported the notion that the TGfU model is grounded in a constructivist learning theory (Butler, 1997; Grehaigne et al., 2005; Grehaigne, & Godbout, 2021; Metzler, 2017; Mitchell et al., 2021). Scholars have made the case that instructional approaches (i.e., models) should have at their foundation a learning theory (Metzler, 2017; Rink, 2001). Understanding the learning theory allows the teacher to have a better sense of the learning process and overall expected outcomes (Kirk & MacPhail, 2002; Rink, 2001). Therefore, aligning a game-based approach (GBA) to constructivist learning theory gives the teacher the opportunity to examine assumptions such as why it works and how it works (Rink, 2001). The purpose of this chapter is threefold. First, we will define constructivist learning theory. Second, describe how social constructivist learning theory aligns with the GBA. Third, we will provide an overview of the Tactical-Decision Learning Model (T-DLM) an example of a social constructivist learning perspective. Finally, we share some chapter takeaways.

Constructivist learning theory

The origins of constructivism date back to the time of Socrates, who contended that teachers and learners should talk with each other and interpret and construct knowledge through asking questions (Amineh & Asl, 2015). Socrates was one of the earliest constructivist teachers employing a questioning approach to teaching and learning (Brooks & Brooks, 1993).

Constructivism has multiple roots in psychology and philosophy (Perkins, 1992). The "constructivist stance maintains that learning is a process of constructing meaning; it is how students make sense of their experience" (Merriam & Caffarella, 1999, p. 260). Constructivism describes the way that students can make sense of the material and how the materials can be taught effectively. There are two main strands of constructivist learning perspectives: (a) cognitive constructivism, and (b) a social-cultural perspective. Piaget proposed cognitive constructivism, in which learners progress through universal stages of cognitive development through maturation, discovery practices and social transmissions of assimilation and accommodation (Amineh & Asl,

DOI: 10.4324/9781003298298-10

2015). Vygotsky emphasised the sociocultural theory of development, which described learning as a social process that facilitates the learner's potential through social interactions and their context and/or culture (Huang, 2021).

In a constructivist view of learning, Hoover (1996) presented two common principles to situate the complexities and diversity of constructivist perspectives.

1   The learners' prior knowledge influences their new knowledge.
2   Learning is an active process in which learners negotiate their understanding based on their experiences with a new learning situation.

The notion of negotiating the curriculum is defined as learners asking questions and trying to find answers themselves, thus giving the curriculum a sense of ownership (Cook, 1992). Constructivist learning is an active process and a personal representation of the world. Problem-solving, authentic tasks, experiences, collaboration, and assessment are important aspects in this learning perspective (Christie, 2005).

From a constructivist view of teaching, Hoover (1996) presented some pedagogical implications for the teacher. Constructivist teachers:

1   Take on the role of facilitator or guide.
2   Consider the role of prior knowledge.
3   Must engage learners in the learning process.
4   Allow sufficient time to build new knowledge in an active manner.

We have provided you with a broad view of constructivist learning theory.

In this next section we focus on social constructivism and a GBA. We believe that GBA is well situated within social constructivism.

Social constructivism and GBA

Understanding the learning theory that foregrounds an instructional approach is important to help teachers better understand how learners will live the curriculum of the instructional approach (Rink, 2001). In this section, we describe social constructivism and show how it aligns to a GBA.

With respect to social constructivism, Vygotsky and Cole (1978) stated that cognitive growth occurs first on a social level, and then it can occur within the individual. Social constructivism is based on three assumptions (Kim, 2001).

1   Reality: Reality is constructed through human activity.
2   Knowledge: Learners create meaning when they interact with each other and with the environment.
3   Learning: Meaningful learning occurs when learners are engaged in social actions such as interaction and collaboration.

Social constructivists view learning as an active process in which individuals make meaning through interactions with each other and their environment (Brown et al., 1989). A key construct related to social constructivism is the Zone of Proximal Development (ZPD) which is defined as the space between what learners can do without assistance and what learners can do with guidance and collaboration (Vygotsky & Cole, 1978; Wood et al., 1976). From this viewpoint it is important to consider the learner's background and culture during the learning process.

A social constructivist teacher takes on the role of facilitator with an emphasis on approaches such as reciprocal teaching, peer collaboration, cognitive apprenticeships, and problem-based instruction (Schunk, 2012). These instructional models highlight the need for collaboration or cooperation among learners and the teacher (Lave & Wenger, 1991). The teacher facilitator carefully scaffolds learning experiences (i.e., easy, and manageable steps) to making connections between concepts and/or achieve a goal, thus working in partnership with peers and the teacher facilitator. Effective scaffolding includes the following processes: (a) make the task easier, (b) increase and uphold learner interest in activity, (c) explain the task, (d) highlight aspects that lead to the solution, and (e) control frustration in the learner (Wood et al., 1976).

Kirk and MacPhail (2002) presented a revised version of the TGfU model that is grounded in a situated learning perspective, a constructivist approach. Situated learning, like social constructivism, refers either to families of learning theories or pedagogical strategies. Situated learning is closely related to socio-culturalism and distributed cognition and to cognitive apprenticeship. Learning is situated in the activity in which it takes place. In other words, learning through doing. In situated learning theory there is a need to explore the relationships among numerous physical, social, and cultural dimensions of the learning context (Lave & Wenger, 1991). Lave and Wenger (1991) describe two major constructs in situated learning:

1 Communities of practice emphasise the context-bound nature of learning in relationships between people (i.e., connection between knowledge and action).
2 Legitimate peripheral participation identifies learning as a social phenomenon in which practice involves genuine participation by the learner engaged in communities of practice that are meaningful to the learners (Kirk & Macdonald, 1998).

Kirk and MacPhail (2002) elaborated on the original TGfU model by making explicit some of the implicit learning principles. Specifically, focused attention to the learner related to the learner voice (i.e., perception), game concepts, thinking strategically, cue recognition, technique selection, and skill development. These constructs form the basis for strategies and techniques and situated performance as legitimate peripheral participation in games (Kirk & Macdonald, 1998; Kirk & MacPhail, 2002). MacPhail et al.

(2008) employed the revised Bunker-Thorpe model to conceptualise the nature of situated learning in the context of learning to play an invasion game in school physical education using a tactical games model. Findings from this study, (a) support the notion that the two situated dimensions (i.e., physical-perceptual, and social-interactive) may be constructs that are robust enough to explore further, and (b) identify how models-based instruction can help situate learning context for teachers and learners. An implication of this study regarding assessment is the importance and relevance of the game as a unit of analysis. Researchers value exploring GBA from a constructivist learning perspective.

We argue that a GBA has strong connections with social constructivism. In a GBA, the emphasis is placed on tactical aspects of the game in relation to modified game situations (e.g., 3v3, 3v2, 4v4). At the beginning of every lesson, the teacher sets up different learning situations by presenting a tactical problem to the students. In this approach, offensive aspects of the game are emphasised. The teacher guides learners in this process by helping them to get organised, read game configurations, and decide on a response. The teacher then helps learners to regulate their learning. In this next section, we present the T-DLM for games teaching and learning which we highlight as a rich example of socio-constructivist learning theory.

The Tactical-Decision Learning Model (T-DLM)

The following section provides an excellent example of a GBA closely aligned with a social constructivist learning theory (i.e., reality, knowledge, and learning). The development of the T-DLM began in France in the 1970s and 1980s. Our French colleagues' work is based on the use of the tactical approach (Rink, 1996) as a framework with contributions from a constructivist and cognitivist perspective, and their research on tactical knowledge in team sports (Grehaigne & Godbout, 1995, Grehaigne et al., 1997, 2001). T-DLM is a learner-centred model that foregrounds small-sided games to facilitate tactical learning, where skills and movements are introduced and practised as needed by the teacher and learners. The key pedagogical strategies of the model include game play, game play observation and peer assessment, debate of ideas (DoI), and action plans.

Game play

Learners are placed in mini-games (i.e., small-sided games) that are modified (i.e., representation, exaggeration, or adaptions) to foreground a tactical emphasis for the lesson/unit. For example, game constraints might include the number of players, boundaries (i.e., size of court or pitch), ways to score and/or type of equipment. Nadeau et al. (2017) also shared the game exaggeration of adding a player (i.e., 2v3, 3v4) such as a "joker" as a support player either offensively or defensively. During game play, there is a game play cycle (i.e., approximately 7-minute games) – players in the game and players as observers of the game then rotate roles from player as observer to player in game.

Game play observation and peer assessment

The observation phase of the game-observe-DoI cycle involves three distinct roles. Role 1 involves the learners, as players in the game, reflecting on their actions and tactical decisions (i.e., what worked, what did not, and how to change). Role 2 involves the teacher's observation noting players' skills, movements, and tactical performances. Role 3 involves the learners in the role of observer of their peers in game play. In the game, observers record game play occurrences using various assessment tools such as Team Sport Assessment Procedure (TSAP) (Grehaigne & Godbout, 2021).

The TSAP was developed by Grehaigne et al. (1997). The TSAP provides information that quantifies a learner's overall offence performance in selected invasion games or net/wall games that reflects technical and tactical aspects of game play. The indicators are all related to successful game play (Richard & Griffin, 2003). The TSAP is based on two concepts (see Table 7.1):

1   How a player gains possession of the ball (two variables), and
2   How a player disposes of the ball (four variables).

Table 7.1 Observation variables and operational definitions

A. Gaining Possession of the Ball	Operational Definition
1 Conquered ball (CB)	Player is considered having conquered the ball if they intercepted it, stole it from an opponent, or recaptured it after an unsuccessful shot on goal or after a near loss to the other team.
2 Received ball (RB)	Player receives the ball from a teammate and does not immediately lose control of it.
B. Disposing of the Ball	**Operational Definition**
1 Lost ball (LB)	Player is considered having lost the ball when they lose control of it without having scored a goal.
2 Neutral ball (NB)	A routine pass to a partner which dies not truly put pressure on the other team.
3 Pass	Pass to teammate which contributes to the displacement of the ball towards the opposing team's goal.
4 Successful Shot on Goal (SS)	A shot is considered successful when it scores or possession of the ball is retained.

Table 7.2 TSAP performance indices

Index	Formula
Volume of play	CB + RB
Efficiency index	$\dfrac{CB + P + SS}{10 + LB}$
Performance score	(Volume of play/2) + (Efficiency index × 10)

Table 7.2 provides the computation for performance indexes and performance score.

The different variables and indices from the TSAP can be broken down into simpler forms based on the tactical problem to be addressed as well as the developmental needs of the learners. The flexibility of the TSAP is a critical feature as this instrument integrates learners in the role of observers as an assessment task. Research has indicated that learners (grades 5-8) are able to record data with a moderate to good level of inter-observer reliability (Godbout & Desrosiers, 2005; Richard et al., 2000; Richard et al., 1999). In sum, the TSAP has been shown to be a valid and reliable peer assessment tool that truly engages the game observer in this observation phase. All three roles are important to the game observation phase which leads to a robust DoI for the teacher and learners.

Debate of Ideas (DoI)

After game plays stops, the teacher sets up a DoI period (i.e., three minutes) for each team to discuss problems during game play. Learners can share their playing experiences, reflections, or opinions based on informal or formal observations using the TSAP. For example, some teams might be struggling with maintaining possession, or offensively the team has limited attacks on goal. Based on the players' observations or playing experience, the team comes up with possible tactical changes for the next game. DoI is the central component or the essence of the model. DoI involves students sharing ideas based on observations or game participation after a teaching and learning situation (i.e., scenario) (Grehaigne et al., 2005; Grehaigne & Godbout, 2021). The underlying questions are asked, "Was there success? If not, what can we do about it?". During this segment, the asking of questions matters. Questions can range from gathering and recalling information from games played, to interpretation of formal data collection based on various observational variables, to questions that focus on learner perspective and/or experience. Asking questions can be the challenging part of a GBA. The DoI episode can be viewed as time-consuming, however, exploring, and reflecting on learners' thinking is important to help guide learning. Therefore, the debates should be limited to about three minutes (Grehaigne, & Godbout, 2021). DoI considers all observers' and players' observations to consider choices for the next objectives to be implemented. The teacher is not excluded from the DoI cycle as the teacher has their own goals for the unit and may need to navigate unit goals with learners' observations. The teacher's questions and highlighting of the problems to be solved (i.e., loss of possession, increase number of attacks) become critical to establishing the action plan. For example, when analysing a group of students' team efficiency index (EI), the teacher can help the discussion for the team to realise that the problem pertaining to efficiency revolves around their collective capacity to successfully take a shot on goal. The teacher can then further guide these students and help them discover if the problem is more technical or tactical in nature. Hence, the observation-DoI cycles build on each other and assist teachers with scaffolding, which breaks up learning into small chunks.

Action plans

The action plan (i.e., project), or what Grehaigne and Godbout (2021) referred to as the "road map concept", is a pedagogical strategy that formalises decisions made at the time of DoI. The road map describes the essential feedback from quantitative and qualitative data, and feedback from teacher and learner observers that comes from the DoI session. The action plan presents the teacher and learners with new skills, movements, tactics, and strategies for improved game play. The notion of tactical knowledge is basically "knowledge in action" (i.e., linking of tactical awareness and performance). The three categories of knowledge are action rules that lead to principles of action, play organisation rules, and skills and movements. What is critical is that the teacher requires learners to discuss, and that decision-making is tracked in a written document (Grehaigne et al., 2005) (see Figure 7.1). This road map concept provides for scaffolding of learning experiences that allows learners to build confidence, which helps them grapple and tackle more difficult tasks.

The T-DLM provides a research-based model for games teaching and learning situated in socio-constructivist learning. There is an important connection among decision-making, problem-solving, understanding, and learning in games education. Having stated that, we acknowledge that learning games is social, complex, and situated; and this model shows this complexity and helps teachers scaffold games learning through game play, game play observation, DoI, or action planning.

Chapter takeaways

In this chapter we explored constructivist learning theory and GBA. Why is understanding learning theory important? As Rink (2001, p. 123) stated "Each learning theory is used to support an approach to instruction … The advantage of using learning theory to talk about pedagogy is that you get to test the assumption of the theory—what is it based on." We believe that this chapter provides insight into social constructivist learning theory and its

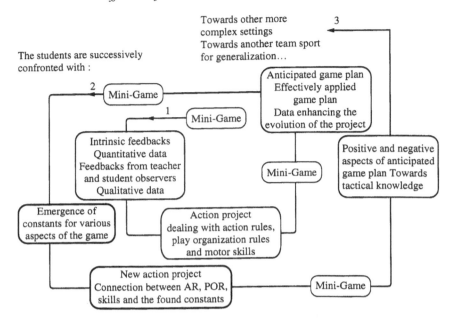

Figure 7.1 Illustration of the Tactical-Decision Learning Model. (With permission from Gréhaigne et al., 2005.)

value to teachers in understanding the why, what, and how that supports GBA. We broadly defined constructivist learning theory and provided an example of a GBA grounded in social constructivism.

The following are 'takeaways' from this chapter. Takeaways for us are the clear and concise messages that we want you to really consider in your GBA teaching. First, a constructivist perspective promotes social and communication skills by creating a learning environment that emphasises collaboration and exchange of ideas. Learners are given the opportunity to learn how to articulate their ideas and collaborate on tasks effectively by sharing in group projects. Vygotsky's social constructivism (1978) emphasised the collaborative nature of learning by the construction of knowledge through social negotiation. Common features of the constructivist teacher include (a) embracing the role of prior knowledge, (b) soliciting and valuing learners' views, (c) designing experiences that challenge learners' assumptions, (d) posing relevant problems, and (e) assessing learning in context on a regular basis.

Second, T-DLM is a research-based example of a GBA grounded in social constructivism. The T-DLM focuses on learners' exploration of the many possibilities of game play and the construction of reasonable responses in small-sided games. The pedagogical strategies of (a) game play, (b) game play observation and assessment, (c) debate of ideas (DoI), and (d) action plans (i.e., road maps) align with key features of a social constructivist perspective. The DoI must be carefully planned by the teacher to help guide the debates but also keeping in mind the focus of the lesson. DoI is at the heart of this model, which brings together all learners gathering data from several perspectives (i.e., playing the game, observing the game, and collecting data on the game). DoI spotlights the power of the peer in learning and assessing which along with the ecological validity of the learning context, is essential to authentic assessment and learning (Zessoules & Gardner, 1991). The debates help to create a scaffolded learning environment for games learning. For learners to truly construct new knowledge (i.e., knowing and doing) teachers need to allow more time and more progressions (i.e., scaffolding) in games units.

DoI can also provide a space for debates related to social emotional learning as well as issues related to equity, diversity, and inclusion. Issues related to these topics can be based on the game play observation episode in the lesson. Intentionally planning for such debates will allow the teacher time to reflect and design thoughtful questions.

Finally, from a social constructivist perspective, understanding and learning are closely linked. In other words, you cannot have shared construction of knowledge or learning without a shared understanding. These shared understandings help further learners' development as competent games players.

References

Amineh, R. J. & Asl, H. D. (2015). Review of constructivism and social constructivism. *Journal of Social Sciences, Literature and Languages, 1*(1), 9–16.

Brooks, J. & Brooks, M. (1993). *In search of understanding: the case for constructivist Classrooms.* ASCD. NDT Resource Center database.

Brown, J. S., Collins, A. & Duguid, P. (1989). Situated cognition and the culture of learning. *Educational Researcher, 18*(1), 32–42.

Butler, J. (1997). How would Socrates teach games? A constructivist approach. *Journal of Physical Education, Recreation & Dance, 68*(9), 42–47.

Christie, A. (2005). *Constructivism and its implications for educators.* http://alicechristie.com/edtech/learning/constructivism/index.htm

Cook, J. (1992). Negotiating the curriculum: Programming for learning. In G. Bloomer, N. Lester, C. Onore & J. Cook (Eds.), *Negotiating the curriculum: Educating for the 21st century* (pp. 15–31). Falmer.

Godbout, P. & Desrosiers, P. (2005). Students' participation to the assessment process in physical education. In F. Carreiro da Costa, M. Cloes & M. Gonzalez Valeiro (Eds.), *The art and science of teaching in physical education and sport* (pp. 227–248). Universidade Tecnica de Lisboa.

Gréhaigne, J. F. (1988). Game Systems in soccer. In T. Reilly, A. Lees, K. Davids & W. J. Murphy (Eds.) *Science and football* (pp. 316–321). E. & F.N. SPON.

Gréhaigne, J. F. & Godbout, P. (1995). Tactical knowledge in team sports from a constructivist and cognitivist perspective. *Quest, 47*(4), 490–505.

Gréhaigne, J. F. & Godbout, P. (2021). Debate of ideas and understanding with regard to tactical learning in team sports. *Journal of Teaching in Physical Education, 40*(4), 556–565.

Gréhaigne, J.-F., Godbout, P. & Bouthier, D. (1997). Performance assessment in team sport. *Journal of Teaching in Physical Education, 16*(4), 500–516.

Gréhaigne, J. F., Godbout, P. & Bouthier, D. (2001). The teaching and learning of decision making in team sports. *Quest, 53*(1), 59–76.

Gréhaigne, J. F., Richard, J. F. & Griffin, L. L. (2005). *Teaching and learning team sports and games.* Routledge.

Hoover, W. A. (1996). The practice implications of constructivism. *SEDL Letter, 9*(3), 1–2.

Huang, Y. C. (2021). *Comparison and contrast of Piaget and Vygotsky's theories.* In 7th International Conference on Humanities and Social Science Research (ICHSSR 2021) (pp. 28–32). Atlantis Press.

Kim, B. (2001). Social constructivism. *Emerging Perspectives on Learning, Teaching, and Technology, 1*(1), 16.

Kirk, D. & Macdonald, D. (1998). Situated learning in physical education. *Journal of Teaching in Physical Education, 17*(3), 376–387.

Kirk, D. & MacPhail, A. (2002). Teaching games for understanding and situated learning: Rethinking the Bunker-Thorpe model. *Journal of Teaching in Physical Education, 21*(2), 177–192.

Lave, J. & Wenger, E. (1991). *Situated learning: Legitimate peripheral participation.* Cambridge University Press.

MacPhail, A., Kirk, D. & Griffin, L. (2008). Throwing and catching as relational skills in game play: Situated learning in a modified game unit. *Journal of Teaching in Physical Education, 27*(1), 100–115.

Merriam, S. B. & Caffarella, R. S. (1999). *Learning in adulthood: A comprehensive guide* (2nd ed.). Jossey-Bass Publishers.

Metzler, M. (2017). *Instructional models in physical education.* Routledge.

Mitchell, S. A., Oslin, J. & Griffin, L. L. (2021). *Teaching sport concepts and skills: A tactical games approach* (4th ed.). Human Kinetics.

Nadeau, L., Gréhaigne, J.-F. & Godbout, P. (2017). Developing tactical knowledge with the help of support players: An illustration in ice hockey. *International Journal of Physical Education, 54*(1), 22–33.

Perkins, D. N. (1992). Technology meets constructivism: Do they make a marriage? In T. M. Duffy & D. H. Jonassen (Eds.), *Constructivism and the technology of instruction* (pp. 45–55). Erlbaum.

Richard J-F. & Griffin, L. L. (2003). Assessing game performance: An introduction to using the TSAP and GPAI. In J. Butler, L. L. Griffin, B. Lombardo & R. Natasi, (Eds.), *Teaching games for understanding in physical education and sport: An international perspective.* NASPE.

Richard, J.-F., Godbout, P. & Gréhaigne, J.-F. (2000). Students' precision and inter-observer reliability of performance assessment in team sports. *Research Quarterly for Exercise and Sports, 71*(1), 85–91.

Richard, J.-F., Godbout, P., Tousignant, M. & Gréhaigne, J.-F. (1999). The try-out of a team-sport assessment procedure in elementary and junior high school PE classes. *Journal of Teaching in Physical Education, 18*(3), 336–356.

Rink, J. E. (1996). Tactical and skill approaches to teaching sport and games. *Journal of Teaching in Physical Education, 15*, 397–398.

Rink, J. E. (2001). Investigating the assumptions of pedagogy. *Journal of Teaching in Physical Education, 20*(2), 112–128.

Schunk, D. H. (2012). *Learning theories an educational perspective* (6th ed.). Pearson.

Vygotsky, L. S. & Cole, M. (1978). *Mind in society: Development of higher psychological processes*. Harvard University Press.

Wood, D., Bruner, J. S. & Ross, G. (1976). The role of tutoring in problem solving. *Journal of Child Psychology & Psychiatry, 17,* 89–100.

Zessoules, R. & Gardner, H. (1991). Authentic assessment: Beyond the buzzword and into the classroom. In V. Perrone (Ed.), *Expanding student assessment* (pp. 47–71). Association for Supervision and Curriculum Development.

8 The Tactical versus Technical Paradigm: Scholarship on Teaching Games with a 'Catch-22'

Adrian P. Turner

As a novice teacher in the United Kingdom during the late 1980s, I experienced some of the challenges later outlined in teaching 'physical education-as-sport-techniques' (Kirk, 2010). I witnessed students learning a technique in one phase of a lesson, with limited content progression, and shortly afterwards playing a scrimmage without understanding how to use the skill in the context of the game (Ward et al., 2022). Prior to my employment, I studied as an undergraduate student at Exeter University, where I learned about Teaching Games for Understanding (TGfU) during the Physical Education Teacher Education (PETE) programme from Dr. Martin Underwood. I also experimented with the approach during my teaching internship and initial years of secondary school teaching in Taunton, Somerset. Upon my arrival in the United States in 1989, as a graduate student at the University of North Carolina Greensboro, I studied under the tutelage of Dr. Tom Martinek and was introduced to the concept of scholarly inquiry in sport pedagogy. In their seminal text, Van Dalen and Bennett (1971) suggested that one of the primary tenets that characterised study in both education and physical education from colonial times through the 20th century was the development of the scientific movement, comprised of objective testing, mathematical procedures to solve educational problems and the interpretation of results on a normal distribution. Contemporary texts on educational research also highlighted the importance of this mode of inquiry, 'the experimental method is both the most demanding and the most productive method of research. Well conducted, experimental studies produce the soundest evidence concerning hypothesised cause-effect relationships' (Gay, 1987, p. 260). It is within this backdrop that it may be helpful to comprehend the initial impetus behind a rookie scholar's research vein, that was part of a larger line of inquiry into TGfU, beginning in the 1990s, that focused on the tactical versus technical paradigm to study games instruction.

Empirical investigation

While Bunker and Thorpe's (1982) model made intuitive sense as an alternative to traditional technique-based teaching, there existed little

DOI: 10.4324/9781003298298-11

empirical evidence to support its validity (Turner & Martinek, 1995). Predominantly in North America, experimental studies began to contrast game-based models (TGfU) with technique instruction by measuring their impact on criteria that included sport technique assessments, declarative and procedural knowledge, and game performance components (control, decision-making and execution). Research also contrasted off-the-ball player movements in accordance with these pedagogical approaches (Mitchell et al., 1995). Below is a brief synopsis of the findings from these early comparative studies. (For a comprehensive review of empirical research on TGfU/game-based approaches, see Barba-Martín et al., 2020; Harvey & Jarrett, 2014; Oslin & Mitchell, 2006; Stolz & Pill, 2014).

Technique outcomes

Research using the technical versus tactical paradigm to examine secondary school students learning in basketball (Allison & Thorpe, 1997), badminton (French et al., 1996a, 3-week study) and field hockey (Turner, 1996; Turner & Martinek, 1992; Turner & Martinek, 1999) indicated no significant differences between technique and game-based teaching approaches on tests of specific sport techniques. Several studies (Turner, 1996; Turner & Martinek, 1992) showed a significant improvement over time in specific game skill tests (e.g., dribbling) but not others (e.g., shooting accuracy) for both teaching approaches. A second badminton study (French et al., 1996b, 6-week study) also revealed significant gains over time for tactical, technique and combination teaching groups on tests of badminton techniques in contrast to a control group.

Knowledge development

For declarative knowledge (e.g., game rules) in middle school students learning field hockey, the TGfU group showed significant gains in comparison to a technique group (Turner, 1996). For procedural knowledge (where students matched specific game conditions with an appropriate response), the TGfU group scored significantly higher than a control group but not significantly more than the technique group (Turner & Martinek, 1999). This finding replicated the outcome of a comparative study examining students' knowledge development in badminton (French et al., 1996a).

Game performance

Student game performance was measured on elements of control, decision-making and execution. Two studies indicated that students undertaking TGfU instruction were significantly better at controlling a ball during field hockey game play than the technique group (Turner, 1996; Turner &

Martinek, 1999). In analysing students' game decision-making, the results were equivocal. Several studies did not find significant differences between game-based approaches and technique instruction groups in invasion sports (Mitchell et al., 1995; Turner & Martinek, 1992). In their badminton study, French et al. (1996b) found a combination teaching group made inferior game decisions when compared to tactical and technical instructional groups. Other research indicated that game-based instruction produced a significant improvement in decision-making in net/wall games (Griffin et al., 1995) and invasion sports (Mitchell et al., 1997; Turner, 1996). There were no significant differences between game-based and technique groups in terms of game execution in studies of soccer (Mitchell et al., 1995) and field hockey (Turner, 1996; Turner & Martinek, 1992). In a subsequent study (Turner & Martinek, 1999), students in the TGfU group exhibited significantly better passing execution during post-test field hockey game play than both technique and control groups. Dribbling and shooting execution, although trending higher, were not statistically significant in the same study.

In addition to examining decision-making and execution, the Game Performance Assessment Instrument (GPAI) (Oslin et al., 1998) was developed to measure game involvement and support play (offensive and defensive off-the-ball movements). In a comparative study on middle school soccer taught using tactical and technique approaches pre-test to post-test gains for game involvement and off-the-ball support play indicated the effectiveness of the tactical approach over the technique model (Mitchell et al., 1995). As noted by Kirk (2010):

> The first studies of TGfU unsurprisingly sought to compare TGfU with the so-called 'traditional' (skill-based) approach … . This rush of studies may have been a sign of enthusiasm for the idea of TGfU or a symptom of researchers' dissatisfaction with the dominance of the technique-led molecular approach. Whatever these researchers' motivation, these comparative studies proved to be disappointingly inconclusive. (p. 52)

Rationale for enigmatic findings

While experimental research attempted to control for extraneous variables, a variety of reasons have been proffered for the equivocal nature of findings from comparative studies that incorporated multifarious research designs. Game-based models were unlikely to be effective if students were taught for only a brief learning segment. To test a hypothesis concerning the impact of an instructional model accurately, an experimental group should be exposed long enough for the treatment to produce a measurable effect (Mills & Gay, 2019). In an analysis of research on the impact of game-based approaches (across 25 years), an intervention volume of at least 8 hours, or 10 sessions, was warranted to support the development of individual decision-making and skill execution outcomes during game play (Miller, 2015). An emergent issue with the technical versus tactical paradigm was ensuring the approaches were sufficiently different. While comparative studies employed protocols that reported the fidelity of technique and TGfU/tactical approaches to instruction (French et al., 1996a; French at al., 1996b; Mitchell et al., 1995), several validation protocols were based around treatment lesson structure to distinguish the pedagogical practices (Turner & Martinek, 1992; Turner & Martinek, 1999). Specific lesson scenarios potentially existed where TGfU teachers permitted students to engage in a modified scrimmage without carefully shaping the modified game via teacher intervention to facilitate student learning (Kinnerk et al., 2018). Additional studies have suggested inexperienced instructors (inadvertently) 'tinkered' with the intended TGfU teaching approach (Turner, 2014).

TGfU/tactical approaches incorporated skill practice once the need was recognised through tactical awareness and understanding in the game context (Kirk, 2010); so individual skill learning components during TGfU/ tactical instruction treatments sometimes overlapped with specific lesson elements used during effective content progression during technique teaching approaches; suggesting potential treatment diffusion (Mills & Gay, 2019). In the technique approach, students may have developed some level of tactical understanding and decision-making capability from participating in game play at the culmination of their lessons and pre-test sensitisation was an additional threat to assessment of student's knowledge development in comparative research (Mills & Gay, 2019). Game-based approaches were also defined and measured differently. For example, in the Mitchell et al. (1995) soccer study utilising the tactical approach, the lesson structure followed a learning sequence of modified game (with student questioning), skill practice, modified game (a game-practice-game sequence) with game performance outcomes measured on the GPAI. It represented a conceptualisation of game-based teaching that differed from TGfU which was delineated and measured in an alternative format during other experimental research (Turner & Martinek, 1992; Turner & Martinek, 1999).

The precise differences in various game-based approaches and measurement instruments (specificity of variables) within varied research designs across a number of sports reduced clarity during the interpretation of results (Stolz & Pill, 2014). Some scholars also suggested that studies attempting to ascertain the viability of a solitary games teaching model over another, represented an invalid research design because each approach promoted different instructional outcomes (Metzler, 2005). For example, TGfU focuses on educating the learner to become skilful within the game context where decision-making and efficient movement execution are all elements of effective game play. Traditional teaching emphasises the learning of individual techniques, with concerns for class control and safety underpinning the approach (Kirk, 2005). An attempt to examine products of TGfU and technique teaching that 'promote different kinds of outcomes with processes they do not hold in common is the empirical equivalent of comparing apples to oranges' (Metzler, 2005, p. 190).

Although scholars called for an end to comparative experimental studies that attempted to discern which approach was optimal (Oslin & Mitchell, 2006), research efforts attempting to draw generalisations from empirical scientific testing, employing the tactical versus technical paradigm, continued in the 21st century. A meta-analysis aimed at analysing both approaches on game performance variables (2006–2018) revealed the tactical approach achieved significant improvements in game decision-making in five of seven studies (Abad Robles et al., 2020). Their systematic review did not indicate similar improvements in game execution. In only two of six studies, the tactical model showed amelioration for game execution while the technique approach failed to show significant development in any investigation.

A comparative 'catch-22'

The tactical versus technical paradigm necessitates a meticulous approach to scholarship; it requires investigators to restrict threats to the internal validity of the research (i.e., both teachers taught using both TGfU and technique approaches in several studies to prevent a 'teacher effect' from confounding the treatments) and sports were selected because participants had no previous experience with the activity (Turner, 1996; Turner & Martinek, 1992, Turner & Martinek, 1999). However, the more a research environment is narrowed and controlled, the less generalisability its findings apply to real-world settings. This scenario represented a 'catch-22' for sport pedagogy scholars employing this paradigm. The empirical scientific testing of the effectiveness of TGfU and technique approaches attempts to make causal connections and predictions by carefully controlling the teaching environment, but potential generalisations to pedagogical practice are unlikely to account for the contextual nature of teaching and learning in varied physical education environments in schools (Stolz & Pill, 2014). TGfU instruction may work effectively with one group of students, during one sport activity, in a specific instructional setting, but the outcomes may be different with other students undertaking an alternate curricular unit in another school (Stolz & Pill, 2014). For example, an essential criterion for an effective learning experience in physical education is the provision of maximal activity for participants at an appropriate level of difficulty (Rink, 2020). Comparative studies in invasion sports (Turner, 1996; Turner & Martinek, 1999) frequently employed small-size teaching groups (10 students) for both technique and TGfU instruction to compensate for a restrictive instructional space and facilitate student learning. The provision of an adequate playing area is essential to effective learning where sufficient time and space facilitate skilful game performance, including effective decision-making and execution (Launder & Piltz, 2013). However, the impact of a less expansive area on game-based approaches (where students spend significant amounts of time in modified games) is potentially greater than on practice components in technique-based lessons (Turner, 2005). Research has suggested that teachers perceive a barrier to teaching some field-invasion sports (e.g., lacrosse), when utilising game-based approaches in authentic environments, due to restrictive instructional space (Barrett & Turner, 2000).

Know-how (and why) for TGfU

In his examination of game-based research, Miller (2015) indicated the majority of studies undertaken by research teams used a prescribed curriculum designed by the investigators. Scholars contend that TGfU places greater demands on teachers' and coaches' subject matter knowledge than technique teaching (Kirk, 2010; Turner, 2021; Turner & Martinek, 1995) and that this expertise goes well beyond common content knowledge (CCK) of game rules, strategies and skills frequently obtained through playing the game (Ward et al., 2018). High-quality game-based teaching incorporates specialised content knowledge (SCK) that includes advanced understanding of game content progression and learning tasks to teach game tactics and skills (Ward & Ayvazo, 2016). In the technical versus tactical paradigm, researchers attempted to equip teachers with SCK (via prescribed curricular content) but the pedagogical content knowledge (PCK) that includes comprehending individual student's needs, their prior learning experiences and learning context (Ward et al., 2018) was minimally accounted for in most pre-set curricula. For example, students' learning styles were not systematically examined in reference to TGfU and technique teaching approaches (Turner & Martinek, 1995). Studies on learning to use TGfU in naturalistic settings highlighted the importance of teachers comprehending the needs of their students in planning for relevant game tactics and skills requiring extensive PCK (O'Leary, 2016). Research by Roberts (2011) with participation cricket coaches using TGfU, also identified inadequate PCK as limiting coaches' questioning strategies.

Most technical versus tactical studies did not address the nuances encountered during 'real-world' teaching engagement and their ecological validity has been subject to question (Kirk, 2010; Metzler, 2005). Research using a practice-referenced or teaching experiment was posited as a viable alternative to examine TGfU (Kirk, 2005) or tactical instruction in a school-based setting (Lee & Ward, 2009). Student learning outcomes for game-based teaching could be derived from contextualised circumstances and data collected in reference to specified outcomes.

In the past decade, several comparative investigations (Gray & Sproule, 2011; López et al., 2016) identified as 'high in ecological validity' (Gray & Sproule, 2011, p. 16) have continued to examine the impact of TGfU/tactical approaches and technique instruction on student's game performance and knowledge acquisition. Both studies examined an invasion sport (basketball) taught in secondary school gymnasia. In the first study, results suggested the tactical group made significantly better on- and off-the-ball decisions, but not game executions (Gray & Sproule, 2011). The research by López et al. (2016) found no significant differences in game decision-making or execution for either approach, but both studies revealed significant enhancement in students' knowledge development when using game-based approaches. In these investigations ongoing professional learning and support was provided to teachers as they engaged in planning activities for game-based instruction. The salience of active communities of practice to enhance teachers' and coaches' PCK in reference to game-based instruction (Turner & Turner, 2022), in light of potential support made available via educational technology, offers considerable promise in future research endeavours (Harvey & Jarrett, 2014).

In the quest to provide clear guidance on how to effectively teach children to play games, some scholars contend the technical versus tactical paradigm still has much to offer (Abad Robles et al., 2020). For example, in the affective domain, results have consistently shown students experienced increased involvement, motivation and enjoyment as a result of a TGfU/ game-based intervention, as opposed to technique instruction (Gray et al., 2009; Kinnerk et al., 2018). In comparative studies (contrasting a technique/control group with TGfU), the utilisation of a clustered research design also permits increased generalisability of findings pertaining to game-based approaches with potentially increased statistical power than in a 'teaching experiment' (Miller, 2015).

Conclusion

As I look back at the initial study Tom Martinek and I undertook 30 years ago to investigate TGfU within the technical versus tactical paradigm, I am struck by the recent scholarship of Dr. Brené Brown (research professor at the University of Houston) and number one *New York Times* bestselling author. Her definition of social comparison has clear application to the technical versus tactical paradigm. Brown (2021) indicates that 'comparison is the crush of conformity from one side and competition from the other—it's trying to simultaneously fit in and stand out. Comparison says, be like everyone else, but better' (p. 20). In its infancy, we were attempting to help TGfU gain legitimacy by comparing it to technique instruction and measuring both approaches against specific dependent measures (technique, knowledge and game performance variables). We hoped to illustrate that TGfU did not mean 'roll out the ball' and let children play games (as it was sometimes initially misinterpreted in the United States), but instead offers a viable alternative to technique instruction that can impact student learning. We now understand that TGfU requires sophisticated teacher SCK and PCK to contextualise learning for students during modified game play. TGfU aims to develop game understanding, help players acquire tactics to make good decisions and learn to effectively execute skills during game-related practices and games, that enable them to enjoy playing and perform better. Future research using the technical versus tactical paradigm is advised to acknowledge that comparison also has the potential to restrict creativity (Brown, 2021), a concept that TGfU espouses as integral to cultivating thinking games players.

References

Abad Robles, M. T., Collado-Mateo, D., Fernández-Espínola, C., Castillo Viera, E. & Giménez Fuentes-Guerra, F. J. (2020). Effects of teaching games on decision making and skill execution: A systematic review and meta-analysis. *International Journal of Environmental Research and Public Health*, *17*(505), 1–13.

Allison, S. & Thorpe, R. (1997). A comparison of the effectiveness of two approaches to teaching games within physical education. A skills approach versus a games for understanding approach. *British Journal of Physical Education*, *28*(3), 9–13.

Barba-Martín, R. A., Bores-García, D., Hortigüela-Alcalá, D. & González-Calvo, G. (2020). The application of the teaching games for understanding in physical education. Systematic review of the last six years. *International Journal of Environmental Research and Public Health*, *17*(3330), 1–16.

Barrett, K. R. & Turner, A. P. (2000). Sandy's challenge: New game, new paradigm. *Journal of Teaching in Physical Education*, *19*(2), 141–161.

Brown, B. (2021). *Atlas of the heart: Mapping meaningful connection and the language of human experience*. Random House.

Bunker, D. J. & Thorpe, R. D. (1982). A model for the teaching of games in secondary schools. *Bulletin of Physical Education*, *18*, 7–10.

French, K., Werner, P., Rink, J., Taylor, K. & Hussey, K. (1996a). The effects of a 3-week unit of tactical, skill, or combined tactical and skill instruction on badminton performance of ninth-grade students. *Journal of Teaching in Physical Education*, *15*(4), 418–438.

French, K., Werner, P., Taylor, K., Hussey, K. & Jones, J. (1996b). The effects of a 6-week unit of tactical, skill, or combined tactical and skill instruction on badminton performance of ninth-grade students. *Journal of Teaching in Physical Education*, *15*(4), 439–463.

Gay, L. R. (1987). *Educational research: Competencies for analysis and application* (3rd ed.). Merrill.

Gray, S. & Sproule, J. (2011). Developing pupils' performance in team invasion games. *Physical Education and Sport Pedagogy*, *16*(1), 15–32.

Gray, S., Sproule, J. & Morgan, K. (2009). Teaching team invasion games and motivational climate. *European Physical Education Review*, *15*(1), 65–89.

Griffin, L., Oslin, J. & Mitchell, S. (1995). An analysis of two instructional approaches to teaching net games. *Research Quarterly for Exercise and Sport*, *66*(Suppl.), A-64.

Harvey, S. & Jarrett, K. (2014). A review of the game-centred approaches to teaching and coaching literature since 2006. *Physical Education and Sport Pedagogy*, *19*(3), 278–300.

Kinnerk, P., Harvey, S., MacDonncha, C. & Lyons, M. (2018). A review of the game based approaches to coaching literature in competitive team sports settings. *Quest*, *70*(4), 401–418.

Kirk, D. (2005). Future prospects for teaching games for understanding. In J. Butler & L. Griffin (Eds.), *Teaching games for understanding: Theory, research, and practice* (pp. 213–227). Human Kinetics.

Kirk, D. (2010). *Physical education futures*. Routledge.

Launder, A. & Piltz, W. (2013). *Play practice: Engaging and developing skilled players from beginner to elite* (2nd ed.). Human Kinetics.

Lee, M.-A. & Ward, P. (2009). Generalization of tactics in tag rugby from practice to games in middle school physical education. *Physical Education and Sport Pedagogy, 14*(2), 189–207.

López, I., Práxedes, A. & del Villar, F. (2016). Effect of an intervention teaching program, based on TGfU model, on the cognitive and execution variables, in the physical education context. *European Journal of Human Movement, 37*, 88–108.

Metzler, M. W. (2005). Implications of models-based instruction for research on teaching: A focus on teaching games for understanding. In J. Butler & L. Griffin (Eds.), *Teaching games for understanding: Theory, research, and practice* (pp. 183–197). Human Kinetics.

Miller, A. (2015). Games centred approaches in teaching children & adolescents: Systematic review of associated student outcomes. *Journal of Teaching in Physical Education, 34*(1), 36–58.

Mills, G. E. & Gay, L. R. (2019). *Educational research: Competencies for analysis and applications* (12th ed.). Pearson.

Mitchell, S., Griffin, L. & Oslin, J. (1997). Teaching invasion games: A comparison of two instructional approaches. *Pedagogy in Practice: Teaching and Coaching in Physical Education and Sports, 3*(2), 56–59.

Mitchell, S., Oslin, J. & Griffin, L. (1995). The effects of two instructional approaches on game performance. *Pedagogy in Practice: Teaching and Coaching in Physical Education and Sports, 1*(1), 36–48.

O'Leary, N. (2016). Learning informally to use the 'full version' of teaching games for understanding. *European Physical Education Review, 22*(1), 3–22.

Oslin, J. & Mitchell, S. (2006). Game-centred approaches to teaching physical education. In D. Kirk, D. Macdonald & M. O'Sullivan (Eds.), *The handbook of physical education* (pp. 627–651). SAGE Publications.

Oslin, J., Mitchell, S., & Griffin, L. (1998). The game performance assessment instrument (GPAI): Development and preliminary validation. *Journal of Teaching in Physical Education, 17*(2), 231–243.

Rink, J. (2020). *Teaching physical education for learning* (8th ed.). McGraw-Hill.

Roberts, S. J. (2011). Teaching games for understanding: The difficulties and challenges experienced by participation cricket coaches. *Physical Education and Sport Pedagogy, 16*(1), 33–48.

Stolz, S. & Pill, S. (2014). Teaching games and sport for understanding: Exploring and reconsidering its relevance in physical education. *European Physical Education Review, 20*(1), 36–71.

Turner, A. P. (1996). Teaching for understanding: Myth or reality? *Journal of Physical Education, Recreation and Dance, 67*(4), 46–55.

Turner, A. P. (2005). Teaching and learning games at the secondary level. In J. Butler & L. Griffin (Eds.), *Teaching games for understanding: Theory, research, and practice* (pp. 71–89). Human Kinetics.

Turner, A. P. (2014). Novice coaches negotiating teaching games for understanding. *University of Sydney Papers in Human Movement, Health and Coach Education Special Game Sense Edition, 3*, 67–89.

Turner, A. P. (2021). Learning to be a game-changer. In S. Pill (Ed.), *Perspectives on game-based coaching* (pp. 77–85). Routledge.

Turner, A. P. & Martinek, T. J. (1992). A comparative analysis of two models for teaching games (technique approach and game-centered (tactical focus) approach). *International Journal of Physical Education*, *29*(4), 15–31.

Turner, A. P. & Martinek, T. J. (1995). Teaching for understanding: A model for improving decision-making during game play. *Quest*, *47*, 44–63.

Turner, A. P. & Martinek, T. J. (1999). An investigation into teaching games for understanding: Effects on skill, knowledge and game play. *Research Quarterly for Exercise and Sport*, *70*(3), 286–296.

Turner, A. P. & Turner, T. W. (2022). Coach education in United States youth soccer: Same game: New paradigm – Play-practice-play. In T. M. Leeder (Ed.), *Coach education in football: Contemporary issues and global perspectives* (pp. 236–248). Routledge.

Van Dalen, D. B. & Bennett, B. L. (1971). *A world history of physical education* (2nd ed.). Prentice Hall.

Ward, P. & Ayvazo, S. (2016). Pedagogical content knowledge: Conceptions and findings in physical education. *Journal of Teaching in Physical Education*, *35*(3), 194–207.

Ward, P., Dervent, F., Iserbyt, P. & Tsuda, E. (2022). Teaching sports in physical education. *Journal of Physical Education, Recreation and Dance*, *93*(1), 8–13.

Ward, P., Piltz, W. & Lehwald, H. (2018). Unpacking games teaching: What do teachers need to know? *Journal of Physical Education, Recreation and Dance*, *89*(4), 39–44.

9 Teaching Games and Sport for Understanding as a Spectrum of Teaching Styles

Brendan SueSee and Shane Pill

In this chapter, we use The Spectrum of Teaching Styles (The Spectrum: Mosston, 1966; Mosston & Ashworth, 2008) to identify the teaching styles used to implement the six-step Teaching Games for Understanding (TGfU) model as a cluster of teaching styles, to show that teaching games for understanding require use of more teaching styles than guided discovery, problem solving or discovery teaching. We clarify TGfU as a model directed at student understanding by explaining that asking students questions may not be guided discovery, or any other type of discovery process. Depending on the objective of the teaching episode, and the instructional language used by the teacher, discovery of new understanding may not be the operant behaviour the teacher is seeking, requesting or being used by the player. We believe that TGfU and game-based approaches (GBAs) generally are a cluster of teaching styles, and not a style (SueSee et al., 2016; SueSee et al., 2020), as lessons and coaching sessions using a GBA are episodic (Pill et al., 2021).

We use an example of a GBA to identify the pedagogical decision making which is apparent in the description: that is, who is making the decisions, when the decisions are being made, and the intent of these decisions, will be considered. We do this from a 'non-versus' perspective in so far as evaluative claims about the episode being 'good' or 'bad' will not be made. Further, we will explain using teaching for effective learning ideas that the episodic nature of GBAs (SueSee et al., 2016; SueSee et al., 2020) means that inquiry episodes attached to game play may be purposefully used by teachers and sport coaches for recall and retrieval practice (Pill & SueSee, 2021). When this intentionally occurs by teacher or coach (by deliberate design), the teaching style aligns with Style B from The Spectrum.

Discovery teaching styles

It is beyond the limits of this chapter to explain The Spectrum in physical education (PE). For a detailed explanation and examples, we direct readers to SueSee et al. (2020) and Pill et al. (2021). Briefly however, in The Spectrum, discovery teaching styles are associated with production of knowledge and understanding rather than reproduction of knowledge or

DOI: 10.4324/9781003298298-12

skills. The term 'guided discovery' is attached to Style F of The Spectrum (Mosston & Ashworth, 2002), which is described as 'the logical and sequential design of questions that lead a person to discover a predetermined response' (Mosston & Ashworth, 2002, p. 212). This response would be unknown to the student and require more than one step or question to discover the response. Mosston and Ashworth (2008) cautioned that in group situations, Style F may not allow all students to discover as learners discover at different speeds. Further, if other students hear or see a response from another student in answer to a question, they can no longer be considered as discovering the answer as they have become receivers of the information from the other player, or imitators of the behaviour they observed (SueSee et al., 2016).

From the perspective of The Spectrum, a question-and-answer experience might be a variation of the Practice style (a review or 'practice' of existing understanding) (Mosston & Ashworth, 2008). If this is the intention of the use of the teaching style, then this is a worthwhile teaching impact. Therefore, the presumption that a teacher is doing Guided Discovery and all the students are discovering as the teacher is asking questions, is uncertain at the least and hard to determine if students' existing thinking and knowing has not previously been made visible. This point is claimed for two reasons. First, in any learning episode it is unlikely that all students are starting from the same knowledge point with respect to the knowledge or skills they possess about a topic. Therefore, if the same questions were asked of 25 students, then some would recall answers and others would discover the answer. The second reason which makes Guided Discovery unlikely is the cognitive processing of the 25 students when thinking and responding to the questions from the teacher. The students' processing speeds would all need to be identical (an unrealistic assumption) so that when the teacher asked the questions associated with using Guided Discovery all students would be able to discover the exact same predetermined response and discover it at the same time (SueSee et al., 2020).

An example of a GBA considered as a spectrum of teaching styles

We use Style F of The Spectrum in a game teaching episode in the form of a striking/fielding game based on cricket, called Super Twos (Pill, 2013). The emphasis of Super Twos is ball placement and the concept of hitting the ball away from fielders to score runs. Four pairs (eight students or four sets/teams of two) play with one pair batting whilst the other three pairs share the bowling and fielding duties. Bowler's bowl one over each and the batting pair face 36 balls between them (six students bowl six balls each).

To identify the possible teaching styles which emerged from this game scenario, we will presume that there are students who have minimal knowledge of striking and fielding games, and some who have a large amount of experience, and therefore knowledge of the game. We will use The Spectrum to view the episode and identify the potential teaching styles. We will presume that the teacher has explained the game and the rules, etc. This would have included the phrase 'the goal of the game when batting is to score as many runs as possible'. It is also presumed that the teacher will have explained the ways to get 'out' (e.g., bowled, caught, run out, etc.).

Suggested questions to ask (Pill, 2013, p. 71) include:

- When do you try to hit the ball along the ground?
- When do you try to hit the ball in the air?
- How do you place the ball to score a run?

For the novice students, an opportunity for a Guided Discovery episode may emerge when they are not scoring runs as they keep hitting the ball to the fielders. The teacher may ask a series of questions to create this episode, as seen below (Figure 9.1, Table 9.1).

In this episode, the teacher asked the student a series of questions to guide them to a single response to a problem which the student did not know the

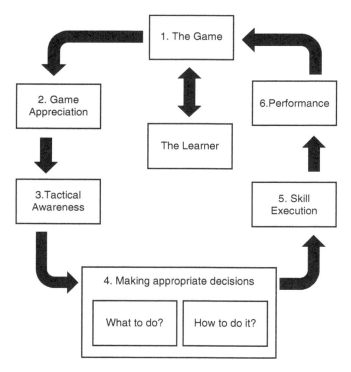

Figure 9.1 The TGfU six-step model from game form to performance (see Bunker & Thorpe, 1982).

Table 9.1 Super Twos' cricket (Pill, 2013)

Super Twos

Game emphasis: Ball placement—batter hits the ball away from fielders to make runs.

Safety
- Ensure adequate distance between games so fielders in one game do not become a hazard in another.
- Use tennis balls and plastic bats and stumps.

Modified cricket rules and the following
- Groups of eight (four pairs).
- One pair bat and the other pairs share bowling and fielding duties.
- Batting pair remain 'in' for six overs (one over from each fielder, or 36 balls if using a batting tee).
- Scoring: At the end of their six overs, the batting pair divide their combined runs by the number of times they were collectively 'out'.

Game progression
- Begin using a batting tee or small witches' hat to hit from, to enhance batter's success.
- Students can be caught, run out or stumped.
- Focus batting concepts, e.g., place the ball in the field, run between wickets.
- Focus on fielding concepts.
- Introduce Bowling a Ball accurately using a 'rock and bowl' technique (set a batting tee to the side of the batting crease so batters still have the opportunity to make a hit even if a ball is bowled wide).
- Introduce a Walk Up and Bowl.

---

solution to. Thus, the student discovered a possible solution. However, if a student with a lot of striking and fielding knowledge was asked these questions, they would more than likely recall known responses as they have some familiarity with the tactical concepts of this game (e.g., hitting to space, safer hitting the ball on the ground). There would be no 'searching' for a response, rather, there would be the recalling of a known response from their previous experiences playing such games. This episode provides an example of the concept that merely asking open ended question does not guarantee Guided Discovery is occurring.

We argue that in our experience of working with teachers and coaches one of the conceptual errors made in discussion about GBAs is that they are 'game-only' and that 'the game is the teacher'. Further, we suggest that careful consideration of examples put forward as TGfU, constraints-led approach, and GBAs generally is that it cannot be assumed to be providing a discovery orientated environment when the published instructions provided to the students are examined from a critical literacy lens, as the structure of the questions do not align to Style F: Guided Discovery requirement of the student to discover or create new understanding (Table 9.2).

Discussion: TGfU as a spectrum of teaching styles

To further highlight the cluster of teaching styles that may be used in the TGfU six-step cycle (Figure 9.1), let us presume that there are students in

Table 9.2 An example of Style F of The Spectrum in a game teaching episode

Teacher: You are having trouble scoring runs Tracey.
Tracey: Yeah, the fielder always gets the ball, and I can't run.
Teacher: How can you make it harder for the fielder?
Tracey: I don't know. Make them run?
Teacher: How can you do that?
Tracey: Hit the ball away from them? But how do I do that? The ball is always in a difficult position? Can I ask the bowler to bowl it where I want it, on my leg side (left)?
Teacher: You can, but I don't think that will work. What else could move so the ball is in a better position?
Tracey: Me? So, if I move to my right the ball may be in a better position?
Teacher: Give it a go and see what happens!

class who have some striking and fielding skills at a level that allows them to consistently strike the ball but have limited game play knowledge or tactical awareness. If we think back to the Super-Twos example (Pill, 2013), Steps 1 (The Game) and 2 (Game Appreciation) may represent Practice Style B from The Spectrum. Bunker and Thorpe (1982) proposed that in Steps 1 and 2 the teacher would explain the game, the rules and how to play. During Step 1, the teacher constructs a modified game for the students to understand the rules of the game. Step 2, or game appreciation, aims to occur in a modified game form that enables the students to develop an appreciation of the rules that shape the game. The aim during this stage is to determine the repertoire of skills required and the tactical problems to be appreciated by the students. If the teacher explains the game, the rules and how to play then we presume that the students will use known skills to play the game. The students will reproduce ways they have thrown, caught and struck balls before in their attempt to play. They have not been directed to discover new skills by the teacher. The students have been told rules and how to play so that they replicate the rules and how to play. It is possible to consider that the students will create a new way; however, as The Spectrum describes teaching as a deliberate chain of decision making (and the teacher has not deliberately instructed the students to discover or create) then it is the student's choice and not because of deliberate instruction.

With regards to Step 2 (Game Appreciation), there is a presumption made that by playing the modified game, the students will develop an appreciation for the rules. This is most likely to take place upon reflection or attempting to understand the rule after playing. In both Steps 1 and 2, there is a reliance on recalling known movements and a presumption that students will reflect on the game which will lead to an appreciation of the rules. Both of these steps, as described here, can be met with practice style as the learning experiences require the students to use known knowledge to play the game and reflect (denotes memory) about what has happened.

If students with some developed skills were to participate in this environment, they would be recalling known skills of striking the ball.

Similarly, if the teacher has created some modified rules new to the student, it is not assured that the new rules would require new movement abilities to promote game development based on the modified game. The new modified game may be new to the students; however, the students may still be re-calling known skills to play the game.

The teacher may notice with a particular student that they are able to hit the ball; however, they are frequently getting out as they always hit the ball in the air. This situation provides a segue for Step 3 (tactical awareness) and Step 4 (decision making). Students are taught tactical awareness through playing a modified game during Step 3 if the students are guided by the teacher to develop tactical awareness of how to gain an advantage over their opponent. Referring to one of the questions asked when playing Super Twos ('When do you try to hit the ball along the ground?'), it helps to see that the teacher encourages the students to consider the increased risk of getting out (caught by a fielder) if the ball is hit in the air. This situation, where the teacher asks a question at the beginning of the playing of this game, may represent a Convergent Discovery Episode—that being, there is one correct answer to the question. This is supported by SueSee et al. (2020) when they suggested, 'if players do not know this information, then it may be that this learning episode will provide them with the opportunity to discover the relationship and cues' (p. 82). Convergent Discovery Style's defining characteristic is to 'discover the correct (predetermined) response using the convergent process' (Mosston & Ashworth, 2008, p. 237). Furthermore, the learner's role is to 'engage in reasoning, questioning, and logic to sequentially make connections about the content to discover the answers' (2008, p. 237). As the batter cannot get out if the ball is fielded on the ground (it must be caught), it means that the student (through attempting to discover) can exploit this rule to their advantage by hitting the ball on the ground when a fielder is near, thus reducing the chance of getting out by being caught. The desire to implement this tactic leads to Step 4—the 'how' to do it. Or as Bunker and Thorpe (1982) suggested, tactical awareness allows the students to recognise cues of what to do (skill selection) and the how to do the skill based on the circumstances of the game. During Step 4, our student (s) may not have ever considered the 'how to' of hitting the ball on the ground. This point in time on the six-step model may create an opportunity for the teacher to use a Guided Discovery episode to guide the student to discovering how the angle of the bat face determines the trajectory that the ball leaves the bat with. Another style that could be used for the student to discover how to hit the ball on the ground could be the use of Convergent Discovery. For example, if the teacher asked the students to play a game in pairs where Student A tosses a half-volley to the batter, who is tasked with hitting the ball over a marker 10 metres away, then asked to hit the half-volley on the ground to the marker. The teacher can then ask the question, 'What do you do differently with the bat to get the ball to go over the marker when compared to on the ground?' If students do not directly focus on the angle of the bat, then the teacher may 'guide' through questions student awareness (convergent discovery) that bat angle is different.

The penultimate stage of the TGfU six-step model, Step 5, is skill execution. During this stage the execution of the skill in the context of the game is practiced. This stage is characterised by students developing problem solving skills which help them to understand the purpose for practicing either a technical skill needed to play the game with more tactical sophistication, or a strategic manoeuvre practiced gaining a tactical advantage (Hopper & Kruisselbrink, 2001). Using the sport of football (soccer) as an example, let us assume the student has not yet learnt to kick the ball to make it bend with accuracy, or in the case of a tactical concept, they do not recognise the cues (some might say affordances) from the game moment 'when' to use this kick. From a cognitive perspective the cues that help the student know 'when' to bend the ball will help the student develop pattern recognition. Pattern recognition can only be learnt in a game or in the context of a modified game where the occasion arises for the need of such a skill to be recalled at the appropriate moment. Game play therefore creates the environment for the player to learn to identify the situation (cues and pattern) and then recall the appropriate skill (the 'how') to match the situation. Stage 5 presents an environment that might be seen to necessitate the use of a cluster of styles or at least two episodes to be used—Divergent Discovery and Practice Style.

By way of a scenario to explain: An opportunity to use Divergent Discovery arises as the teacher realises that the player is unaware of how to solve the problem of being a striker outside the 18-yard box with the ball and moving towards goal. Let us presume they are coming from a central position on the pitch, and they see the keeper standing in the middle of goal. A defender is between the keeper and the striker. The teacher can pose the problem/question for players to solve, 'In this situation, create as many ways as possible to score'. The player may think firstly they will kick the ball hard at the defender and hope the defender does not touch the ball. Secondly, they may consider bending the ball around the defender, hoping the defender may obscure the keeper's view for a while. Finally, they may consider striking the ball to the left side of the goal. The teacher may then give the player an opportunity to practice these three scenarios and ask them to decide which one is the most effective. This would represent a Convergent Discovery episode as the teacher is asking the player to decide on one correct response to the question. The teacher may then ask the player if there is a skill that they need to improve to execute their chosen scenario with more success. The player may conclude that they need to work on bending of the ball with more accuracy and consistency. This now presents the opportunity for a variety of Practice Style B episodes, depending on the player's skill level and ability to identify and respond to the cues associated with the game scenario. The reason that Style B would be selected is the desired outcome is twofold: (a) it is to bend the ball with accuracy and consistency, and (b) when the attacker recognises the cues (open goal on their right with a defender in front) and choses to execute that strike. A Practice Style B episode allows for the rehearsal and retrieval of both the skill (bending the ball) and the recognition of the pattern which is based on the position of the attacker and defenders. The Recognition Primed Decision (RPD) model suggests that 'as individuals become more experienced within a domain, they automatically recognise situational patterns as familiar which, in turn, activates an associated situational response' (Ward, 2011, p. 2). From a cognitive perspective, pattern recognition provides a priming mechanism for the desired behaviours.

Step 6, the final stage of the TGfU six-step model, is performance of the skill or strategy and where what is learned is 'measured against criteria that are independent of the learner' (Hopper & Kruisselbrink, 2001, p. 10). This criteria focuses upon the appropriateness of responses as well as efficiency of technique. The reference to the word 'learned' from a cognitive perspective implies memory or a gained movement ability, therefore it might be concluded that the six-steps end with a Practice Style B teaching episode as the player(s) are recalling learned skills and strategies from Steps 4 and 5 in a game-like environment, while the teacher provides feedback about the performance. Alternatively, the six steps can be seen as a series of teaching episodes ending with assessment (Step 6) through a Practice Style B episode.

Conclusion

This chapter has viewed the six-step TGfU model through The Spectrum, which has provided a lens to highlight the micro-pedagogies or different learning episodes which occur when using a TGfU approach. The Spectrum has shown that the six-step model is more than one teaching style and it has highlighted the complexities of the model in terms of how different teaching styles are needed to create learning episodes to achieve the aims of the model. We suggest The Spectrum can assist the teacher in describing the behaviour needed of both the teacher and student in the learning episode created (by the teacher) to meet the objective beyond 'play a game' and use of 'guided discovery'. We have provided an explanation to demonstrate that one teaching style alone could not meet all the goals of the six-step model. This however is not a claim that The Spectrum replaces the six-step TGfU model (or is better than it) as this would not be congruent with The Spectrum's valuing of all teaching styles for their utility in student learning (SueSee et al., 2021) in a non-versus approach (Mosston & Ashworth, 2008). Whilst Hopper and Kruisselbrink (2001) explained that all teaching styles described by Mosston and Ashworth (1994) can be applied to any technique being learned, we suggest that this comment is contextual. The teaching styles may be applied, however, the challenge for the teacher is knowing for what purpose they should be applied. If teachers do not align their intent (goals) with their behaviour (teaching style), then the learning episode will undoubtedly be confusing, inefficient and not meet the objects the teacher desired. We argue that having Spectrum knowledge can assist teachers in aligning their goals and their pedagogy to create a learning experience which leads to the outcome they desire.

References

Bunker, D. & Thorpe, R. (1982). A model for the teaching of games in secondary schools. *Bulletin of Physical Education, 18*(1), 5–8.

Hopper, T. & Kruisselbrink, D. (2001). Teaching games for understanding: What does it look like and how does it influence student skill acquisition and game performance? *Journal of Teaching Physical Education, 12*, 2–29.

Mosston, M. (1966). *Teaching physical education: From command to discovery.* Charles E. Merrill.

Mosston, M. & Ashworth, S. (1994). *Teaching physical education* (4th ed.). Macmillan.

Mosston, M. & Ashworth, S. (2002). *Teaching physical education* (5th ed.). Benjamin Cummings.

Mosston, M. & Ashworth, S. (2008). *Teaching physical education* (1st ed.). Online: Spectrum Institute for Teaching and Learning. www.spectrumofteachingstyles.org/e-book-download.php

Pill, S. (2013). *Play with purpose: Game sense to sport literacy.* Australian Council for Health, Physical Education and Recreation (ACHPER).

Pill, S. & SueSee, B. (2021). The game sense approach as play with purpose. In S. Pill (Ed.), *Perspectives on game-based coaching* (pp. 1–10). Routledge.

Pill, S., SueSee, B., Rankin, J. & Hewitt, M. (2021). *The spectrum of sport coaching styles.* Routledge.

SueSee, B., Pill, S., Davies, M. & Williams, J. (2021). "Getting the tip of the pen on the paper": How the spectrum of teaching styles narrows the gap between the hope and the happening. *Journal of Teaching in Physical Education* (published online ahead of print 2021).

SueSee, B., Pill, S. & Edwards, K. (2016). Reconciling approaches – a game centred approach to sport teaching and Mosston's spectrum of teaching styles. *European Journal of Physical Education and Sport Science, 4*(2), 70–96.

SueSee, B., Pill, S. & Hewitt, M. (2020). Reconciling approaches: Mosston and Ashworth's Spectrum of Teaching Styles as a tool to examine the complexity of any teaching (or coaching) approach. In B. SueSee, M. Hewitt & S. Pill (Eds.), *The Spectrum of Teaching Styles in physical education* (pp. 73–84). Routledge.

Ward, P. (2011). Prediction and situational option generation in soccer. In *10th International Conference on Naturalistic Decision Making*, 31st May–3rd June 2011, Orlando, Florida.

10 A Constraints-Led Approach as a Theoretical Model for TGfU

Jia Yi Chow, Ian Renshaw and Brendan Moy

Teaching Games for Understanding (TGfU), when presented in the early 1980s, was indeed a breath of fresh air in regard to how physical education (PE) teachers could make games teaching fun and engaging for school children. However, although embraced by university academics, TGfU has had limited uptake by PE practitioners in schools (Moy et al., 2021). Why so? Is it because of the challenges to properly enact TGfU in the schools? Or is it because of a lack of the 'How' to deliver TGfU lessons? Or perhaps, there is a gap in practitioners' understanding of not just the 'How' of TGfU but importantly, the 'Why' of TGfU in making it so popular in its acceptance as a way to teach game skills.

Let's first take a closer look at TGfU itself. The TGfU model uses four pedagogical principles: sampling, modification-representation, modification-exaggeration, and tactical complexity, to guide teachers in TGfU learning design and delivery (Thorpe & Bunker, 1989). This model contains embedded assumptions about learning but was not explicitly underpinned by a theoretically based learning framework (Kirk & MacPhail, 2002). As highlighted by Rod Thorpe and Dave Bunker on numerous occasions, TGfU was developed as an operational model proposed as a way of improving the teaching of games in schools (see Bunker, 2012; R. Thorpe, personal communication, March 2015). Over time, advocates for TGfU have proposed a variety of theoretical models to retrospectively explain how learning occurs when adopting the approach in practice (Stolz & Pill, 2014). Many of these theories have their roots in the educational learning theory of cognitive constructivism, which conceptualises students as active learners who individually construct knowledge and understanding (or cognition) controlled at a conscious level using the mind while engaging with the environment (Eggen & Kauchak, 2006). However, many contemporary motor learning researchers have expressed concerns about the ability of cognitive theoretical frameworks to examine the efficacy of TGfU (e.g., Tan et al., 2012). This is because the primary focus on the internal conscious mental processes controlled within an individual's mind has neglected the role of both the environment and the subconscious control mechanisms of the body in movement and learning (Araújo & Davids, 2011).

DOI: 10.4324/9781003298298-13

In contrast to a cognitive perspective, an ecological perspective, based on the contemporary motor learning theory of Ecological Dynamics, recognises the continuous interaction between the mind, the subconscious control mechanisms of the body, and the environment in learning (Araújo et al., 2006). An alternative PE teaching approach, the constraints-led approach (CLA), is distinguished by the grounding of its learning design in Ecological Dynamics. The CLA and TGfU have similar operational principles in practice as both approaches challenge learners to solve common tactical problems through active exploration in modified representative environments (Bunker & Thorpe, 1986; Renshaw et al., 2009). Subsequently, advocates of an ecological perspective have proposed the contemporary motor learning theory of Ecological Dynamics to provide a comprehensive theoretical framework that effectively explains why and how TGfU works (see Chow et al., 2022).

The aim of this chapter is to show how the teaching and learning mechanisms for TGfU can be underpinned by a CLA. We want to give practitioners a 'familiarity and ease' with the key theoretical ideas behind the CLA, to help them use the pedagogical methodologies associated with TGfU appropriately, effectively, and efficiently. Specifically, we propose that modified and scaled games through the use of a CLA based on a theory of affordances can help practitioners better understand why and how TGfU works even though they may know the 'what' of TGfU.

Understanding the development of movement behaviours through ecological dynamics

Ecological Dynamics is underpinned by ideas from both Ecological Psychology and Dynamical Systems Theory. Ideas pertaining to the role of affordances in guiding actions is a central concept within Ecological Dynamics. The emergence of goal-directed behaviours as a consequence of the interactions among constraints is also a key feature in using Ecological Dynamics to understand the control and coordination of the human movement system (Button et al., 2020). The emphasis of using Ecological Dynamics to support our understanding of movement is pegged to a focus on learner-environment mutuality (beyond learner-centredness) (Renshaw & Chow, 2019). The interactions among constraints in the learning context are instrumental in shaping the emergence of movement behaviours. Learners search, explore, and exploit movement possibilities among a myriad of movement opportunities (Button et al., 2020). It is through these processes that the learners can discover their own ways of moving 'functionally' (i.e., by making movements that work) that is specific to the individual.

What is the link of these learning or skill adaptation processes with the perceived efficacy of TGfU? We believe the games designed in a typical TGfU lesson would offer opportunities for learners to discover for themselves movement possibilities that are representative of how the skills are to be performed. Therefore, games in TGfU need to be designed such that the perceptual information available in the games represents what is available to the learners in actual performance contexts. However, we are not prescribing that these games need to be the actual adult/mature form of the game. But rather, the dynamics in these games should be present so that the movement opportunities and decision-making aspects are made available to the learners. And certainly, some form of exaggeration of affordances would be present in the design of some of these games to make certain behaviours more inviting and attractive to the learners. In this way, the leaners are afforded opportunities to search, explore, and exploit their own individual movement solutions.

Through the CLA, practitioners can intentionally design games that cover the four pedagogical principles espoused in TGfU. Modifying rules, equipment, and task goals can shape different learner behaviours to attempt to achieve certain desired outcomes of learning. Learners are not told specifically what to do and how to do it, but rather, through their involvement in the games, certain behaviours become more attractive for them. The human movement system can be organised to move in many different ways but the constraints in the learning environment shapes the search, exploration, and exploitation of certain movement behaviours for the individual learner (Chow et al., 2022). The focus is on encouraging learners to find their own individualised way of moving and learning such that learners can satisfy the interacting constraints that are present in the specific learning contexts (Chow et al., 2021). Development of skills could also be seen as a form of 'wayfinding' underpinned by Ecological Dynamics (Woods et al., 2020). This is seen as a search process with reference to developing movement skills that is intentional and self-regulated (Woods et al., 2020). The practitioner is seen as a designer of practice, and this is evident in how games in TGfU are set up. In this sense, the teacher designs the practice landscape, and the learners are actively acquiring and adapting their skills through their involvement in the games. Knowledge of the environment (rather than knowledge about the environment) is heightened such that the learner couples the emergent behaviour with the environment (through the games in the TGfU context). Knowledge of the environment refers to the context where there is strong coupling between perception and action that reflects the embodied-embedded knowledge developed by and exemplified in activities (Gibson, 1966). This is distinct to 'knowledge about the environment' which reflects an abstracted and indirect response to things or states of affairs (Gibson, 1966). From an Ecological Dynamics perspective, the direct involvement in the games within TGfU affords these valuable opportunities for the learners to develop movement solutions and behaviours that are situated within the games itself and thus develop 'knowledge of the environment' (and beyond knowledge about the environment).

TGfU is not CLA: Differences between TGfU and CLA

Misconceptions

First of all, we need to make clear that a CLA is much more than 'just' a games-based model and is a theoretically-based approach to skill acquisition and motor learning that informs learning design in the whole spectrum of exercise, health, PE, sport performance and physical activities, as well as now being adopted by academics and practitioners outside of these areas, including diverse content areas such as mathematics teaching (Abrahamson & Sánchez-García, 2016).

Perhaps, the biggest misconception from those who argue that a CLA cannot be viewed as a comprehensive model to support skill acquisition or in particular one that fits with TGfU is that Ecological Dynamics fails to account for cognition (see Harvey et al., 2018). It should be clarified that the role of cognition in an Ecological Dynamics approach has been discussed and explained in many research papers and book chapters over the years. For example, the organising role of intentional constraints from an ecological perspective was described in detail as long ago as 1988 (Shaw & Kinsella-Shaw, 1988). Further, Kelso (1995) viewed *intentions* as an important informational constraint that can act to stabilise or destabilise existing system organisation, depending on needs or desires of an individual (or teams) (Araújo et al., 2019). In games, *intentionality* in interaction with task and environmental constraints frames the actions of individual players as well as interactions between players as they search to achieve the task goals set by games. Action is, therefore, the manifestation of cognition and is an emergent process under individual, task, and environmental constraints (Araújo et al., 2009) and trying to separate the mutually constraining influences of cognitions, actions, and perception is, therefore, a futile exercise because they are so deeply intertwined in human behaviour. This is the fundamental essence of decision-making in sport, which teachers can harness in curriculum design. In summary, rather than neglecting cognition, Ecological Dynamics views processes such as emotions, cognitions, perception-action as having a central role in shaping performance behaviours as they interact with the task and environmental constraints (Araújo et al., 2019).

Another misconception is the view that a CLA promotes a 'game is the teacher' approach (Harvey et al., 2018). While we agree that an ideal teaching scenario would be one where no teaching interventions would be needed and the well-designed game form would allow functional self-organisation to occur, in reality, games are so complex and getting the design exactly right is incredibly challenging (Rovegno et al., 2001). This means that there is a need for the teacher to play a central role in facilitating learning, and this may be achieved via verbal informational constraints in conjunction with game design. For example, not every learner will immediately pick up the affordances available to be exploited in a game form so would need to be guided towards the available information. While questioning is one of viable way to support this process at appropriate teachable moments in the game, this is just one strategy. The key point here is that rather than simply setting up games and stepping back, a CLA proposes that what teachers say acts as an important informational constraint that shapes intentions, perceptual search, and the coupled actions.

Support for TGfU: Some ideas from ecological dynamics though CLA

In this chapter, we want to be able to share insights on why aspects of TGfU can be supported by ideas from CLA and therefore, the relevance of CLA beyond the construct of games teaching as espoused by TGfU. To that end, next, we explore how CLA can support TGfU through Ecological Dynamics. One key aspect of CLA is to adopt Representative Learning Design. From TGfU, the incorporation of modified games, especially through exaggeration to invite attunement to specific affordances, and task simplification to ensure the maintenance of perception-action couplings can create situations where learners are channelled towards certain behaviours.

The design of such modified games is purposeful and creates a representative learning environment where the coupling between perception and action are further strengthened. In some instances, the modified games in TGfU can also be simplified. For example, the use of tennis racquets in badminton is an example of *task simplification*. Manipulating task constraints such as equipment can be potentially effective to reduce the complexity of the task such that the learners can still achieve success while ensuring that the perception-action coupling is not compromised. Task simplification is undoubtedly grounded in how constraints are manipulated, and this is key in supporting how practitioners design games and practice task. While it is easy to manipulate constraints, it does not necessarily mean that all *constraints manipulation* will lead to effective learning and the emergence of functional movement behaviours. Games can be designed that may lead to learners searching and exploring movement behaviours that do not meet the task goal for the session. Therein lies the demand on the practitioner to understand the dynamics of the game well enough to purposefully design suitable games for the learners to channel them to search, explore, and exploit individualised movement solutions in TGfU. Importantly, games offer significant amounts of *practice variability* that such variability can be functional as well. Game play is inherently dynamic in nature and potentially affords large volume of practice variability. From an Ecological Dynamics perspective, infusion of practice can encourage exploratory behaviours (Button et al., 2020; Chow et al., 2022). Learners could be placed in situations where they may need to try different pathways of trying to problem solve a movement challenge. Variability in practice (e.g., using different size projectiles) could help learners to explore a larger area of their perceptual-motor workspace. In TGfU, infusion of practice variability can be incorporated into the game and practice task. Nevertheless, one should also note that there are aspects of TGfU that are not CLA (especially with regards to the need to look for one solution if that is emphasised by the teacher). Indeed, the practice task can still be repetitive and not representative. Thus, there are many opportunities for CLA to be infused within a TGfU context where learners can search, explore, and exploit functional movement solutions. This further highlights how TGfU is not CLA and vice versa. The key point is to avoid being overly prescriptive even within the TGfU context and provide opportunities for the learners to explore and find their own individualised ways to move.

An exemplar of a CLA informed TGfU game for junior cricket

Rovegno and colleagues highlighted the interdependence of motor skill execution and decision-making as well as the relational character of games (Rovegno et al., 2001). It is only through playing games that players can learn to attune to their action capabilities, such as how far they can pass a ball or learning to recognise the opportunities provided by the movements and action capabilities of, or positions of opponents. Tactical decisions to exploit opportunities provided by opponents are, therefore, predicated on knowledge of one's action capabilities in interaction with available affordances. Consequently, if a player lacks the specific skill capability, they may not be aware of the presence of the affordance. For example, if a junior cricketer lacks the ability to hit the ball softly to deflect it into spaces in front of and between fielders, they may not be aware that these spaces provide run scoring opportunities. Here we will show how manipulating the task constraints of number of fielders, boundary size, and shape, along with *task simplification* to remove the rate limiter of not being able to re-direct the ball with a bat, can invite young beginner level cricket batters to first develop an awareness that run scoring is possible even when the ball is hit softly and does not travel far from the wicket. Let us explain.

The singles game

Background: When first learning to bat in cricket, young players usually score the majority of their runs by hitting the ball to the leg-side as they can swing the bat across their body to harness as many body parts as possible to generate force and hit the ball 'hard'. This shot works as most beginner level bowlers bowl many 'bad' short balls at the player's legs to enable run scoring. However, when the opposition bowlers improve, there are less opportunities to score in this way and players need to learn to score by deflecting the ball into gaps between fielders to score singles. An important consequence of scoring runs by hitting the ball hard means that players have not needed to find other ways of scoring and hence limiting the development of other technical skills to provide other scoring methods. In fact, typically, young players do not realise there are opportunities to score runs when they hit the ball (relatively) 'close' to the wickets as they think it will be easy to run them out as the fielder does not have to throw the ball very far to hit the wicket. The teacher therefore modifies the game to help youngsters to begin to recognise these opportunities by building awareness by providing a fun yet representative way of helping players learn to decide when to and when not to run. Essentially, the teacher adopts the following approach (1) No bat: Instead of using a bat, the 'batter' is allowed to 'catch' a softly bowled tennis or plastic ball delivered by a team-mate and must immediately throw the ball underarm into spaces for runs. Allowing the batter to throw the ball means that they can quickly build their awareness of where to throw the ball and how hard to throw it. (2) Rule: Introducing a rule that the batter is out if they hit the ball over the reduced-sized boundary (25 m × 30 m). The first consequence of this change is that players know they cannot throw the ball hard. (3) Reduced fielders: The number of fielders is reduced to six plus a wicketkeeper. These fielders must initially stand in 'proper' fielding positions as they would in a game to make sure the positions are representative of those in a 'standard' game (i.e., mid-off, extra cover, backward point, backward square leg, midwicket, mid-on, see Figure 10.1). Of course, the game allows fielding and captaincy skills to be

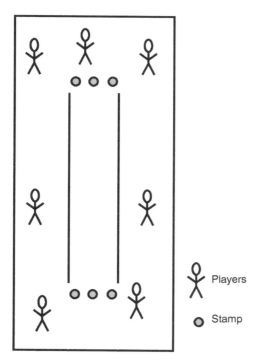

Figure 10.1 The singles game with various levels of force (i.e., softly or hard).

developed at the same time and the principle of co-adaptation (see Renshaw et al., 2009) will apply. The feedback from this game has been extremely positive with a junior co-ordinator contacting me (Ian) to tell me that the U8 coaches and players love the game and even better, it has resulted in them scoring up to 40 more runs per game.

- 7 v 7 (two batters as per cricket).
- Stumps should be placed so that the 'batting' stumps are 2 m from the rear boundary.
- Initially fielders must start on the set 'marker' but eventually the teacher will allow them to stand anywhere in the field (but this *MUST NOT* stand within 10 m of the 'batter' as this is a 'safety' zone enforced in all junior games).
- The batters MUST run at least ONE run but may run more if they choose. Batters can run, over throws (even if the ball goes over the boundary via a fielder's throw).
- Batters are out if they are caught, run-out or throw the ball over the boundary.

An extension to this game is to introduce hitting using tennis rackets, and then batting against co-operative feeds (the batting team provide the bowler), before eventually playing competitive games.

Conclusion

The focus of this chapter is to share how teaching and learning mechanisms for TGfU can be supported by CLA. We note that there are indeed various theoretical approaches that can be related to TGfU, and we are cognisant that TGfU was not developed with a theoretical framework in mind originally. Nevertheless, we hoped that we have been able to share adequately within a brief chapter here that aspects of TGfU can be supported by ideas from Ecological Dynamics and by demonstrating its relevance to CLA.

References

Abrahamson, D. & Sánchez-García, R. (2016). Learning is moving in new ways: The ecological dynamics of mathematics education. *Journal of the Learning Sciences*, 25(2), 203–239.

Araújo, D. & Davids, K. (2011). What exactly is acquired during skill acquisition? *Journal of Consciousness Studies*, 18(3-4), 7–23.

Araújo, D., Davids, K., Chow, J. Y. & Passos, P. (2009). The development of decision making skill in sport: An ecological dynamics perspective. In D. Araújo, H. Ripoll & M. Raab (Eds.), *Perspectives on cognition and action in sport* (pp. 157–169). Nova Publishers.

Araújo, D., Davids, K. & Hristovski, R. (2006). The ecological dynamics of decision making in sport. *Psychology of Sport and Exercise*, 7(6), 653–676.

Araújo, D., Davids, K. & Renshaw, I. (2019). Cognition, emotion and action in sport: An ecological dynamics perspective. In G. Tenenbaum & R. Eklund Hoboken (Eds.), *Handbook of sport psychology*. John Wiley & Sons.

Bunker, D. (2012). *The roots of TGfU*. Paper presented at the 5th International Teaching Games for Understanding Conference, Loughborough University, July 14–16.

Bunker, D. & Thorpe, R. (1986). The curriculum model. In R. Thorpe, D. Bunker & L. Almond (Eds.), *Rethinking games teaching* (pp. 7–10). Loughborough University of Technology.

Button, C., Seifert, L., Chow, J. Y., Araújo, D. & Davids, K. (2020). *Dynamics of skill acquisition: An ecological dynamics approach* (2nd ed.). Human Kinetics.

Chow, J. Y., Davids, K., Button, C. & Renshaw, I. (2022). *Nonlinear pedagogy in skill acquisition: An introduction* (2nd ed.). Routledge.

Chow, J. Y., Komar, J. & Seifert, L. (2021). The role of nonlinear pedagogy in supporting the design of modified games in junior sports. *Frontiers in Psychology, 12*, 744814.

Eggen, P. & Kauchak, D. (2006). *Strategies and models for teachers: Teaching content and thinking skills*. Pearson Education.

Gibson, J. (1966). *The senses considered as perceptual systems*. Houghton Mifflin.

Harvey, S., Pill, S. & Almond, L. (2018). Old wine in new bottles: A response to claims that teaching games for understanding was not developed as a theoretically based pedagogical framework. *Physical Education and Sport Pedagogy, 23*(2), 166–180.

Kelso, J. A. S. (1995). *Dynamic patterns: The self-organization of brain and behavior*. The MIT Press.

Kirk, D. & MacPhail, A. (2002). Teaching games for understanding and situated learning: Rethinking the Bunker-Thorpe model. *Journal of Teaching in Physical Education, 21*(2), 177–192.

Moy, B., Rossi, T. & Russell, S. (2021). Supporting PETE students to implement an alternative pedagogy. *Physical Education and Sport Pedagogy*. 10.1080/17408989.2021.1958178

Renshaw, I. & Chow, J. Y. (2019). A constraint-led approach to sport and physical education pedagogy. *Physical Education and Sport Pedagogy, 24*(2), 103–116.

Renshaw, I., Davids, K., Shuttleworth, R. & Chow, J. Y. (2009). Insights from ecological psychology and dynamical systems theory can underpin a philosophy of coaching. *International Journal of Sport Psychology, 40*(4), 540–602.

Rovegno, I., Nevett, M., Brock, S. & Babiarz, M. (2001). Teaching and learning basic invasion-game tactics in 4th grade: A descriptive study from situated and constraints theoretical perspectives. *Journal of Teaching in Physical Education, 20*(4), 370–388.

Shaw, R. & Kinsella-Shaw, J. (1988). Ecological mechanics: A physical geometry for intentional constraints. *Human Movement Science, 7*(2-4), 155–200.

Stolz, S. & Pill, S. (2014). Teaching games and sport for understanding: Exploring and reconsidering its relevance in physical education. *European Physical Education Review, 20*(1), 36–71.

Tan, C. W. K., Chow, J. Y. & Davids, K. (2012). "How does TGfU work?": Examining the relationship between learning design in TGfU and a nonlinear pedagogy. *Physical Education and Sport Pedagogy, 17*(4), 331–348.

Thorpe, R. & Bunker, D. (1989). A changing focus in games teaching. In L. Almond (Ed.), *The place of physical education in schools* (pp. 42–71). Kogan/Page.

Woods, C. T., Rudd, J., Robertson, S. & Davids, K. (2020). Wayfinding: How ecological perspectives of navigating dynamic environments can enrich our understanding of the learner and the learning process in sport. *Sports Medicine-Open, 6*(1), 1–11.

11 Positive Pedagogy for Sport Coaching: A Game Changer?

Richard L. Light and Stephen Harvey

The need for Positive Pedagogy (PPed) for sport coaching or something similar can be traced back to the first publication on Teaching Games for Understanding (TGfU; Bunker & Thorpe, 1982) and perhaps even further, but the seeds for the idea were planted during a lecture at Sydney University in 2008. During a lecture delivered by the first author to graduating year four physical education students, one said that the whole cohort believed in Game Sense (an Australian derivative of TGfU) but asked what they could do when teaching non-game sports like swimming and athletics. The first author paused and after thinking about it, replied by saying that he could not be sure, but felt that the underpinning principles of Game Sense could probably be modified and applied to individual sport(s). Over the next few years, he read, thought about the idea, and volunteered to coach/teach in primary, high school, universities, and in sport clubs. He focused on individual sports such as swimming where he worked with a local coach (see, Light, 2021b); the 4 × 100 track relay (see Light, 2019) and beach sprinting (see Light, 2021a) to develop his ideas from practice and reflection on it as well as connecting them with appropriate theory.

After his first presentation on PPed at the 2018 British Educational Research Association (BERA) conference, the first author was asked by the session chair 'do we need another game-based model'. His answer was to say that Game Sense is not a model and to then ask the chair what teaching or coaching approach(es) there were for teaching individual sports using the student-centred, inquiry-based approach of a game-based approach (GBA). The silence emphasised the need for an approach to teaching the skill and technique that is so central to individual sport(s) without abandoning the very effective pedagogical features of all GBA and that is the aim of PPed.

The rationale

Although there were a few similar proposals for a learner-centred approach to teaching sport in the 1960s and 1970s (see Mahlo, 1973; Wade, 1967), Bunker and Thorpe's publication is generally accepted as the starting point for the development of GBAs with PPed having direct lineage to it. PPed

DOI: 10.4324/9781003298298-14

built upon the same philosophical foundations and pedagogical principles of Game Sense (Light & Light, 2021) that is derived from TGfU (see Chapter 1 for more detail), like so many GBAs. PPed is, however, very different due to its focus on the teaching and learning associated with skill and technique development.

Over the 1990s, there was considerable debate over the relative importance of technique and tactics with TGfU in the tactical corner and seen to be anti-skill or anti-technique. From the new millennium onward, thinking about TGfU, Game Sense, and similar approaches to games teaching moved on from the simplistic tactics vs. technique debate to recognise the complexity of games. This more holistic view involved recognising how skill and technique were important but no more important than the other aspects and abilities needed to play games such as decision making, awareness, anticipation, and tactical understanding. This recognition of game complexity is because coaching and teaching physical education using a GBA focuses on the game as a whole instead of reducing it to independent components practised outside the game.

Recognising the complexity of games and team sport(s) highlights the efficacy of GBA and provides cause to question why anyone would adopt the traditional skill-drill approach, but it is a different story when considering individual sports like athletics, swimming, rock climbing, or martial arts. In these sports, skill is of undeniably central importance with the tactical dimensions of secondary concern or sometimes even negligible. The argument we present above for the holistic approach of GBAs and their focus on the whole game does not apply to sport in which skill must be the focus, but this does not mean teachers or coaches must abandon the philosophical foundations and pedagogical features of GBA.

The development of PPed

The development of PPed began with modifying the pedagogical features that Light (2013) suggests underpins the practice of Game Sense to make them applicable to activities beyond team sport(s) and games. Its early development included establishing a dialectic between theory and practice that involved applying ideas to teaching young people skills and technique, reflecting on the outcomes, modifying the idea or ideas, and trying again. This approach to developing the idea was very much like the inquiry-based approach originally proposed by Dewey (see Dewey, 1933) and later developed in different ways such as in discovery learning (see Bruner, 1961). It is also a feature of Game Sense, other GBAs, and PPed.

The initial stages of developing PPed focused on its application to individual sport(s) and its ongoing development through collaboration with scholars, PhD students, and practitioners such as teachers and sport coaches across a wide range of cultures and sports. The subsequent development of PPed maintained a focus on individual sports ranging from swimming, javelin, triathlon and gymnastics to karate, boxing, rock climbing and beach sprints in different cultural and institutional settings across the United Kingdom, Europe, the United States, Asia, and Australasia (see Light, 2017; Light & Harvey, 2019; Light & Harvey, 2021) with feedback from practitioners assisting in the ongoing development of PPed.

Making it positive

The pedagogical features of Game Sense encourage positive learning experiences that PPed maximises by appropriating Antonovsky's (1996) work on well-being and Positive Psychology, and in particular, its focus on happiness (see Seligman, 2012). Game Sense and other GBAs can provide positive experiences for learners due to their learner-centred, inquiry-based approaches and the ways in which they empower learners. They also retain some of the play element that is so important in learning culture (Huizinga, 1938) and which requires making learning fun.

The traditional skill-drill approach to teaching and coaching can be seen as an essentially negative approach because the pursuit of mastering technique involves telling learners what they are doing wrong and how they need to improve their performance to get closer to performing the ideal technique. Within the diversity of abilities, dispositions, and motivations in physical education classes, being on show and judged by classmates makes pursuing the mastery of skills and technique particularly negative for many students. Discovering good technique or how to execute a skill through collaboration with peers, interaction, reflection, and taking an inquiry-based approach can empower the learner to make learning satisfying, or even joyful. In doing so, this approach to helping students and athletes learn skill and technique provides a very positive learning experience and one that lies in sharp contrast to the skill-drill approach that dominates teaching and coaching across the globe.

There are sport teaching approaches that use sport specifically as a medium for achieving positive personal development such as Sport Education (Siedentop, 1994), Teaching Personal and Social Responsibility (Hellison, 2003), and Positive Youth Development (see Holt et al., 2012) but positive learning in PPed is slightly different. Although PPed emphasises positive experience, its focus is on learning to play the sport or game, with positive moral, social, and personal learning a consequence of the pedagogical approach. Positive experiences of learning also make a major contribution to learning how to play the game or perform a skill for students and young people.

The name of Positive Pedagogy for sport coaching was chosen to capture the importance placed on positive learning experiences. Positive Pedagogy is used to broadly describe what is basically a discovery-learning approach across a range of activities, such as music, that the idea of PPed aligned with, and particularly in relation to teaching skill and technique. Emphasising positive learning experiences in PPed involved building on the inherent positive approach of Game Sense by appropriating the work of Antonovsky

(1996) and Positive Psychology (see Seligman, 2012) which included Csikszentmihalyi's (1997) concept of flow. It was so successful that we collaborated on applying the modified principles and the emphasis on positive experiences of learning to team sport(s), in addition to individual sport(s). This was much like going full circle back to a slightly modified version of Game Sense, but it included teaching or coaching individual sports with a focus on skill and technique, and in which games are not necessarily used.

The features of PPed

In PPed, there is a guiding framework like that suggested by Light (2013) for Game Sense that we briefly describe here. In PPed the teacher or coach:

Designs an engaging physical activity/learning experience

In team sport(s), this is typically a small-sided game that builds from simple (with high success rate) to being more complex and more challenging. PPed draws on Csikszentmihalyi's (1997) notion of flow which suggests that to achieve flow as a state of optimal experience and learning, learners/athletes need to be challenged to the point where they are lost in the flow. This state of flow is not only optimal learning but usually very enjoyable and can be applied to individual sport(s) and a focus on skill. When focused on a skill or technique the teacher or coach may create a problem to be solved by imposing a constraint such as asking a learner to run with hands behind their back or swim butterfly with one arm. This aimed at creating awareness of a particular aspect of the skill such as the use of the arms in sprinting or the execution of the two kicks per stroke in butterfly (see Light, 2021a, b) and leading them to discovering the most efficiency through trial and error. It is also aimed at providing something to reflect upon in dialogue focused on the problem and on feel. In individual sports such as javelin, boxing, or swimming, for example, feel is of pivotal importance with PPed questioning typically focusing on it. For example, if we constrain hip rotation when throwing a javelin by asking students to stand with feet parallel when throwing we would typically ask them how it feels and why, and what the problem is? If we then allow them to drop one foot back to throw, we will ask them questions like 'how did that feel?', 'why does it feel better?', and 'what can you learn from that about throwing a javelin as efficiently as possible?'. Comparing how far the javelin travels would add to the reflections on how important hip rotation is and how to make it most efficient.

Adopts an inquiry-based approach to learning

Game Sense, other GBAs, and PPed tend to adopt an inquiry-based approach to learning that involves the athlete(s) identifying, formulating, testing, and evaluating solutions to problems or challenges. As we have pointed out, these may be naturally occurring problems to solve that occur as part of practice, or problems that are intentionally created by imposing a constraint that dealing with will enhance awareness and direct the students or athletes toward discovering the objective of the lesson or session. This typically involves the learner: (1) identifying the problem, (2) discussing the problem and formulating a possible solution, (3) testing the solution, (4) evaluating it, and (5) acting on it or abandoning it. When focusing on skill or technique, groups are typically small and as suggested earlier, it can also be between one athlete and the coach.

Uses questioning to stimulate thinking and dialogue instead of instructing directly.

The questioning in PPed for team sport(s) is no different to Game Sense, or other GBA, but it is also applied when teaching a specific skill or technique. Using the example from above, the teacher or coach will shape and encourage discovery (through cycles of trial and error) of the most suitable and efficient execution of a skill and in a way that allows a degree of adaptation by the student or athlete of the skill. In work on skill, he/she/they will typically ask how it feels as a type of kinaesthetic feedback and a very important aspect of skills like throwing (anything), jumping, punching, kicking, turning, and so on. With this approach 'getting it right' typically involves a positive feeling like hitting a ball on the sweet spot of the bat in cricket or baseball. In skill work, the groups are usually small and can even be with only one athlete and a coach that develops a productive relationship and conversation.

For all the above features to work for students or athletes, the PPed coach or teacher must establish and develop a suitable environment that is supportive, collegial, and in which there is no fear of failure. By this, we mean that all involved accept that we learn from mistakes. This does not mean we want learners to intentionally make mistakes but instead, that we challenge them enough for errors to occur and that they reflect upon, think about, and discuss to learn from. PPed also encourages the development of creativity that cannot happen if students or athletes are worried about making mistakes. PPed, Game Sense, and other GBAs should promote curiosity, learning how to learn and the ability to solve problems that arise in competition at any level, from physical education classes to the Olympics.

Applying PPed

When PPed is applied to team sport(s) and games it looks much like Game Sense but offers a little bit more. This includes increased enjoyment, happiness, positive well-being, and what the flow approach can offer, as well the more humanistic relationship it encourages between teacher and students or coach and athletes at all levels. These are positive additions for teachers or coaches using a Game Sense approach, but it is the use of PPed for teaching skill and technique that offers the most for those involved in physical education and sport coaching at any level. What we mean is that the most distinct feature of PPed is its ability to use a learner-centred approach to teaching skill and technique.

Here we provide a brief explanation of how to apply PPed but for those who might be interested in reading more about its application, we suggest reading Light and Harvey (2017), Light (2017), and Light and Harvey (2021). To provide an example of using PPed to teach skill and technique we focus on karate as a martial art that also has a sporting dimension. It is known for its militaristic approach to drilling and attempting to perfect basic skills such as the reverse punch (*gyakuzuki*), which is a technique that can be seen as the workhorse of karate. It offers a good example of how PPed can be used in place of, or in combination with, the traditional skill-drill approach.

The reverse punch is a straight punch delivered from the side of body that is opposite the front foot, which is why it is called reverse punch (in English). The session we outline here puts students in pairs or in groups of three to adopt an approach that is similar to reciprocal teaching (Mosston, 1966) but with a more collaborative relationship between students in the teacher and learner roles, and in which feel is of prime importance for learning. In this activity, the puncher strikes a hit pad held by his/her/their partner. This activity would follow practising by punching in the air and focusing on technique for generating power from the ground, efficient timing of hip rotation, having a straight back and snapping the punch on impact but all in one movement. The puncher gets subjective feedback on the strike from how it felt and how it sounded. The holder provides more objective feedback on the basics of technique and how the strike feels to him/her/them, and how it sounds. The two learners then swap roles and when the timing is right, the teacher or coach pulls the group into one big circle for all learners to share what they learned and suggest what they need to work on.

This format can be changed to include an extra learner and an extra role of objective observer viewing the punching technique from the side with all three rotating through the roles. For further detail on teaching reverse punch using PPed, please see Light (2017).

Concluding thoughts

To our knowledge, this is the only systematic teaching approach that applies all the benefits of Game Sense and other GBA pedagogy to individual sport(s). This is an exciting development and an answer to the question asked to the first author about individual sport pedagogy at The University of Sydney, especially that focused on a holistic and humanistic approach to individual sport pedagogy.

Clearly, individual sport(s) teaching and coaching would benefit greatly from PPed because skill and technique are so important in them but, PPed also offers an attractive option for teachers or coaches using a GBA, when they decide that a skill needs attention. When the first author attended one of Rod Thorpe's TGfU workshops in 1996 (one of the main developers of TGfU), he said that a skill only needed to be good enough to allow the game to progress, which is placing skill in context. When a modified, small-sided game breaks down because a required skill is not good enough, the teacher/coach normally has two options. The first is to lower the demands of the game and let the skill develop in context. The second is to work on the skill to get it up to the standard required for the game. This development of the skill normally occurs out of the game, involving a reversion to the skill-drill approach and with the expectation that the improved skill will work back in the context of the game. In the tactical games approach, this is embedded in a process that focuses on skill developed in and through games.

What PPed offers is a way of working on skills when needed, that maintains the learner-centred pedagogy used and all it has to offer. It challenges the unquestioned dominance of repetitive skill drills when focusing on skill or technique as what could be its last stronghold. For this reason, we suggest that, when focused on skill and technique, PPed could be a game changer.

References

Antonovsky, A. (1996). The salutogenic model as a theory to guide health promotion. *Health Promotion International, 11*(1), 11–17.

Bruner, J. S. (1961). The act of discovery. *Harvard Educational Review, 31*(1), 21–32.

Bunker, D. & Thorpe, R. (1982). A model for the teaching of games in secondary schools. *Bulletin of Physical Education, 18*(1), 5–8.

Csikszentmihalyi, M. (1997). *Finding flow: The psychology of engagement with everyday life.* Basic Books.

Dewey, J. (1933). *How we think: A restatement of the relation of reflective thinking to the educative process.* Heath & Co Publishers.

Hellison, D. R. (2003). *Teaching responsibility through physical activity* (2nd ed.). Human Kinetics.

Holt, N. L., Sehn, Z. I., Spence, J. C., Newton, A. S. & Ball, G. D. C. (2012). Physical education and sport programs at an inner city school: Exploring possibilities for positive youth development. *Physical Education and Sport Pedagogy, 17*(1), 97–113.

Huizinga, J. (1938). *Homo Ludens.* Random House.

Light, R. L. (2013). *Game sense: Pedagogy for performance, participation and enjoyment.* Routledge.

Light, R. L. (2017). *Positive pedagogy for sports coaching.* Routledge.

Light, R. L. (2019). Relay baton changeover. In R. Light & S. Harvey (Eds.), *Positive pedagogy for coaching* (2nd ed.). Routledge.

Light, R. L. (2021a). Beach sprint starts. In R. Light & S. Harvey (Eds.), *Applied positive pedagogy in sport coaching: International cases* (pp. 146–152). Routledge.

Light, R. L. (2021b). Coaching swimming technique: The second kick in butterfly. In R. Light & S. Harvey (Eds.), *Applied positive pedagogy in sport coaching: International cases* (pp. 99–105). Routledge.

Light, R. & Harvey, S. (2017). Positive pedagogy for sport coaching. *Sport Education and Society, 22*(2), 271–287.

Light, R. & Harvey, S. (2019). *Positive pedagogy for coaching* (2nd ed.). Routledge.

Light, R. L. & Harvey, S. (Eds.) (2021). *Applied positive pedagogy in sport coaching: International cases.* Routledge.

Light, R. L. & Light, A. (2021) Holism and humanism: The philosophical foundations of game sense. In R. L. Light & C. Curry (Eds.), *Game sense for coaching and teaching* (pp. 15–24). Routledge.

Mahlo, F. (1973). *Act tactique en jeu* [Tactical action in play]. Vigot.

Mosston, M. (1966). *Teaching physical education: From command to discovery.* Charles E. Merrill Books.

Seligman, M. E. P. (2012). *Flourish: A visionary new understanding of happiness and wellbeing.* Random House.

Siedentop, D. (1994). *Sport education: Quality PE through positive sport experiences.* Human Kinetics.

Wade, A. (1967). *The FA guide to training and coaching.* Heineman.

12 Teaching Games for Understanding and Athlete-Centred Coaching

Shane Pill and Ellen-Alyssa F. Gambles

The pedagogies chosen by sport teachers and coaches are a powerful way to influence athletes' development and sense of themselves. Athlete-centred coaching has emerged as a humanistic approach developed to engender empowerment and agency within the player/athlete and enhance their performance by adopting a holistic approach to the athlete. The purpose of this chapter is threefold. Firstly, to explore game-based approach research and practice related to coaching and player development (e.g., game sense). Secondly, to examine and reflect on athlete-centred coaching as an approach that promotes an educative and holistic process for players' sporting experiences. We will outline the sporting experience (i.e., sport as a form of play, the athletes and coach). Finally, to discuss the possibilities and challenges of implementing an athlete-centred approach to coaching and player development.

Game-based approach research and practice related to coaching and player development

The pedagogical choices of coaches are central to player development (Ford et al., 2010). Kinnerk and colleagues' (2018) review of game-based approaches to coaching supported the efficacy of game-based approaches in the development of player/athlete decision-making and tactical awareness, the promotion of personal and social development, and fostered positive affective outcomes for athletes. O'Connor et al. (2021) reviewed game-based approaches and asserted that a key aspect of game-based approaches is promoting player learning, not just performance. This means that the practice environment of the player/athlete fosters problem-solving, analysing information, devising solutions to problems, and evaluation of the outcomes of this thinking and action. Considering player/athlete motivation, O'Connor and colleagues argued that adopting a game-based approach required a coach to intentionally consider the needs of their player/athlete in creation of an environment promoting enjoyment, engagement, and autonomy. Light and Harvey (2017) similarly referred to these characteristics of environments created by game-based approaches. They expand upon the explanation by including consideration of the central role that

DOI: 10.4324/9781003298298-15

collaborative and co-constructed dialogue, reflection and purposeful social interaction play in the deep understanding of self and self as player that game-based approaches can promote. Light and Harvey therefore described game-based approaches as athlete-centred. Game-based approaches align with the requirements of athlete-centred coaching which 'promotes athlete learning through athlete ownership, responsibility, initiative and awareness, guided by the coach' (Pill, 2018b, p. 1).

Athlete-centred coaching

The traditional coaching approach has been described as coach-centred, where the player has no active role in their learning, training, and competition (Kidman & Lombardo, 2010). In this instance, the coach is directive and employs a commanding coaching style typical of the autocratic coach (Ahlberg et al., 2008). This is coaching solely for the transmission of information for the reproduction of coach expectation or demonstration. The coach controls players/athletes who are not empowered as owners of their performance (Pill, 2018a), as the player/athlete is reliant on the coach to facilitate all aspects of training and performance. This coach-centred approach has been debated within academia and the wider sporting community, which has resulted in the emergence of, and developments in, athlete-centred coaching.

Being athlete-centred has been identified as central to contemporary coaching practice (Gilbert, 2017). Coaching is now considered 'a relational, dynamic social microcosm' (Cushion, 2007, p. 397) involving a community of practice, called a 'team' (Jones & Ronglan, 2018). The adoption of an athlete-centred coaching approach is characterised by coaching to develop and encourage player self-determination, initiative, and responsibility both as a person and as a player, which requires that the coach adopts a specific 'way' of being a coach. The coach moves from the traditional role of director of player/athlete behaviour, to a facilitator of environments and opportunities by asking questions in preference to being commanding (Kidman & Davis, 2006). Coaches creating player/athlete inquiry environments with opportunities for the development of thinking players is observed as the coach asks questions and creates moments for player reflection on play. This environment puts the responsibility for development of the player/athlete on the player/athlete: 'In an athlete centred environment, the athlete owns the direction, is accountable for that direction and thus takes responsibility for their actions and performance' (Penney & Kidman, 2014, pp. 2–3). In summary, in an athlete-centred coaching environment the player/athlete is encouraged to participate in developmentally appropriate co-construction through invitation to decision-making and problem-solving (Pill, 2018b).

Kidman and Lombardo (2010) suggested three core practices of athlete-centred coaching: (a) teaching games for understanding or a game-based approach; (b) use of questions to develop player 'game sense'; and (c) development of team culture. A game-based approach employs the game for the purposes of developing players' knowledge and understanding of tactics or strategies to solve the problems that the game raises (Bunker & Thorpe, 1982). Teaching Games for Understanding (TGfU) is compatible with an athlete-centred philosophy as players employ problem-solving capabilities which promotes motivation and can enhance their performance (Kidman & Lombardo, 2010). A key feature of game-based approaches is that of using questioning to educate players with regard to their options at critical moments of gameplay, to improve their decision-making capabilities and game sense. The use of questions in the context of athlete-centred coaching is not limited to the coach's use of questioning strategies and creation of inquiry moments led by the coach. It includes the coach's encouragement of players/athletes to see themselves as learners and therefore also responsible for asking and considering questions to develop, extend, or create their own knowledge and understanding, as indicators of ownership of their learning (Griffin et al., 2018). Learning and success are inextricably linked to the establishment of a quality team culture where players' autonomy allows them to share a common vision, expectations, and values (Kidman & Lombardo, 2010).

Griffin et al. (2018) provided a holistic and process-oriented model for athlete-centred coaching, building on Kidman and Lombardo's three tenets, to integrate the factors of democracy in action and life skills. The model retained the 'signature pedagogy' (Griffin et al., 2018, p. 13) of athlete-centred coaching as TGfU (Bunker & Thorpe, 1982) to educate player/athletes in their roles, responsibilities, and ways of behaving in an active learning practice. The concept of 'democracy in action' is central to the model, as the way coach and player/athlete gain ethical understanding and life skills, and game play development through well-designed group processes (Figure 12.1). The collective agreement of individual rights and responsibilities between players and coach based on group process, decision-making, social justice, free inquiry, and personal and social responsibility incorporates democratic citizenship and moral action firmly into the team culture (Griffin et al., 2018). Coaches need to purposefully design environments that promote the development of key social and life skills with their athletes for example collaboration, critical thinking, and communication (Griffin et al., 2018). The fostering of a conscious agency will be enhanced by the incorporation of social dimensions in athlete-centred coaching to support the holistic development of athletes throughout their lives.

Teaching games for understanding as a process (as distinguished from TGfU, the game-based pedagogy) provides for player empowerment and as such has contributed to a change in understanding of how player/athletes learn in context (Garner et al., 2022). Further, in how coaches intentionally can influence practice design to generate player/athlete capacity for, and opportunity to develop, independent self-regulated learning (Garner et al., 2022). An athlete-centred coach will use a game-based approach, such as TGfU, to teach in and through games for player understanding which

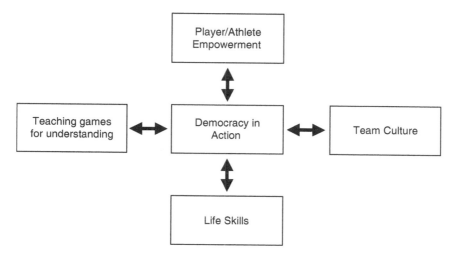

Figure 12.1 A holistic and process-oriented model for athlete-centred coaching. (Adapted from Griffin et al., 2018.)

enables players to learn on three levels. Namely, about themselves as a player/athlete and understand the team's culture and playing style (macro level), in addition to the tactics (meso level) and skills/decisions required to enact this style in the emergent game situation (micro level) (Harvey, 2018).

An athlete-centred coaching approach fosters the players as learners and therefore, the coach as educator is developing a process for player/athlete holistic development (Kidman & Lombardo, 2010) of physical, cognitive, social, and emotional learning. Here, we see a possible connection between athlete-centred coaching and the domains of the development of physical literacy (Sport Australia, 2022). Sum et al. (2016) identified three attributes of player/athlete perceived physical literacy: (1) knowledge and understanding; (2) self-expression and communication with others; and (3) sense of self and self-confidence. Li et al. (2019) investigated the influence of student athlete physical literacy on their perception of coach efficacy and their leadership behaviour and found that it influenced both positively. In Australia, physical literacy attainment is positioned as an element of the Playing for Life philosophy which is pedagogically underpinned by the game-based approach known as Game Sense (Sport Australia, 2022).

The possibilities and challenges of implementing an athlete-centred approach

Harvey's (2018) investigation of two coaches' adoption of athlete-centred coaching found that the first step of developing a philosophy associated with athlete-centred coaching is critical to the transition of practice. However, developing the ability to design games as teaching tools that enabled learning to transfer from practice to match play was critical in succeeding with the approach. Bowles and O'Dwyer's (2020) self-study of adoption of athlete-centred coaching suggested that coaches often articulate views and values aligned with athlete-centred coaching but lack surety about how to apply tenets of athlete-centred coaching in practice. In a similar vein, Hewitt's research provided insights into coaches' beliefs that they were delivering game-based coaching, which was not evident in observations of coaching practice, and that appeared more behaviourist by the dominance of command and practice pedagogy (Hewitt & Edwards, 2013; Hewitt et al., 2016; Pill et al., 2016). Additionally, junior sport coaches have been observed to struggle with athlete-centred coaching due to insufficient pedagogical content knowledge inhibiting the use of game-based pedagogy (Roberts, 2011).

Studies have reported a challenge with athlete-centred coaching is that some players/athletes do not want the responsibility of having to think and reflect, and just want to be told what to do (Harvey, 2018; Pill, 2016). However, some coaches have experienced uplifts in team performances and an enhanced relationship with players once adopting an athlete-centred approach (e.g., Pill, 2018c). In addition, academics studying youth sports have noted that for many coaches, focusing on learning and player development rather than on immediate observable performance, presented a challenge when interacting with parental expectations of their children's performance (Turner, 2018). However, Turner (2018) suggests that with developments in initiatives to support and educate parents, the perspectives towards athlete-centred coaching may increase.

Pill and Hyndman (2018) described a challenge that applies to athlete-centred coaching and the connection to teaching games for player/athlete understanding. That is, the concept of 'understanding' is largely implicit in much of the extant literature. They argued for a framework to approach conception of understanding developed from player/athlete experience of game-based coaching underpinned by meaning-making, which is 'deep and personal' knowledge, developed over time, involving reflection, and agency. Pill and Hyndman suggested pedagogy that enabled a focus on the player/athlete states of mind that are drawn from the player/athlete experiences in sport teaching/coaching environments is what makes a game-based approach 'athlete-centred'. It is therefore the type of meaning-making stemming from experience of athlete-centred coaching that creates the long-term enduring 'value' for the individual.

The creation of player/athlete inquiry and reflection for learning from performance at practice is central to game-based coaching, and therefore as game-based coaching is an inherent feature, it is also central to athlete-centred coaching. However, in attempting to be an athlete-centred coach the use of questioning strategies to stimulate learning is an area often not experienced by players/athletes (Preston et al., 2016). For other coaches, it has been found that creating an athlete-centred culture tested the coaches as the pedagogy of engaging players in active dialogue and movement performance through questioning scenarios was found to be challenging (Turner, 2018). Often, coaches are observed to use questioning that retrieves existing player understanding when the intent is to guide discovery of new or further understanding, or coaches pose a question and leave insufficient time for player thinking for development of a response before providing the answer to the players/athletes. Athlete-centred questioning engages players/athletes more often with well-considered and focused questions aimed at developing player thinking, rather than it does using questions to check for understanding (Vinson & Bell, 2019).

Another challenge and a possibility in athlete-centred coaching is how to use game-based pedagogy in teaching games for understanding to enable the consideration of, and connection to, disability and inclusion. Townsend and Cushion (2018) argued that to apply athlete-centred coaching practices inclusively is to consider the cultural and social construction of disability as a base for coaching practice. They argued that if by athlete-centred coaching it is meant that the player/athletes' needs are paramount, then the premise of the approach is appealing to inclusion and disability discourses. However, applied uncritically within an intent of normalising certain coaching behaviours, athlete-centred coaching may divert attention away from the impact that impairment has on the lives of people with a disability, diminishing player/athlete agency. Context is therefore of importance in athlete-centred coaching use of game-based approaches. Further research is needed on what it means to be an athlete-centred coach in the context of para and disability sport.

Teaching games and sport for understanding in the context of an athlete-centred approach has been explained in the literature for junior, adult, and masters swimming (Light, 2017b; Magias, 2018; Penney & Zehntner, 2018), a range of individual sports and outdoor pursuits (e.g., Javelin, Karate: Light, 2017a; Light & Harvey, 2019), and a range of team sports (Harvey, 2018; Kidman & Lombardo, 2010; Light & Harvey, 2019, 2021; Pill, 2018a). Athlete-centred coaching encompassing game-based pedagogy, to teach in and through the game for holistic player development across all domains of learning (physical, social, emotional, cognitive), is consistent with coaching for the development of player/athlete learning across the domains of physical literacy (Sport Australia, 2022). Game-based approaches are thus part of a humanistic and holistic approach to coaching (Kidman, 2005) and contemporary directions encouraging coaching for the development of the 'whole' person (Light, 2017a). It is therefore important in becoming an athlete-centred coach that coaches not only monitor the observation of player/athlete performance in practice but also make visible player/athlete subjective and affective emotive experience to gain comprehensive understanding of what the player/athlete is learning.

Conclusion

While athlete-centred coaching places the coach-athlete relationship at the core of coaching (Jowett, 2017), it is important to acknowledge that the pedagogical behaviour of coaches is only one aspect of athlete-centred coaching (Garner et al., 2022). Consistent with a holistic, process-oriented model for athlete-centred coaching centralised on democracy in action, (Figure 12.1), Kihl et al. (2007) explained that realising athlete-centred coaching required sporting bodies to put structural mechanisms in place that provided and supported opportunities for player/athletes and their coaches to be empowered to exercise their autonomy. In practice, this means empowerment of players and coaches to contribute deliberately to the policies of their sport through ethical, consultative, communicative, and analytical discussions. In this way, athlete-centred is both an approach to coaching and a guiding principle in the development and application of standards, outcomes, and processes serving a sport.

References

Ahlberg, M., Mallett, C. & Tinning, R. (2008). Developing autonomy supportive coaching behaviours: An action research approach to coach development. *International Journal of Coaching Science*, *2*(2), 3–22.

Bowles, R. & O'Dwyer, A. (2020). Athlete-centred coaching: Perspectives from the Sideline. *Sports Coaching Review*, *9*(3), 231–252.

Bunker, D. & Thorpe, R. (1982). A model for the teaching of games in secondary schools. *Bulletin of Physical Education*, *10*(1), 9–16.

Côté, J., Bruner, M., Erickson, K., Strachan, L. & Fraser-Thomas, J. (2010). Athlete development and coaching. In J. Lyle & C. J. Cushion (Eds.), *Sports coaching: Professionalisation and practice* (pp. 63–83). Elsevier.

Cushion, C. J. (2007). Modelling the complexity of the coaching process. *International Journal of Sports Science and Coaching*, *2*(4), 395–401.

Ford, P. R., Yates, I. & Williams, A. M. (2010). An analysis of practice activities and instructional behaviours used by youth soccer coaches during practice: Exploring the link between science and application. *Journal of Sports Sciences*, *28*(5), 483–495.

Garner, P., Roberts, W. M., Baker, C. & Côté, J. (2022). Characteristics of a person-centred coaching approach. *International Journal of Sports Science & Coaching*, *17*(4), 722–733.

Gilbert, W. (2017). *Coaching better every season*. Human Kinetics.

Griffin, L., Butler, J. & Sheppard, J. (2018). Athlete-centred coaching: Extending the possibilities of a holistic and process-oriented model to athlete development. In S. Pill (Ed.), *Perspectives on athlete-centred coaching* (pp. 9–23). Routledge.

Harvey, S. (2018). Developing an athlete-centred coaching high performance field hockey. In S. Pill (Ed.), *Perspectives on athlete-centred coaching* (pp. 79–92). Routledge.

Hewitt, M. & Edwards, K. (2013). Observed teaching styles of junior development and club professional tennis coaches in Australia. *ITF Coaching and Sport Science Review*, *59*, 6–8.

Hewitt, M., Edwards, K., Ashworth, S. & Pill, S. (2016). Investigating the teaching styles of tennis coaches using The Spectrum. *Sport Science Review*, *25*(5/6), 350–373.

Jones, R. & Ronglan, L. T. (2018). What do coaches orchestrate? Unravelling the 'quiddity' of practice. *Sport, Education and Society, 23*(9), 905–915.

Jowett, S. (2017). Coaching effectiveness: The coach–athlete relationship at its heart. *Current Opinion in Psychology, 16,* 154–158.

Kidman, L. (2005). *Athlete-centered coaching: Developing inspired and inspiring people.* Innovative Press Communications.

Kidman, L. & Davis, W. (2006). Empowerment in coaching. In W. Davis & G. Broadhead (Eds.), *Ecological task analysis perspectives on movement* (pp. 121–140). Human Kinetics.

Kidman, L. & Lombardo, B. J. (2010). *Athlete-centered coaching: Developing decision makers* (2nd ed.). IPC Press Resources.

Kihl, L. A., Kikulis, L. M. & Thibault, L. (2007). A deliberative democratic approach to athlete-centred sport: The dynamics of administrative and communicative power. *European Sport Management Quarterly, 7*(1), 1–30.

Kinnerk, P., Harvey, S., MacDonncha, C. & Lyons, M. (2018). A review of the game-based approaches to coaching literature in competitive team sport settings. *Quest, 70*(4), 401–418.

Li, M-H., Sum, R. K. W., Wallhead, T., Ha, A. S. C., Sit, C. H. P. & Li, R. (2019). Influence of perceived physical literacy on coaching efficacy and leadership behavior: A cross-sectional study. *Journal of Sports Science & Medicine, 18*(1), 82–90.

Light, R. L. (Ed.) (2017a). *Positive pedagogy for sport coaching: Athlete-centred coaching for individual sports.* Routledge.

Light, R. L. (2017b). Swimming. In R. L. Light (Ed.), *Positive pedagogy for sport coaching: Athlete-centred coaching for individual sports* (pp. 88–94). Routledge.

Light, R. L. & Harvey, S. (2017). Positive pedagogy for sport coaching. *Sport, Education and Society, 22*(2), 271–287.

Light, R. L. & Harvey, S. (Eds.) (2019). *Positive pedagogy for sport coaching* (2nd ed.). Routledge.

Light, R. L. & Harvey, S. (Eds.) (2021). *Applied positive pedagogy in sport coaching: International cases.* Routledge.

Magias, T. (2018). Athlete-centred coaching in swimming: An autoethnography. In S. Pill (Ed.), *Perspectives on game-based coaching* (pp. 161–170). Routledge.

O'Connor, D., Larkin, P. & Höner, O. (2021). Coaches' use of game-based approaches in team sports. In S. Pill (Ed.). *Perspectives on game-based coaching* (pp. 117–126). Routledge.

Penney, D. & Kidman, L. (2014). Opening call for discourse: Athlete centered coaching – a time for reflection on meanings, values and practice. *Journal of Athlete Centered Coaching, 1,* 1–5.

Penney, D. & Zehntner, C. (2018). Athlete-centred coaching tensions and opportunities arising in the masters context. In S. Pill (Ed.), *Perspectives on athlete-centred coaching* (pp. 206–216). Routledge

Pill, S. (2016). Implementing game sense coaching approach in Australian football through action research. *Agora for Physical Education and Sport, 18*(1), 1–19.

Pill, S. (Ed.) (2018a). *Perspectives on athlete-centred coaching.* Routledge.

Pill, S. (2018b). Introduction. In S. Pill (Ed.), *Perspectives on athlete-centred coaching* (pp. 1–5). Routledge.

Pill, S. (2018c). Developing thinking players: A coach's experience with game sense coaching. In S. Pill (Ed.), *Perspectives on athlete-centred coaching* (pp. 93–103). Routledge.

Pill, S., Hewitt, M. & Edwards, K. (2016). Exploring tennis coaches' insights in relation to their teaching styles. *Baltic Journal of Sport and Health Sciences, 3*(102), 30–43.

Pill, S. & Hyndman, B. (2018). Gestalt psychological principles in developing meaningful understanding of games and sport in physical education. *Journal of Teaching in Physical Education, 37*(4), 322–329.

Preston, C., Kerr, G. & Stirling, A. (2016). Elite athletes' experiences of athlete-centred coaching. *The Journal of Athlete Centered Coaching, 1*(1), 81–101.

Roberts, S. J. (2011). Teaching games for understanding: The difficulties and challenges experienced by participation cricket coaches. *Physical Education and Sport Pedagogy, 16*(1), 33–48.

Sport Australia. (2022). *Physical literacy.* https://www.sportaus.gov.au/physical_literacy

Sum, R. K. W., Ha, A. S. C., Cheng, C. F., Chung, P. K., Yiu, K. T. C., Kuo, C. C., Yu, C. K. & Wang, F. J. (2016). Construction and validation of a perceived physical literacy instrument for physical education teachers. *PLoS One, 11*, e0155610.

Townsend, R. & Cushion, C. (2018). Athlete-centred coaching in disability sport: A critical perspective. In S. Pill (Ed.), *Perspectives on athlete-centred coaching* (pp. 47–56). Routledge.

Turner, A. (2018). Athlete-centred coaching and teaching games for understanding-not quite the perfect match. In S. Pill (Ed.), *Perspectives on Athlete-Centred Coaching* (pp. 127–136). Routledge.

Vinson, D. & Bell, J. (2019). Athlete-centred coaching: An applied example from junior international field hockey. In E. Cope & M. Partington (Eds.), *Sports coaching: A theoretical and practical guide* (pp. 40–52). Routledge.

13 Using Global Lesson Study to Promote Understanding of Game-Based Approaches

Naoki Suzuki and Karen Richardson

Lesson Study is a simple idea: If you want to improve instruction, what could be more obvious than collaborating with fellow teachers to plan instruction and examine its impact on students? In Lesson Study, teachers bring their own questions to the table and seek answers from one another, from outside specialists and researchers, and from careful study of students. Global Lesson Study is a professional development opportunity for teachers from multiple countries. We come together to improve our teaching. (Global Lesson Study Workshop Announcement; N. Suzuki, personal communication, January 2021)

Game-based approaches (GBAs) for teaching and coaching have been advocated for use in physical education and sport across the globe (Kinnerk et al., 2018; Light, 2013; Mitchell et al., 2021). Widespread adoption of GBAs among in-service teachers, however, has been uneven (Harvey & Pill, 2016). Evidence of the influence of GBAs is seen in how games are represented in national curriculum documents. For example, the 2010 Japanese National Course of Study (National Curriculum Guide) identified the contents of games by game categories (e.g., net/wall, target) rather than by the names of sports. Despite the focus of GBAs in the Japanese National Course of Study, when Japanese university students in a physical education pedagogy class in 2021 were asked about their experiences in learning games, most had only experienced traditional skill-based game instruction. The results suggest that an understanding of what is taught in the Japanese Courses of Study is not enough to support the implementation of GBAs. Thus, while GBAs are ostensibly the mainstream method advocated for games teaching in Japan, school aged students fail to experience games taught in this manner as teachers are not using GBAs. Lesson Study is a ubiquitous form of teacher professional development in Japan and has promise for supporting the implementation of GBA.

In this chapter, we will explore Lesson Study as a meaningful form of professional development. We will then introduce an innovative Global Lesson Study initiative in physical education that has engaged more than 110 teachers in 15 countries to deepen their understandings of GBAs.

DOI: 10.4324/9781003298298-16

What is lesson study?

Lesson Study, called 'Jugyokenkyu' in Japan, has attracted attention worldwide as an important opportunity to support the professionalisation of teachers. Japan has over a 100-year tradition of Lesson Study (Makinae, 2010). Lesson Study is a form of professional development that involves a collaborative close look at the teaching process. Lewis and Hurd (2011) summarise the Lesson Study cycle to include:

1 *Goal setting.* Consider the long-term goals for student learning and development based on gaps between long-term goals and current progress.
2 *Lesson planning.* Teachers collaboratively plan a research lesson designed to reach the goals in a detailed lesson proposal. The proposal includes the research theme, connections with content to other grade levels, a plan for data collection and more.
3 *Research lesson.* One team member teaches the lesson while other members of the team and school community, and often a knowledge-able outside other, observe and collect data.
4 *Post-lesson discussion.* In a formal lesson meeting, the observers share data from the lesson to highlight student learning, specific content knowledge, lesson and unit design.
5 *Reflection.* Document the cycle to carry forward new understandings, and to identify new questions for the next cycle of Lesson Study. A report is written that includes the lesson proposal, data, and reflections on what is learned.

In the Lesson Study cycle, planning decisions, lesson structure, a guiding question, and scrutiny of student responses are at the centre of the process of *jugyokenkyu*. Lewis and Tsuchida's (1997) research on Lesson Study was an avenue for Lesson Study to spread in North America with the published description of the Lesson Study cycle in English. The effectiveness of the Lesson Study was also featured in the *New York Times*, a major newspaper in the United States, and was the centrepiece of Green's (2015) popular book *Building a Better Teacher*. Tokyo Gakugei University has conducted Project IMPULS (International Math-teacher Professionalization Using Lesson Study) since 2011, which was featured in Green (2015) as a model for teacher professional development. The export of the Lesson Study as Japanese professional development has been carried out positively in other cultural contexts (Lewis et al., 2009).

Stigler and Hiebert's (1999) *The Teaching Gap* brought increased global recognition to classroom research as Lesson Study (Fujii, 2018). Stigler and Hiebert (1999), who focused on mathematics, argued that lesson studies are needed as an opportunity to learn about systems for generating and sharing knowledge about learning and teaching. They identified the following characteristics of Lesson Study that support the generation and sharing of pedagogical knowledge:

1   Lesson Study is based on a long-term, continuous improvement model.
2   Lesson Study keeps the focus on student learning.
3   Lesson Study emphasises the situation in which instruction occurs and focuses on making improvements in response to that situation.
4   Lesson Study is collaborative process.
5   Teachers actively participate in the Lesson Study, and teachers believe that they are contributing not only to their professional development but also to the development of knowledge about learning instruction.

Ono (2009) noted that these five characteristics roughly match the seven conditions for practical primary teacher training described by Darling-Hammond et al. (2017). The formation of teacher competence through such Lesson Study workshops has been the subject of many studies in physical education classes in Japan.

Furthermore, features of Lesson Study can be considered best practice in in-service teacher development, a practice that Japan is trying to transfer to developing countries (Ono, 2009). Lesson Studies are positioned as an initiative to improve the quality of education. Shiga (2017) found that intercultural competencies occurred in language learning, and that attitudes and postures such as acknowledging others, being close to the position of others, accepting self-transformation, escaping from the thinking that 'my view is the only view' (p. 20), and objectifying the situation were observed. Shiga (2017) also suggested that intercultural competencies were a significant learning experience that transcends language learning that occurred through Lesson Studies.

Structure of physical education Global Lesson Study

Global Lesson Study in physical education was developed by Dr. Naoki Suzuki as a means to engage colleagues from around the world in the practice of Lesson Study to improve instruction in GBAs. Global Lesson Study included a study group that combined asynchronous and synchronous distance learning focused on the observation of GBA research lessons, close review of the lesson plans, and post-lesson discussions. In 2021, the Global Lesson Study Workshop series featured lessons developed by physical education teachers from Japan as well as participant teachers from 15 different countries.

As outlined above, the full Lesson Study cycle consists of collaborative lesson planning, presentation of a research lesson for colleagues to observe, formal discussions, and reflection (Stigler & Hiebert, 1999). Global Lesson Study in physical education has evolved to focus on a video observation of the research lessons (with translations into English), review of the detailed lesson plan documents, preparation of questions, and a formal post-lesson discussion.

Even with adjustments in the cycle, barriers to Global Lesson Study that we continue to address included differences in educational content (i.e., lack of shared curriculum goals as provided in the Japanese Course of Study), educational jargon/language, and time zone differences. With the advances and accessibility to free and low-cost technologies, we constructed an online Global Lesson Study series with in-service teachers from across the globe to form a teacher community of practice for professional development which overcame the barriers of language and time.

The Global Lesson Study cycle began by having GBA lesson plans translated into English using features in Word processing software and distributed in advance of the Global Lesson Study Workshop. The accuracy of the automatic translation is becoming more and more accurate, and although there are still some mistakes, the translation allowed participants to understand the content. The class video (Figure 13.1) was accompanied by English subtitles, distributed on YouTube on limited service, and the URL was sent to participants to watch the video in advance. Also, since there are time differences, we used an online tool to check the time and send reminders one day, three hours, or one hour in advance of the workshops. We made extensive use of technology to prepare and deliver the workshop. The Global Lesson Study format has developed over the last five years through trial and error as we will share next.

The first physical education Global Lesson Study took place in 2015. Participants engaged in the complete five-step Lesson Study cycle from planning to reflection. In the 2015 academic year, Tokyo Gakugei University also supported two online Lesson Studies held between several Japanese schools. Attendees had difficulty participating in discussions. To make small discussion groups more appropriate, each online group was then assigned a facilitator, which improved the process. In the 2016 academic year, two international Lesson Studies were held between Japanese and US

Figure 13.1 Recorded lesson with subtitles.

schools. Translation to English was provided as the lesson was conducted in Japanese. The challenge was for non-Japanese speakers to fully understand what they were seeing and hearing to enable them to engage in a deep discussion and reflective process.

For the 2021 Global Lesson Study, more limited elements of the Lesson Study were then used that included: (a) observation of lesson video and review of lesson plan; (b) questions on Padlet; (c) teacher's presentation about the lesson; (d) share prepared comments about the lesson in small group; and (e) develop a shared theme for improvement. In advance of the Global Lesson Study, the participants watched the research lesson video and then posted their questions and perspectives on Padlet (Figure 13.2). The facilitator then set the discussion points based on Padlet content for part of the workshop. The teacher, who was featured in the video, provided supplementary explanations during the plenary session at the beginning of the Lesson Study workshop based on the questions posed on Padlet. We believe it is essential to separate the content to be discussed on the Padlet from the content to be discussed directly in the workshop (based on the observation of the lesson). We now use Padlet to deepen our understanding of the content of the research lesson by asking participants to write only questions. The evaluation of the lesson and discussion of modifications and improvements are then held during the Lesson Study workshop. In addition, since the Lesson Study was designed as a participatory and collaborative learning environment, we asked participants to prepare written comments (limited to two minutes) in advance about their perspectives of the research lesson.

At the Global Lesson Study Workshop, the lesson proposer (teacher) shared basic ideas of the class and reflected on their teaching practice using a

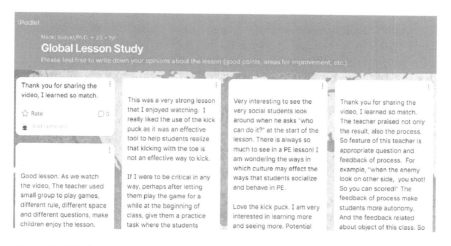

Figure 13.2 Padlet.

It was great to see that students are having fun.

Implementing rackets in addition to bats was a great idea in order to include students who have less ability to hit the ball.

Teacher did a good job on asking questions and having students think (improve decision-making ability).

The most important part of this lesson was that teacher asked qeustions (instead of telling them what to do), have them discuss, make them opportunities to come up with the ideas (i.e., how, what and why..etc.).

This is hybrid of GBA and Sport Educaiton method that having students play different roles....it was helpful to give ownership to the students.

warm up could ccombined with more specific/dynamic warm up that related to the activity (i.e.,cricket)

teacher could have moved around and provide individual feedback (including asking questions) or teach feedback "while" the game is being played so students could understand the game situation better.

teacher need to distiguish when to talk to "individual student" and when to talk to "a whoe team" so the individual student can understand who teacher is talking to.

Since some students was not moving quickly in transition, using whistle was suggested.

Figure 13.3 Jamboard descriptions.

PowerPoint presentation. Based on this presentation, in Zoom breakout rooms, 3–4 participants presented the ideas they had prepared in advance and then decided on a theme to discuss. Each small group organised the contents of this small group discussion using Jamboard (Figure 13.3). This was a way to overcome the language barrier and for all to participate in the discussion. Afterward, we gathered as a whole group to review the discussion, we then separated into new groups to then discuss specific lesson improvements. In this discussion, each person made an entry using Jamboard (Figure 13.3), discussed specific improvements based on the presentation, and summarised the content on a shared Google Document (Table 13.1). Since the group's writings can be viewed on a single sheet, the lesson proposer was able to review and reflect on their teaching practices. After the discussion, in the plenary session, the lesson proposer reflected on the content of the discussion up to that point, and presented what they have reflected on and the directions they intend to improve upon. The workshop was then concluded by having the commentator summarise and make connections to the discussions.

Lessons learned from Global Lesson Study

The two teachers who participated in the 2015 Global Lesson Study had 10 and 12 years of teaching experience and communicated in English, which was not their first language. Data collection included a semi-structured interview, all discussions were audio recorded for analysis and artefacts

Table 13.1 Google Document descriptions

	Small group discussion # 3 including ideas for improving the lesson
Group 1	We must incorporate small-sided games into teaching games. Games should be used for warm-ups and skill practice. Lesson start: <u>Small sided game!</u> For example, throwing and catching game.
Group 2	Warm up could combine with more specific/dynamic warm-up that related to the activity (i.e., cricket). The teacher could have moved around and provided individual feedback (including asking questions) or teach feedback while the game is being played so students could understand the game situation better. Since some students were not moving quickly in transition, using a whistle was suggested. The teacher needs to distinguish when to talk to individual students and when to talk to the whole team so the individual students can understand who the teacher is talking to. Intensity of the class needs to be improved. Too much chatting time.
Group 3	Let the students have the choice of equipment without any comment from the teacher. Were students aiming when they were striking? Did they talk about hitting to open space? Liked using the rackets to allow students to enjoy it (game) more. Need more ways to involve more students. Maybe use smaller teams as mentioned. Both offense and defence can score points. Very interesting and creative approach. Liked the questioning and would encourage more of it.

developed for the Lesson Study were collected. The analysis was interpreted using Shimizu's (2011) theoretical framework that asserted there were three challenges for consideration in doing the *jugyokenkyu* (i.e., Lesson Study). First, 'Why does the teacher teach it to students?'. Second, 'What is the content of the teaching?'. And third, 'How do teachers teach it to students?'. It was evident that a process of professional development occurred through the Lesson Study for the two teachers. The differences in thinking among the teachers and the international colleagues influenced the participants in new ways of thinking, although the openness to new ideas took time. One of the teachers stated in an interview:

At first, I could not understand what the international participants said. I believed that their understanding was wrong (misconception). However, some people who joined the conference said it was a good idea. Those words have impacted me. Then I decided to try it though I was doubtful about it. Surprisingly, it was a fit for the students. I was so excited to teach with such an experience. After that, I began to listen to other ideas and accepted them at once and reflected deeply on my own ideas based on them. (teacher 1)

During the Lesson Study, there was a difference in understanding expected teacher behaviours and in the learning content. According to Shimizu (2011), teachers' interaction (in Lesson Study) is intended to be mainly focused on 'how to teach'. However, the international participants frequently asked, 'Why do you teach it?' or 'What is your purpose?'. The teacher 2 said,

> At first, I was interested in "how to teach." Overseas participants have increased questions about our practice, and I have begun to reflect on my teaching by myself. It has become an opportunity to reflect on myself rather than having new knowledge and new teaching skills. (teacher 2)

Typically, a teacher's lesson plans were not critiqued based on the purpose and the content of teaching, but that was not the case with Global Lesson Study. Asking 'why' or 'what' was not a significant problem focused on in a typical lesson study (with domestic teachers only) because the Course of Study that outlines this for teacher. International participants, however, were interested in this point of view that domestic participants implicitly ignored. Overseas participants had a different schema of physical education from the domestic participants. In the first half of the stage of making the unit plan, domestic participants struggled with this difference in thinking. It seemed that they felt stressed by the differences between other ideas. However, they listened to those ideas and began to accept the ideas of others while noticing the effectiveness of using those ideas through the sharing of the lessons. One of the teachers said:

> Also, by accepting the difference, I had the opportunity to rethink myself. Through this, they came up with a new idea. In other words, Global Lesson Study worked as an opportunity to accept differences and reflect on their teaching, leading to teaching improvement. (teacher 4)

Both teachers described how interactions with international participants led to a reflection of their teaching behaviour rather than creating new ways to teach. Interaction with diverse values was thought to encourage this deep reflection. The teachers were then able to talk about 'how' to teach the GBA content to students, based on the new ideas for the purpose of physical education and its contents generated by that introspection.

By 2021, the format for Global Lesson Study had been refined and participants were able to explore questions essential to using a GBA. International participants in the Lesson Study were not part of the planning process, but rather in the research lesson and discussion. Mr. Fujimoto, a teacher at Masago Elementary School in Niigata City, developed a lesson plan for a first-grade kicking game using a large soft puck. This lesson was focused on a 2 v 2 game, and the discussion centred on game modification and exploring the role of questions in the learning process. One participant from the United States indicated that this was the first time he had seen tactical learning in the lower grades of elementary school, and was surprised that it could be implemented in the lower grades with some game modification. Various suggestions were made on how to ask better questions that would lead to better tactical understanding. Commentators organised how to create questions based on class observations and the results of those observations, which the class participants said were very helpful.

A second lesson was taught by Mr. Kikuchi at Setagaya Junior High School an affiliated school with Tokyo Gakugei University, who developed a lesson plan and research lesson for a striking/fielding game for first grade students. Discussions at this workshop centred on the warm-up and the grouping of students for the lesson. The warm-up provoked a rich discussion with various opinions expressed, which focused on the role of static stretching and dynamic stretching; timing of teacher's intervention; and how small-sided games can be part of preparatory exercises. The participants were able to reflect on the discussions and eventually ways to use small-sided games for preparatory exercises. Another area of discussion was grouping and leadership roles. The class used a hybrid model of Tactical Games (Mitchell et al., 2021) and Sport Education (Siedentop et al., 2020), therefore, students were in four intact teams and all of the team leaders were boys. Team leaders were selected by the teams. Participants discussed how physical education instruction and other cultural factors may have led to girls not being selected into the leadership positions. They also pointed out that there were differences between the boys and girls in how the students interacted during the activity. Through this discussion and reflection, the teacher and participants of the Lesson Study noted that just because games are taught in junior high schools with both boys and girls learning together, that is not innovative teaching. The importance of looking at how boys and girls interacted and contributed to the class in this context, created insights around gender and role expectations. The hybrid model of instruction was a point of discussion that allowed for the exploration of moral education in Japan and the role of the learner. It was a valuable discussion that led to a reexamination of responsible learning in physical education.

The 2020–2021 Global Lesson Study Workshop included 43 participants from 15 countries for the elementary lessons, and 110 participants from 14 countries for the junior high school lessons. In a survey taken after the Global Lesson Study Workshops, 100% of the participants answered that they had benefited from both workshops. These results indicate that the attempt to think collaboratively about a physical education lesson, beyond national borders, is a valuable one. A few participants mentioned the difficulty of verbal communication, and we will continue to take steps to resolve this issue by making better use of technology.

Final thoughts

The Global Lesson Study in physical education has created an important bridge between Japan and colleagues around the world interested in supporting the development of GBAs. The opportunity to learn together with experienced physical education teachers from Japan, and teachers from around the world can be a model for professional development. In addition, this Global Lesson Study in physical education provided unique opportunities for educators outside of Japan to experience Lesson Study for professional development. There remain challenges in providing resources on how best to share class practices as physical educators. We would like to create resources (e.g., lesson plans, videos of research lessons) that are likely to be used in the future to promote the use of GBAs in physical education.

Global Lesson Study worked as an opportunity to accept differences and for all the participants to reflect on their teaching, leading to teacher professional development. In Global Lesson Study, the focus is different from typical lesson study. The focus was the ontology and the epistemology of the unit. Participants were more like philosophers, not teachers at first. Deep thinking contributed to new cross-cultural understandings about physical education.

Technology is a tool that makes the 'impossible' possible. We have made it feasible for Global Lesson Studies to be a place where people far away from each other can come together to share their perspectives and address common problems to improve physical education. We contend that the future of physical education in a global society is best constructed based on different perspectives, and Global Lesson Study supports this aim.

References

Darling-Hammond, L., Hyler, M. E. & Gardner, M. (2017). *Effective teacher professional development*. Learning Policy Institute.

Fujii, T. (2018). Lesson study and teaching mathematics through problem solving: The two wheels of a cart. In M. Quaresma, C. Winslow, S. Clivaz, J. P. da Ponte, A. Ní Shúilleabháin & A. Takahashi (Eds.), *Mathematics study around the world: Theoretical and methodological issues* (pp. 1–21). Springer.

Green, E. (2015). *Building a better teacher: How teaching works (and how to teach it to everyone)*. WW Norton & Company.

Harvey, S. & Pill, S. (2016). Comparisons of academic researchers' and physical education teachers' perspective on the utilization of the tactical games model. *Journal of Teaching in Physical Education, 35*(4), 313–323.

Kinnerk, P., Harvey, S., MacDonncha, C. & Lyons, M. (2018). A review of game-based approaches to coaching literature in competitive team sport settings. *Quest, 70*(4), 401–418.

Lewis, C. & Hurd, J. (2011). *Lesson studystep by step: How teacher learning communities improve instruction*. Heinemann.

Lewis, C. & Tsuchida, I. (1997). Planned educational change in Japan: The shift to student-centered elementary science. *Journal of Educational Policy, 12* (5) 313–331.

Lewis, C., Perry, R. & Hurd, J. (2009). Improving mathematics instruction through lesson study: A theoretical North American case. *Journal of Mathematics Teacher Education, 12*(4), 285–304.

Light, R. (2013). *Game sense: Pedagogy for performance, participation, and enjoyment.* Routledge.

Makinae, N. (2010). The origin of Lesson Study in Japan. In Y. Shimuzu, Y. Sekiguchi & K. Hino (Eds.), *The proceedings of the 5th East Asia regional conference on mathematics education: In search of excellence of mathematics education* (vol. 2, pp. 140–147). Japan Society of Mathematics Education.

Mitchell, S., Oslin, J. & Griffin, L. (2021). *Teaching sports concepts and skills: A tactical games approach* (4th ed.). Human Kinetics.

Ono, Y. (2009). Borrowing lending of educational programs: A case study of class research. *International Educational Cooperation, 1*(22), 69–80.

Shiga, R. (2017). The potential of collaborative learning: From the perspective of inter-cultural education. *The Bulletin of International Education Center at Hitotsubashi University, 8,* 15–26.

Shimizu, N. (2011). A study on professional development of physical education teachers. *Report of Grant-in-Aid for Scientific Research (C) (20500533).* http://hdl.handle.net/2241/115217

Siedentop, D., Hastie, P. & van der Mars, H. (2020). *Complete guide to sport education* (3rd ed.). Human Kinetics.

Stigler, J. & Hiebert, J. (1999). *The teaching gap: Best ideas from the world's teacher for improving education in the classroom.* Free Press.

14 Game-Based Approach and Teacher Reflective Practice

Aspasia Dania

Game-based approaches (GBAs) are inquiry-based teaching approaches that depend on the teacher's capacity to modify instruction, content and tasks as a response to students' learning to play games. By using modified games to develop players' tactical understanding, teachers create learning environments within which decision-making and problem solving are used as strategies to promote peer and social interaction. The ultimate goal is to create a game environment that enhances students' pleasure and enjoyment to play, learn and relate. GBAs entail a human-centred way of practice, which incorporates the teacher's thoughtful and compassionate action to step back, observe and emphasise questioning to stimulate empathy, co-creation, and iteration through players' cooperation and interaction (Light & Mooney, 2014). To this end, reflection has a valuable role in supporting GBA teachers to work more holistically in designing and implementing games so as to achieve not only psychomotor and cognitive goals but also social and affective ones (i.e., good sporting behaviour, social and emotional learning, issues of equity, diversity and inclusion).

Teachers reflect on and in their practice (Schon, 1987) to perceive what has worked well or not and adapt or review established practices by drawing on their values and beliefs (Dewey, 1933), and the way(s) these influence their habitual practices (Ortwein et al., 2015). Reflection is described as a deep-thinking process which goes beyond day-to-day thinking to address practical problems to the processes of determining what one actually knows compared to what they believe or doubt (Greene & Yu, 2016). Therefore, scholars have called for the enactment of reflection as an 'augmented form of higher-order thinking' (Wackerhausen, 2009), and a professional stance which goes beyond self-introspection to a commitment of questioning the taken-for-granted beliefs or topics in their field (Feucht et al., 2017). Within physical education, reflection has been examined in relation to everyday practices, showing that open-mindedness is essential for teachers to recognise contingencies and prompt pedagogical change (Ballard & McBride, 2010; O'Connell & Dyment, 2011; Østergaard, 2018; Standal & Moe, 2013). Further, individual characteristics such as teacher self-awareness, insight, determination, and spontaneity have been examined as important

DOI: 10.4324/9781003298298-17

virtues for enacting reflection in a contextually relevant way across different levels of teaching and professional development (Darling-Hammond, 2009; Hargreaves, 2000).

Teacher selfhood and reflexivity are culturally dependent and changing (Blasco, 2012), which means that inner prejudices cannot always be accessible and fixable. When trying to adapt something that has not worked well in practice, the teacher has to be able to initiate different varieties of reflection (e.g., focusing on the content or the process of instruction) in order to test inferences and engage with new forms of thinking. Especially within games education, the teacher needs to develop a sense-of-self that is thoughtful enough to enact internal dialogue in ways that will advance action towards students' unique socio-emotional, psychomotor and cognitive capacities. To do so, the reflective GBA teacher should be able to consider whether and how his/her/their own personal ways of perceiving, doing and explaining influence his/her/their teaching and learning priorities. Ultimately, the teacher's sensitivity in relation to the different 'anatomical elements' of reflection (Wackerhausen, 2009) will shape instruction in alignment to what is best for the student as a whole human being.

Based on the need to support GBA teachers' reflection, this chapter draws on Wackerhausen's (2009) 'anatomy of reflection' framework, to:

a   Unpack the elements that shape the anatomy of teacher reflection.
b   Problematise on the complexity of teacher reflection within games education.
c   Connect GBA examples of teacher reflection with their relative anatomical elements and parts.

By drawing on the points above, I aim to highlight the circumstances under which reflection can raise instructional awareness and bring positive gains in teachers' professional development, as part of their engagement with human-centred praxis in GBA contexts.

The anatomy of teacher reflection

According to Wackerhausen (2009), ontological, epistemological and ethical perspectives challenge a teacher's ability to enact or support processes of inner dialogue that may lead to the suspension of habit and the development of new routines. The way that teachers interpret the causal background of phenomena in their discipline (e.g., why girls are less physically active than boys), as well as their willingness to reach beyond the 'givens' of their profession, will expand or limit the boundaries of their reflection. The formation of professional identity implies attunement to rules, beliefs and habits that are constituent elements of how a teacher becomes, performs and stays 'one of the kind' both at a macro (i.e., the public level of the profession) and at a micro (i.e., the level of the practitioner) level

(Wackerhausen, 2009). Habitual and embodied ways of perceiving, valuing and behaving at the micro and macro levels may often create barriers to professional development and 'colonise' certain non-effective ways of practice (Shahjahan, 2015).

Wackerhausen (2009) suggested that when reflection is enacted as a conscious and intentional form of internal conversation, it may help circumvent teaching challenges and lead to transformative action.

Regardless of the different forms of reflection, the 'anatomy of teacher reflection' draws upon the following four fundamental elements: (a) *reflection on* a topic or an idea that is typical in the field (e.g., what and why teachers thematise); (b) *reflection with* concepts, beliefs, assumptions; (c) *reflection from* the perspective of tacit interests, motivations and values; and (d) reflection *in* specific settings or contexts (e.g., which are the motivating or constraining surroundings for reflection) (Wackerhausen, 2009). Thus, the renewal of everyday professional practice and the move from self-affirmative to non-conservative forms of thought and action involve a change of perspective in regard to *with, from* and *on* elements of reflection. By engaging with the different elements of reflection, teachers will become acquainted with conceptual, scientific and/or practical resources that will expand the ontological (what knowledge is or is not) and epistemological (how do we evaluate, apply and modify what we know) reach of their field. Overall, such a stance implies professional agility (e.g., recognition that diversity is a virtue) and epistemic humility (e.g., intentional and conscious re-education), with respect to what one may (claim to) know, both inside and outside of their subject domain (Wackerhausen, 2009).

The complexity of teachers' reflection within games education

From a social constructivist point of view, teaching is a dynamic form of cultural practice that cannot be easily predicted. The extent to which teachers may become aware of their purposes, prejudices and orientations depends on the content and nature of their lesson experiences. In the same way, teachers' ability and willingness for internal dialogue is influenced by the spatial and temporal factors that shape the boundaries of their profession (e.g., employment opportunities, professional advocacy, etc.) (Blasco, 2012). Specifically in today's highly developed global societies, teachers may become either hyper-reflective or unreflective about contextual elements of their teaching, as a response to the fragmented nature of learning in modern institutions (Shahjahan, 2015). In this sense, teachers' unconscious underpinnings may not be easily accessible through reflection.

GBA teachers' rumination over ideas is essential and cannot be confined only to thinking how they apply and evaluate knowledge, skills and information in their profession. Such understandings need to be transformed into meaningful praxis. The vision of the reflective GBA teacher encompasses conceptualisation and move-to-action (e.g., increasing student learning and enjoyment through participation in games that cater for diversity), engagement in teaching that depends on relational reasoning (e.g., evaluation of knowledge brought in class, acknowledgement of students' understandings, experiences, personal interests, etc.) and adaptive thinking (e.g., contextual judgement of instructional decisions, use of available resources, task-orchestration in accordance to curriculum goals, etc.). These qualities need time to develop (Murphy et al., 2016). A GBA teacher with limited professional experience will not approach otherness or equity within game activities in the same way that an experienced teacher will. Further, for some teachers' reflexivity and self-interrogation may be self-assuring practices that glorify personal opinions. For instance, some teachers believe that they use modified games in their practice, even though they exhibit limited conceptual understanding of GBA principles (Stolz & Pill, 2014). On the other hand, teacher reflection may be enacted as an overly narcissistic form of introspection, and thus may become less tolerant to student holistic needs (Maton, 2003). A teacher may adopt ways of telling personal stories about GBAs for the purpose of showing professional skilfulness without necessarily understanding what is best for students in practice.

When practice becomes habit (i.e., routine) and professional identity, it is experienced as natural and obvious, and then attention to ineffective or biased habits is not attracted. As a result, the GBA teacher may enact the etiquette and customs of their profession (i.e., ways of speaking, behaving, understanding and explaining) without consciously attuning to biased judgements. According to Alexander (2017), reflection should be examined as a learned disposition to reason about knowledge and action and not simply as a non-conscious, self-dialogic stance. Thus, due to the complexities of teaching, it is important to be cautious in assuming an always-positive effect of reflection in games education. Wackerhausen (2009) suggested that reflection can open up opportunities for professional development only when changes are made to the conceptual and knowledge background that teachers use to reflect with. This means that GBA teachers must become 'strangers to oneself' and thoughtfully (re)consider their goals and understandings before they are ready to transgress the boundaries of their established professional identity (Blasco, 2012). By obtaining knowledge about concepts, ideas, theories and practice 'outside' their profession (e.g., from fields like sport pedagogy, psychology, sociology, etc.), GBA teachers may increase the cognitive resources needed to question the 'naturalness' of their beliefs and enact conscious and human-centred reflection.

Reflection as professional habit within GBAs

The way teachers understand their learners' needs, become conscious of their contextual situatedness and address issues of equity and diversity in teaching, may place biases in their reflective practice (Schon, 1987). Further, social, temporal and affective factors that shape teachers' orientation towards self and others may alter their insightful moments when teaching. When implementing a GBA, teachers focus on the content of the modified games and the characteristics of the context and game-based pedagogical principles. As a result, reflection can range from practices of mindful introspection (i.e., teachers trying to adapt the rules that did not work in practice in a certain game), to practices of internal dialogue that advances inner thought and action (i.e., critical analysis of the challenges encountered during designing lessons with a human-centred focus). Both forms of reflection can raise instructional awareness and advance understanding. Consequently, GBA practitioners will reflect in a transformative manner when both at a micro and macro level they are able to re-think the limitations of their current practice and envision alternatives that are best for the student.

At a macro level, the professional identity of the GBA practitioner is shaped by factors that relate to the general public face of the physical education profession in general (i.e., educational authorisation, duties, regulations, privileges, etc.). These factors define the GBA practitioner's professional identity and the way that he/she/they is expected to fulfil his/her/their 'raison d'etre' in the field. On the other hand, the micro level identity of the GBA practitioner equates with certain ways of questioning, valuing and under-standing, all of which define the customs of good conduct of this specific approach. Until today, the established professional dogmas of the physical education and coaching professions (e.g., multi-sport teaching approaches, high-level performance pathways to elite sport, etc.) do not easily leave space for implementing GBA as human-centred form of teaching practice (Dania, 2021). Teachers' athletic occupational socialisation experiences and embodied coaching-oriented practices prevent them from examining or overcoming previously established coaching trails that may be ineffective (Vollmer & Curtner-Smith, 2016). Research has shown that especially novice teachers encounter difficulties in applying GBA principles in alignment with their learner holistic needs (Harvey et al., 2015; Vollmer & Curtner-Smith, 2016).

Reflection could help teachers to carefully work through areas of GBA practice (e.g., questioning, working with constraints, modifying games in relation to observed student performance, etc.), and identify potential teaching routines or customs that may replicate ineffective instructional practices within GBAs (e.g., use of decontextualised skill practice between games, conservative use of questioning, teacher authority in problem solving activities, etc.). To reflect meaningfully means that the teachers first identify which is their general issue of concern (e.g., they cannot easily leave their teacher-as-authority role) and then engage in internal dialogue to trace those cultural or personal factors that influence the above issue. For this purpose, the next section uses the sketch of Wackerhausen's 'anatomy of reflection' (2009) to provide examples of the instances under which reflection can be enacted as an adaptive form of thinking and making judgements in relation to 'taken for granted' GBA practices. Particularly, for each element of reflection, indicative anatomical parts and GBA reflection questions are presented (Table 14.1).

Table 14.1 Game-based approach reflection for change

Elements of Teacher Reflection	Anatomical Parts of Teacher Reflection	GBA Teacher Reflection for Change
Reflection *on*	Teaching Coaching	• Is teaching with GBAs educational? • What is the nature of coaching when using GBAs? • What is meant by human-centred learning?
Reflection *with*	Concepts Assumptions Knowledge in the field	• What are the benefits of using questioning as an instructional strategy within GBAs? • What kind of constraints do I use to modify my games and why? • How does knowledge in the field of GBAs relate to/is different from neighbouring approaches such as sport-as-techniques approaches?
Reflection *from*	Tacit Interests Motivations Values	• Why do I invest in students' tactical awareness? • What are my personal beliefs concerning player skilfulness? • How are GBAs inclusive teaching/coaching approaches?
Reflection *in*	Context	• Where do I choose to reflect on the above ideas and why (e.g., during conversations with colleagues)? • Whose voices are included in the contexts where I usually engage in different forms of reflection? • How easy/relevant is for reflection to take place in/outside of my daily circumstances?

Reflection on

The ability to use a variety of instructional models and styles is related to teaching effectiveness and needs to be practiced before learning to teach with GBAs. Within university courses, teacher educators could help novice teachers to become aware of the ontological and epistemological background behind each model or teaching style and the conceptual resources that are used when reflecting on its practice. For example, the epistemic aims of direct instruction are different to those of convergent discovery teaching and thus what is privileged as educational within each teaching style has to be questioned both in terms of its structure and in terms of its dynamics (e.g., teacher-student-content relationship). In this sense, the enculturation of desirable habits of reflection among GBA teachers must begin as early as their undergraduate studies (Oliver et al., 2015) and continue throughout the stages of their professional development (induction, early career stages, lifelong learning). Collaborating with other colleagues within networks or micro-communities of practice (Dania & Griffin, 2021), teachers could start by *reflecting on* topics that are typical in the field, such as the nature of teaching or coaching within GBAs (see also Table 14.1).

Reflection with

Practitioners could be encouraged to *reflect with* concepts, assumptions and beliefs inherent in the philosophy of GBA teaching. Teachers' engagement with different GBAs could offer opportunities for intra-professional learning and dialogue that could help them legitimise their knowledge and become more conscious of their professional practice (Casey & MacPhail, 2018; Gutierrez, 2016). Within GBA conferences and workshops teachers could be given opportunities to share views with experts focusing on common issues such as what does it mean in practice to modify games as a response to students' learning, which instructional styles foster tactical understanding and why, what type of problem-based learning promotes peer interaction, how can teachers step back and critically observe students' practice. By visiting the above issues though reflection and dialogic interactions, teachers could problematise on GBA pedagogical principles of reasoning and processes of knowing before applying them in their practice.

Reflection from

Teachers should recognise that they usually reflect from their class, gender, and racial perspectives and interests and thus their reflection is inhibited by their cultural dependent emotions. When such emotions are negative or inferior (e.g., a female GBA teacher negatively reflecting on her ability to teach 'masculine' sports), then reflection may become a form of self-denial that is enacted in consideration to other people's needs. Reflection can enable teachers to circumvent self-corrective consultations like the above, as long as teachers recognise that both their and their students' inner selves are not inner at all, but instead are socially constructed. Thus, instead of looking for 'effective teaching practices', GBA teachers should be encouraged to *reflect from* the way that they symbolically and pragmatically value meanings related to themselves and others. For example, how easily do they accept a 'wrong student answer' to their questioning practices? How can they support all student ideas as equal? How easy is it for them to grapple with diverging views of lesson design and introduce modified games that are not 'the real game'? Such a stance requires confidence to problematise on what, how and why of instruction. A way to achieve this is to engage in practice-oriented research collaborations, participatory action research projects, or teacher self-study networks (Baker, 2021; Ovens & Fletcher, 2014; Tinning, 2016).

Reflection in

Teachers should seize opportunities to *reflect in* settings where teaching takes place, without limiting themselves to GBA settings. As previously stated, teaching is indwelled by the norms and standards of each disciplinary field, which determine the conceptual resources that teachers use to reflect with. By visiting 'foreign teaching domains' and observing or collaborating with practitioners from other disciplines, teachers get acquainted with various practices of instructional design. Such practices help them to recognise the privileges and norms that shape the 'public face' of various professions. In this way, they are more likely to develop a positive intra-professional attitude to inter-professional reflection, which is needed to adjust professional habits and practices.

Final thoughts

In this chapter, reflection was described as the teacher's enculturation of habits of mind (i.e., care, compassion, relationship, and responsibility) that can support human-centred learning. By accepting human-centred learning as the ethical demand of every teaching endeavour, Wackerhausen's (2009) 'anatomy of reflection' was used as a framework to explain the circumstances under which GBA teachers need to reflect to enhance students' holistic development. Engagement in intra and inter-professional dialogue and were suggested as ways for helping teachers to move beyond micro-thinking to higher-order reflection *on, with, from* and *in* practice. Networks of co-operation and teacher partnerships were suggested as appropriate settings for sustaining the above effort. Even though the reflective process takes time to develop as a professional habit/stance, it shows promise for teacher professional learning as it relates to empowering students' holistic potential, in games education and hopefully carry over to everyday life.

References

Alexander, P. A. (2017). Reflection and reflexivity in practice versus in theory: Challenges of conceptualization, complexity, and competence. *Educational Psychologist, 52*(4), 307–314.
Baker, K. (2021). Developing principles of practice for implementing models-based practice: A self-study of Physical Education Teacher education practice. *Journal of Teaching in Physical Education, 41*(3), 446–454.
Ballard, K. K. & McBride, R. (2010). Promoting preservice teacher reflectivity: Van Manen may represent a viable model. *Physical Educator, 67*(2), 58–73.
Blasco, M. (2012). On reflection: Is reflexivity necessarily beneficial in intercultural education? *Intercultural Education, 23*(6), 475–489.
Casey, A. & MacPhail, A. (2018). Adopting a models-based approach to teaching physical education. *Physical Education and Sport Pedagogy, 23*(3), 294–310.
Dania, A. (2021). An autoethnography of becoming critical in physical education teacher education. *Curriculum Studies in Health and Physical Education, 12*(3), 251–267.

Dania, A. & Griffin, L. L. (2021). Using social network theory to explore a participatory action research collaboration through social media. *Qualitative Research in Sport, Exercise and Health, 13*(1), 41–58.

Darling-Hammond, L. (2009). Recognizing and enhancing teacher effectiveness. *The International Journal of Educational and Psychological Assessment, 3*(1), 1–24.

Dewey, J. (1933). *How we think.* D. C. Heath & Co.

Feucht, F. C., Brownlee, J. L. & Schraw, G. (2017). Moving beyond reflection: Reflexivity and epistemic cognition in teaching and teacher education. *Educational Psychologist, 52*(4), 234–241.

Greene, J. A. & Yu, S. B. (2016). Educating critical thinkers: The role of epistemic cognition. *Policy Insights from the Behavioral and Brain Sciences, 3*(1), 45–53.

Gutierrez, D. (2016). Game-centered approaches: Different perspectives, same goals-working together for learning. *Research Quarterly for Exercise and Sport, 87*(S1), S23.

Hargreaves, A. (2000). Mixed emotions: Teachers' perceptions of their interactions with students. *Teaching and Teacher Education, 16*(8), 811–826.

Harvey, S., Cushion, C. & Sammon, P. (2015). Dilemmas faced by pre-service teachers when learning about and implementing a game-centered approach. *European Physical Education Review, 21*(2), 238–256.

Light, R. L. & Mooney, A. (2014). Introduction. In R. L. Light, J. Quay, S. Harvey & A. Mooney (Eds.), *Contemporary developments in games teaching* (pp. 1–12). Routledge.

Maton, K. (2003). Reflexivity, relationism, & research: Pierre Bourdieu and the epistemic conditions of social scientific knowledge. *Space and Culture, 6*(1), 52–65.

Murphy, P. K., Firetto, C. M., Wei, L., Li, M. & Croninger, R. M. (2016). What REALLY works: Optimizing classroom discussions to promote comprehension and critical-analytic thinking. *Policy Insights from the Behavioral and Brain Sciences, 3*(1), 27–35.

O'Connell, T. & Dyment, J. (2011). Health and physical education pre-service teacher perceptions of journals as a reflective tool in experience-based learning. *European Physical Education Review, 17*(2), 135–151.

Oliver, K. L., Oesterreich, H. A., Aranda, R., Archeleta, J., Blazer, C., de la Cruz, K., … & Robinson, R. (2015). 'The sweetness of struggle': Innovation in physical education teacher education through student-centered inquiry as curriculum in a physical education methods course. *Physical Education and Sport Pedagogy, 20*(1), 97–115.

Ortwein, M., Carpenter-McCullough, A. & Thompson, A. (2015). A qualitative analysis of teachers' understandings of the epistemic aims of education. *Journal of Education and Human Development, 4*(3), 161–168.

Østergaard, L. D. (2018). Creation of new routines in physical education: Second-order reflection as a tradition-challenging form of reflection stimulated by inquiry-based learning. *Sport, Education and Society, 24*(9), 981–993.

Ovens, A. & Fletcher, T. (2014). Doing self-study: The art of turning inquiry on yourself. In A. Ovens & T. Fletcher (Eds.), *Self-study in physical education: Exploring the interplay between scholarship and practice* (pp. 3–14). Springer.

Schön, D. A. (1987). *Educating the reflective practitioner: Toward a new design for teaching and learning in the professions.* Jossey-Bass.

Shahjahan, R. A. (2015). Being 'lazy' and slowing down: Toward decolonizing time, our body, and pedagogy. *Educational Philosophy and Theory, 47*(5), 488–501.

Standal, Ø. F. & Moe, V. F. (2013). Reflective practice in physical education and physical education teacher education: A review of the literature since 1995. *Quest, 65*(2), 220–240.

Stolz, S. & Pill, S. (2014). Teaching games and sport for understanding: Exploring and reconsidering its relevance in physical education. *European Physical Education Review*, *20*(1), 36–71.

Tinning, R. (2016). Transformative pedagogies and physical education: Exploring the possibilities for personal change and social change. In C. Ennis (Ed.), *Routledge handbook of physical education pedagogies* (pp. 299–312). Routledge.

Vollmer, C. E. & Curtner-Smith, M. D. (2016). Influence of acculturation and professional socialization on preservice teachers' interpretation and implementation of the teaching games for understanding model. *Physical Educator*, *73*(1), 74.

Wackerhausen, S. (2009). Collaboration, professional identity and reflection across boundaries. *Journal of Interprofessional Care*, *23*(5), 455–473.

15 Game Balance Analysis: A Pedagogical Approach for Designing Rich Learning Environments

Wytse Walinga and Jeroen Koekoek

In this chapter, we present a games teaching framework that focuses on gameplay design. This framework can be used as a lens to analyse the teaching practice in how to move away from a traditional skill-based approach towards a game-based approach (GBA). The key element of this analysis is that observed play is placed within a categorisation of gameplay types to structure possible teaching interventions. Gameplay is about behaviour. It is the interaction of players within the game that can be observed as patterns that emerge under influence of environment, game rules, objectives, and instructions. The main premise in this pedagogy is that the elementary purpose of a game always plays the central role in analysis. This means that the balance of gameplay is charted between the offensive and defensive task complexity that players encounter (Game Balance Analysis). Consequently, gameplay types are distinguished based on the specific outcome of this reciprocal relationship in terms of power balance. Designing games towards a desired gameplay type may support teachers and coaches to better guide their teaching strategies. We will first discuss the relevance of incorporating a game balance analysis in practice and research in the next paragraph. This is followed by how the balance within a game can lead to several gameplay types, and how these may work as cues for design and guided discovery input by teachers.

Today, one of the main challenges for teachers and coaches is the implementation of pedagogical principles into practice (Memmert et al., 2015). Lesson plans, through the selection of appropriate small-sided games, contribute to structure a GBA practice. However, this is only one part in trying to achieve student engagement, motivation, and success in learning outcomes. An important aspect in the teaching process has been often undervalued. Namely, the situation when making decisions as a teacher while players play the game. Many lesson plans and games suggestions pay relatively little attention to the question 'what to do?', in the process for teachers during gameplay. For example, considering several didactical choices regarding number of players, team compositions, field sizes, or other environmental and task constraints relative to observed gameplay. Each gameplay context differs from another. We detect the tendency in Physical Education Teacher

DOI: 10.4324/9781003298298-18

Education that teacher candidates often copy the game situation directly from the textbook without critically analysing the learning context. In other words, the presented game situation is applied in practice as a fixed game situation. Hence, less attention is paid to the teaching process of adapting and modifying the gameplay situation so that a rich learning environment can be achieved and maintained.

From a teacher education perspective, it is important that pre-service teachers recognise that even after introducing the game, and beginning play, many teaching decisions can be made to achieve student engagement and performance. Moreover, *through teaching* the constraints of the game change because the players learn and consequently, the shape of gameplay changes as well. A teacher must monitor this change and decide whether it is still appropriate for the desired learning opportunities. If not, the game needs to be re-modified to enhance learning. Monitoring the shape of gameplay refers to certain gameplay types. These gameplay types provide information about what kind of adjustments are needed or what learning interventions should be selected to further enhance player learning processes. As teachers move away from a skill-based approach that offers rather linear, sequenced, and prescriptive content for students, they take on a new challenge by applying a pedagogy that is situated (Kirk & MacPhail, 2002) and adapted. Therefore, the focus is on expanding gameplay in an increasingly complex manner instead of sequencing pre-structured content (Figure 15.1).

In line with this central aspect in games teaching of adjusting the learning situation during gameplay, information about the shape of gameplay might also be of interest from an academic point of view. The balance of a game can be considered as an important lens for interpreting data that has been revealed from a study. Several review studies of GBAs have shown that researchers often choose the configuration of the game situation as a fixed variable (e.g., Barba-Martín et al., 2020; Harvey & Jarrett, 2014; Stolz & Pill, 2014). For example, 3v3 games are compared to 5v5 games, but reflections about how the game has been played receives relatively little attention. What did players/teams encounter in terms of complexity to

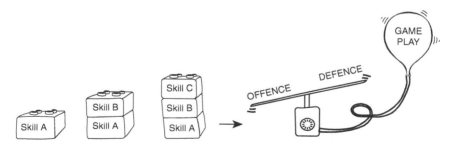

Figure 15.1 Illustrating change in teaching approach: from fixed sequencing of skills (left) towards guiding expansion of gameplay (right).

achieve the central purpose of the game? Was it hard to prevent scoring, or was it easy? What was the balance in the game? Teachers know that every single game of different players has its own unique shape which also progressively changes during teaching. Dividing two seemingly equal groups in a design will consequently lead to completely different gameplay. In other words, determining the situated gameplay, which we call 'shape of gameplay', could be an important but underestimated academic variable.

Defining the shape of gameplay in terms of complexity

Gameplay is the emerging behaviour of players in a game. It can be seen as a complex ecological dynamical system under influence of constraints (Davids et al., 2008). In terms of behaviour, defining the shape of gameplay can be done on its different layers. For example, keeping track of successful on-ball and off-ball decisions for individuals with the use of a game performance assessment instrument (Harvey et al., 2010; Oslin et al., 1998) is picturing player behaviour within a game. Olthof et al. (2019) expressed the quality of player actions in small-sided soccer games. Measures such as the mutual distance between players (Frencken et al., 2012), or the number of touches per player in soccer games (Sarmento et al., 2018), are examples of outcomes that inform practitioners about the shape of gameplay in terms of player behaviour. These outcomes are valuable for the evaluation of teaching processes. The essential performance parameters for individual players in sports games are functional. For the direct impact on situated teaching decisions, these measures can be difficult to directly read and translate into teaching actions.

Game balance analysis

The most fundamental layer that expresses the shape of gameplay judges a game situation on the ability of players to (cooperatively) solve the central purpose of the game. In an invasion game such as basketball or handball, the central purpose when in possession of the ball (i.e., game principle) is getting the playing object past the opponent to score, while the opponent is trying to prevent this and tries to achieve the same. The occurrence of success in these roles can be measured as it maps the ability of teams to solve the given game challenges. It does not yet reveal how this is done, and who takes on what role, but it questions if it is done. The benefit of reasoning from this idea (of teaching in game principles) is that it opens the opportunity to play a game and experience the central meaning of it, irrespective of conditional skills that need to be learned first. Therefore, *Game Balance Analysis* (Koekoek et al., 2023) offers a practical observational method for analysing gameplay. Game balance refers to the ratio between offensive success and defensive success. For example, when basketball teams manage to score only once out of 10 ball possessions, the balance is a 1/10 ratio for the offensive task, and 9/10 ratio for the defensive task. It can be concluded that it is relatively hard in such a game to complete all phases of the game (including the phase of scoring a point) for the attacking task. In the case of a situation that two teams of equal ability play against each other in such a game, the outcome after 20 possessions will be a 1-1 end score. Although the two teams play a fair match, it can be questioned whether the game offers enough opportunities for players to explore all specific elements. The low score shows that players are hardly able to experience the full purpose of the game by going through all phases of the game successfully (i.e., setting the attack, creating chances to score, and scoring a point). To let players discover relevant decisions in all phases of the game calls for the design of a preferred complexity, to solve the central purpose of the game (i.e., the game principle).

Designing the shape of gameplay

The introduction of modified small-sided games allows teachers to design games that fit the abilities of their players. Through adjusting the constraints of a game such as composition of teams, number of players, court sizes, rules, and materials, teachers can search for creating the optimal learning environment. With available game constraints, a teacher can influence the shape of gameplay in terms of balance outcome on the game principle. For example, if a teacher decides to let players play soccer with six attackers versus three defenders on a large pitch with multiple small soccer goals to score on, the chance of gameplay with an offensive dominance is obviously quite high (i.e., it is relatively easy to score points and hard to defend). In this example, the teacher is designing the game by exaggerating specific gameplay for the offensive or defensive task of teams. However, if the task is too easy, the teacher will fail to achieve their objectives. With respect to the teaching practice, it is thus required to determine the preferred ratio in scorings that benefits the learning processes in gameplay. To develop a pedagogical viewpoint on this principle, a distinction can be made between five different gameplay types (shapes) that derive from game balance outcomes.

Gameplay types

Gameplay types express the balance between offensive complexity and defensive complexity for all players (i.e., both teams) in a game (Figure 15.2). This can be determined for the specific group that plays a game. If players in, for example, an invasion game are not able to convert ball possession into scores, then there is a unilateral power for the defensive task. The offensive task is too hard to solve, and the defensive task is relatively easy. This gameplay type is called a *Defensive Power Game* (DPG). The complete opposite is also possible. If all ball possessions lead to scores, then gameplay is called an *Offensive Power Game* (OPG). The latter means that the success of attacking is very easy, and the defensive task is too hard. If, however, the defence prevents some attempts and the absolute offensive power is reduced, but still

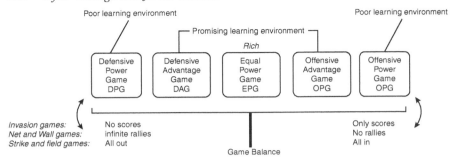

Figure 15.2 Overview of the different gameplay types related to the learning environment.

significant, then gameplay is called *Offensive Advantage Game* (OAG). In this situation, players find it relatively easy to create chances and to score points and, consequently, it is quite hard to prevent this. The counterpart of an offensive advantage game is a *Defensive Advantage Game* (DAG) in which few scores are present, and the defensive task is relatively easy compared to the offensive task. Finally, if both tasks are of similar complexity and the success of scores is in balance with successful prevention of scores, gameplay is called an *Equal Power Game* (EPG).

For net and wall games, a similar approach can be applied but with different outcomes. The most straightforward measure for net and wall games can be expressed through rally length (e.g., the average number of net passages in badminton or volleyball). Rallies provide insight into the ability of players to place the object into the opponent's field (offensive task), and at the same time, their ability to prevent this (defensive task). It expresses the ability of teams to deal with an incoming ball. If the average rally length is short (e.g., only one net passage), the complexity of gameplay is that bringing the ball to the other side of the net is enough to score a point. When a valid serve is not returned successfully by the opposing team, it is concluded that the offensive task is relatively easy (i.e., simply passing the net is enough). The prevention of a ball from falling on the court is quite hard, if not, almost impossible. Of course, the defensive actions are inseparable from offensive plans. The way a player prevents a ball from falling on the ground has direct effect on the way the attack has been set up. Attack and defence are always intertwined in that sense. A long rally length demonstrates that players must force the opponent to make an error, whereas short rallies show that forcing errors is relatively easy. For striking and fielding games, the ratio between players' ability to get safely to a base or being forced out is the most straightforward measure of balance in the game principle.

Designing the game towards a rich learning environment

The gameplay types mentioned in the previous paragraph make it possible to discuss the shape of gameplay that is formed by teaching decisions. The amount of defensive power in a game defines the chances for learning offensive solutions and vice versa. If not all phases of gameplay are regularly completed in both roles (e.g., setting the attack, creating chances, scoring a point), players will hardly be able to experience the full meaning of the game. Gameplay with no scores might, in the long run, be seen as a poor environment to learn unique elements of a game. At the other end of the spectrum lies gameplay where all attempts by players result in a score which can also be seen as a poor learning environment. To enable students to undergo a discovery learning process in a situation where the game takes on meaning in the central purpose of the game, it is preferred that game design leads to gameplay in the zone between offensive advantage and defensive advantage. These gameplay types provide opportunities to explore and develop problem-solving behaviour in a meaningful context for both tasks.

Aim for continuous balance shifts

In a GBA students learn to play games while playing games and find solutions for problems they encounter. One of the interesting features in games teaching is that the solution for the offensive strategy is the next problem for the defensive task. The objective in designing games for a preferred gameplay is eventually not to create a *status quo*, but rather to make the gameplay shift around the wanted outcome (Figure 15.1). If defensive strategies lead to a decrease in scores, the players are challenged to find new offensive strategies. When found, a new defensive problem occurs that can be countered with another defensive strategy. This evolution of the game, that consists of constant shifts around a preferred outcome, is what learning in games is about. Teachers may enhance these shifts by discussing strategies (e.g., through debate of ideas settings), providing playing opportunities, or by creating sufficient time to discover solutions.

From quantitative to qualitative analysis

In this chapter, we have introduced a game-based pedagogy including the application of game balance analysis and game design when observing gameplay. A numeric outcome of the balance between the offensive and defensive roles of two teams does not shed light on the cause of emerged gameplay. The teaching example (see Figure 15.3) shows that it is also important to search for qualitative indicators with respect to observed gameplay. The phases of gameplay can provide teachers with a structure for choosing appropriate interventions. The idea is that after determining the gameplay type, teachers also evaluate what the possible reasons were for this indication. For example, a teacher may conclude that there is a defensive power game due to the inability of players to score a point from many created chances in the last phase of the game. This situation indicates that interventions should be centralised to this last phase of gameplay to restore any

Example of teaching when using a game balance analysis

A teacher prepares a lesson plan for a modified hockey game. Given the abilities of the players, the teacher chooses to make some modifications to enable players to be successful to score, but at the same time not leaving the defence with no chance to prevent scores. Therefore, a rather wide pitch is chosen, and the teacher decides to let players score in two small goals that stand 10 metres apart on the back line of the pitch. Initially, the teacher decides to play a 4v4 match. In practice after several minutes of play, the teacher concludes that no scores have been made despite the modifications. It is concluded that in the first phase of the game the defence can disturb the setup of the attack in such a way that the game is characterised by frequent turnovers and no scores.

This defensive power game is not expected by the teacher. To change the unilateral power for the prevention of scores, the teacher decides to play a 3v3 game with the adding of one extra player who supports the team in ball possession. The result is a 4v3 powerplay when in possession of the ball. The modification immediately results in different gameplay. Players of both teams are better able to setup the attack, create chances and even score some of these chances. From ten ball possessions, both teams on average score two goals. The teacher decides that an intervention to upgrade the number of scores is still appropriate. During the game it became clear that successful chances are often made when the team in possession of the ball can play a ball to a team member that is in the centre of the pitch near the goals. From this position, the player can play a last pass (assist) to one of the goals. To make players aware of this attacking skill, the teacher shortly discusses with players the way successful attempts are created. After summarising the discussion, the teacher starts another round of gameplay and players try to use the plan to increase scores.

The next round of play, players increasingly succeed in using a central player to create chances and score. The balance shifts towards an offensive advantage in the game and the defence is struggling to prevent scores. The teacher then decides to ask about how to prevent the central player near the goals from receiving the ball. Players come up with a plan to support each other in a zone defence and take out the pass through the middle.

Figure 15.3 Example of teaching decisions through a game balance analysis lens.

unwanted imbalance. There is no reason to choose interventions that further enable players to set-up an attack or to create chances when the analysis shows that the last phase of the game is the major cause of the established imbalance.

Game design for exaggeration

An often-applied pedagogical principle in Teaching Games for Understanding (TGfU) is that games are purposefully designed to evoke either offensive advantage or defensive advantage to exaggerate tactical problems for a specific role (Thorpe & Bunker, 1989). For example, when a badminton court is made longer, it exaggerates the possibility of offensive advantage and challenges the defensive skill of preventing the shuttle drop on the court. If a teacher decides, however, to shorten the court it becomes easier to defend the court half. For the attacking role, players are challenged to find solutions to score (e.g., using a smash). Even within this exaggeration, gameplay with endless rally length (i.e., defensive power game) loses its meaning for this discovery learning process. In addition, rallies that instantly end after serving also offer less meaningful discovery. It can be questioned whether this type of exaggeration then falls outside of the players 'zone of proximal development' (Vygotsky, 1978). Exaggerated tactical problems or samples of tactical problems that are highlighted by a teacher through specific designs are still important aspects of teaching. For example, if a teacher wants to make players aware of how to make use of a switch of ball position from left to right to open the defensive lines in a soccer game, the width of the field may be enlarged to provide players with more space to split up the defensive players. These game design decisions are elementary within a GBA. Still, if the central purpose of the game constantly lies outside the gameplay zone of defensive advantage to offensive advantage, the exaggeration of this tactical problem will tend to be a meaningless trick instead of a meaningful skill to solve the essence of the game.

Game balance for scholars

Gameplay types may also be used to clarify research findings in studies investigating games teaching. If researchers were to inform on the shape of gameplay that occurred in terms of balance, this would provide insights in how possible effects have emerged. For example, studies on youth volleyball performance may report the shape of gameplay by reporting the outcome of average net passages per serve. If research was, for example, to reveal that most of the games had short rallies, the reader will have a more profound understanding of what the effects of the experimental conditions were on a fundamental level, before learning about the effects on other outcomes such as successful bump set spike sequences. For invasion games, researchers may report that modification of the number of players led to a high-score game (OAG). Then the reader more profoundly understands how other measures like 'covering space' and or 'time in ball possession' can be interpreted. A fundamental scholarly application of gameplay types is when the independent variable in an experimental set up is not the fixed game form, but the shape of gameplay due to adaptive modifications. The shape of gameplay can be kept constant within a bandwidth of gameplay types and thus serve as a variable within or between groups.

In summary, this chapter was designed to picture the threefold contribution of game balance analysis and accompanied gameplay types to GBAs. This game-based pedagogy serves as a model for analysis in Physical Education Teacher Education programs. It also has much to offer for research and scholarly discussions. Most of all, teachers in particular may benefit from this pedagogy as they are enabled to create meaningful learning opportunities for children by design of rich learning environments.

References

Barba-Martín, R. A., Bores-García, D., Hortigüela-Alcalá, D. & González-Calvo, G. (2020). The application of the teaching games for understanding in physical education. Systematic review of the last six years. *International Journal of Environmental Research and Public Health*, *17*(9), 3330.

Davids, K., Button, C. & Bennett, S. (2008). *Dynamics of skill acquisition: A constraints-led approach.* Human Kinetics.

Frencken, W., Poel, H. D., Visscher, C. & Lemmink, K. (2012). Variability of inter-team distances associated with match events in elite-standard soccer. *Journal of Sports Sciences*, *30*(12), 1207–1213.

Harvey, S. & Jarrett, K. (2014). A review of the game-centred approaches to teaching and coaching literature since 2006. *Physical Education and Sport Pedagogy*, *19*(3), 278–300.

Harvey, S., Cushion, C. J., Wegis, H. M. & Massa-Gonzalez, A. N. (2010). Teaching games for understanding in American high-school soccer: A quantitative data analysis using the game performance assessment instrument. *Physical Education and Sport Pedagogy*, *15*(1), 29–54.

Kirk, D. & MacPhail, A. (2002). Teaching games for understanding and situated learning: Rethinking the Bunker-Thorpe model. *Journal of Teaching in Physical Education*, *21*(2), 177–192.

Koekoek, J., Dokman, I. & Walinga, W. (2023). *Game-based pedagogy in physical education and sports. Designing rich learning environments.* Routledge.

Memmert, D., Almond, L., Bunker, D., Butler, J., Fasold, F., Griffin, L., Hillmann, W., Huttermann, S., Klein-Soetebier, T., Konig, S., Nopp, S., Rathschlag, M., Schul, K., Schwab, S., Thorpe, R. & Furley, P. (2015). Top 10 research questions related to teaching games for understanding. *Research Quarterly for Exercise and Sport*, *86*, 347–359.

Olthof, S. B., Frencken, W. G. & Lemmink, K. A. (2019). A match-derived relative pitch area facilitates the tactical representativeness of small-sided games for the official soccer match. *Journal of Strength and Conditioning Research*, *33*(2), 1557–1563.

Oslin, J. L., Mitchell, S. A. & Griffin, L. L. (1998). The game performance assessment instrument (GPAI): Development and preliminary validation. *Journal of Teaching in Physical Education*, *17*(2), 231–243.

Sarmento, H., Clemente, F. M., Harper, L. D., Costa, I. T. D., Owen, A. & Figueiredo, A. J. (2018). Small sided games in soccer—a systematic review. *International Journal of Performance Analysis in Sport*, *18*(5), 693–749.

Stolz, S. & Pill, S. (2014). Teaching games and sport for understanding: Exploring and reconsidering its relevance in physical education. *European Physical Education Review*, *20*(1), 36–71.

Thorpe, R. & Bunker, D. (1989). A changing focus in games teaching. In L. Almond (Ed.), *The place of physical education in schools* (pp. 52–79). Kogan/Page.

Vygotsky, L. S. (1978). *Mind in society.* Harvard University Press.

Section III

Future Directions

16 Promoting Justice, Equity, Diversity and Inclusion (JEDI) through Game-Based Approach (GBA) in Physical Education

Kanae Haneishi, Teng Tse Sheng, Bruce Nkala and Korey Boyd

We have all witnessed numerous incidences related to inequity and discrimination as well as racial and social injustices in our society, such as the Black Lives Matter movement, and violence against Asian people during the COVID-19 pandemic. The recent Russian invasion in Ukraine has shown the world an ultimate scene of social injustice. In the school setting, students in Generation Z (born in 1997–2012) and Alpha (born in 2010–2025) face a wide variety of challenges. Cyberbullying, school shootings, mental health, and an increase in suicide attempts/deaths are just some of those challenges (Mitchell & Walton-Fisette, 2022). These are challenging times in the world, and now more than ever young adults and adolescents need quality education. The physical education (PE) curriculum in many countries remains a legacy of schooling as an instrument of colonisation. Decolonisation is necessary for a more just and inclusive, perhaps even restorative, games curriculum (Race et al., 2022). Therefore, we suggest a need to renew and transform games teaching and learning.

Injustice practices and oppression toward persons of minoritised backgrounds (i.e., race, gender, language, age, religion, socioeconomic status, ethnicity, nationality, ability, and sexual orientation) have challenged physical educators to expand the PE learning environment and promote equitable and just practices. "PE offers the opportunity to navigate challenging tasks through face-to-face negotiations and discussions and in a context where it becomes difficult to smooth over or ignore such problems as inequity, unfairness and injustice" (Butler, 2016, p. 13). PE teachers can create learning environments where JEDI outcomes are embedded in the learning experience. PE offers students opportunities to observe, experience, and discuss inequity around difference and power. Rather than talking about JEDI matters in the abstract, students can explore and learn the importance of JEDI first-hand as they practice these democratic principles and skills required to develop an ethic of care (Butler, 2016). PE teachers, thus, play an important role in the social justice movement as they address human dynamics and complexity in our society through movement during their lessons. Although the contents of

DOI: 10.4324/9781003298298-20

social justice differ in international contexts, striving for quality PE (McLennan & Thompson, 2015) and offering just practice in PE settings appears to be an urgent matter in many countries, such as Australia (Williams & Pill, 2019), the United Kingdom (Evans & Davies, 2015), and the United States (Block et al., 2021).

In this chapter, we discuss how PE teachers can promote JEDI through a GBA in lessons. Butler (2016) indicated the lack of intentional focus on affective learning in PE lessons even though many PE teachers agreed that PE is a perfect platform for 21st century learning (Mitchell & Walton-Fisette, 2022), including educating on JEDI. This chapter is an urgent call for PE professionals for implementing intentional teaching to teach the affective domain of learning and address JEDI as social injustice and issues on democracy have become more apparent in recent years (Light & Harvey, 2017).

Addressing democracy and social justice during Game-Based Approach

A GBA offers a venue for physical educators to foster JEDI where all students are respected and feel a sense of belonging. By nature, games reflect our society. Since games (i.e., invasion, net/wall, fielding, and target games) are social, we have found dynamic, public, and social issues (i.e., discrimination and inequity) often emerge during game play and among students' interaction. Using the key pedagogical features of a GBA (i.e., modified game, problem solving, student-centred, and critical dialogue) offers a practical tool for PE teachers to address social issues and foster JEDI in their game teaching. Use of a GBA values "the ability to work cooperatively and make smart, democratic decisions as much as it does the performance of physical skills" (Butler, 2016, p. 55). A GBA facilitates interaction and brings out the social aspects of games by offering the potential for increasing students' emotional, cognitive, and social engagement as they discuss, and problem solve when playing the game (Mitchell et al., 2021). Students taught using GBA are provided the opportunities to create a space where they discuss, problem solve (i.e., adjusting rules for inclusion and equity), and collaborate with each other. Through GBA, teachers deliberately facilitate a safe learning space where all students genuinely belong, are valued, and relied upon, empowered and ultimately matter (Block et al., 2021). When planned and delivered carefully and intentionally by teachers, we suggest that the GBA learning space can promote JEDI, where differences such as race, age, gender, sexual orientation, (dis)ability, religion, ethnicity, and socioeconomic status are addressed and the game learning space becomes inclusive, equitable, and just for all students. Games, when well-designed, provide students with many opportunities to learn new skills and concepts. Players will also be confronted with situations salient to JEDI, where they will have opportunities to experiment with and discuss the situations with their peers (Butler, 2016). In this section, we introduce the idea of Democracy in Action through Inventing Games and the Social Justice Education framework and how it ties with a GBA.

Butler (2016) previously advocated Democracy in Action through Inventing Games (IG), a GBA approach to teaching PE. IG is introduced as a variation of GBA, and it is an innovative pedagogy to address bullying, teach democracy, and promote social justice. In the IG pedagogy, students are the ones who develop their own modified games in certain sports based on a set of frameworks and parameters specified by the teacher; for example, an invasion game or net/wall game. Teachers ask questions and facilitate critical dialogue among students so games being developed and played are fair, safe, inclusive, challenging, and fun. The IG model (Butler, 2016) provides teachers with a structure, guided by IG principles, to seize the opportunities in the learning process to teach students not just to play the game, but also important values and life skills. In the IG model, the process is equally, if not more, important than the product. When students invent games, debates and disagreements happen. Issues on power and inclusivity become more apparent and pressing. Through inventing games, students are provided "opportunities to examine, discuss, and reflect on content; grapple with ethical responsibility; analyse critically; and enact the democratic ideals of equality, freedom, and justice" (Butler, 2016, p. 19). As students confront these issues, they discover more about themselves and their teammates, guided by questioning, discussions, and reflections completed as individuals and in groups. Although more research is needed, a Master Teacher from Singapore, who has provided professional development for PE teachers on the implementation of the IG model, indicated that results so far looked "promising" (T. Sheng, personal communication, February, 2022).

Hackman's five essential components of social justice education

Heather Hackman's five essential components of social justice education (Hackman, 2005), one of several social justice frameworks, uses a social justice camera to introduce five lenses: (1) content mastery, (2) tools for critical analysis, (3) tools for social change, (4) tools for personal reflection, and (5) multicultural group dynamics. We now explore how each lens can be related to the pedagogical strategy in GBA lessons.

Lens 1: Content mastery

If we want students to critically think about game content, they first must understand the game from multiple perspectives, not just memorising rules and skills. Why do students make certain decisions at certain moments of the game? Are there several possibilities of decisions at the moment? When Bunker and Thorpe first introduced the original version of GBA, Teaching Games for Understanding (TGfU) in 1982 (Bunker & Thorpe, 1982), the model included the game appreciation where students gain a deep understanding of game content, which can be further extended to social justice as a content.

Lens 2: Tools for critical analysis

Hackman (2005) contends that whenever students receive information, they should be encouraged to critically analyse the information and be challenged to think beyond their own interpretation or perspective and consider how others may perceive the same information. For example, what are power differences and group dynamics in the decision-making process? Access to this information could be influenced by power differences and group dynamics, which may have implications on the decision-making process. Through modifying games and asking questions in GBA lessons, teachers can facilitate students in critical dialogue and analysis and propose possible solutions, such as how to address equality and equity in game playing (Figure 16.1). Students can be encouraged to modify games using exaggeration, representation, and adaptation pedagogical principles (Bunker & Thorpe, 1982).

Lens 3: Tools for social change

To explore the Hackman (2005) social justice framework's third lens (i.e., tools for social change), a GBA provides learning environments where students can apply tools for social change through game situations. GBA is a student-centred instructional model and uses an approach of empowerment where students take ownership of their learning and are encouraged to

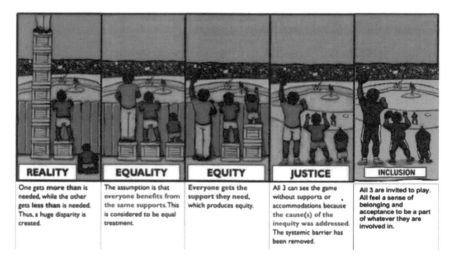

Figure 16.1 Reality, equality, equity, justice, versus inclusion (see Kanae Haneishi et al., 2021).

transfer their learning into their daily lives. For example, a GBA (i.e., Game Sense) was reported to be an effective opportunity for the PE teacher and the students to explore Indigenous perspectives in PE and highlight issues of social justice while learning a traditional Australian Aboriginal game (Williams & Pill, 2019).

Lens 4: Tools for personal reflection

The fourth tool of social justice framework (Hackman, 2005) is personal reflection by teachers and students. The issue of power and dominant group privilege needs to be critically reflected on because oftentimes members of the dominant groups are unaware of their inherent privilege and are taught their life and privilege are the norm/standard (Hackman, 2005). Self-reflection by students (and teachers) has the potential to reinforce lessons within a GBA. For example, teachers can ask more skilled players what access they might have outside of class in comparison to others. How can they use their higher skills to help others in game play? Teachers can dig deeper into social issues by asking critical social questions, such as do boys have more access to physical activity and sport than girls? How does the sociocultural background influence physical activity and sport participation for children?

Lens 5: Multicultural group dynamics

The fifth tool of the social justice framework, teachers need to be aware of multicultural group dynamics. For example, dynamics of game play and student interaction during GBA lessons can be different when the game is being played with students from dominant backgrounds or if it is being played from marginalised backgrounds. Because a GBA provides opportunities for students to work with others in group settings when addressing game problems and inquiries, teachers can intentionally raise awareness of the dynamics of the class. Teachers can address power and/or multicultural dynamics in the class by asking a question like, "in what ways can your popularity and/or cultural background be used to shift the climate of the game play from exclusive to inclusive?" Table 16.1 provides an overview of how GBA lessons can fit with Hackman's (2005) social justice framework.

What does the GBA and JEDI lesson look like? – practical implication

Although PE teachers agree to include more of the affective domain of learning and address JEDI, there are yet limited practical resources for PE teachers to apply JEDI into their lessons (Lynch et al., 2022). In this section, we explain the practical implication of GBA into a PE lesson for promoting the JEDI perspectives. While JEDI can be addressed in all game categories (i.e., invasion, target, fielding, and net/wall games), we use an invasion game

Table 16.1 Overview of social justice framework and GBA/JEDI pedagogy

Five Essential Components of Social Justice (Hackman, 2005)	GBA and JEDI Pedagogical Strategies and Considerations
1 Content mastery	Intentionality and design considerations (i.e., exaggeration and representation to highlight the issue, create aporia that mimic the issues in society). Game appreciation.
2 Tools for critical analysis	Asking critical questions; how others might perceive the same information differently. Game modification pedagogical principles (i.e., exaggeration, representation, and adaptation).
3 Tools for social change	Problem solving towards just practice and fair game play. Relevance by relating the lesson to outside the class.
4 Tools for personal reflection	Critical reflection/dialogue through problem solving and group discussion.
5 Multicultural group dynamics	Democratic engagement in lessons through and exchange of ideas and opinions. Intentionally created opportunities for self and group reflection on various dynamics.

(i.e., soccer) because it is universal, and more students' interactions can be observed. Several GBA models include a skill practice portion of the lesson (Bunker & Thorpe, 1982; Mitchell et al., 2021); however, we stay focused on the game playing parts of the lesson to show how PE teachers can address different aspects of JEDI during the GBA lesson.

The example lesson plan (Tables 16.2 and 16.3) targets secondary PE and teaching soccer/football. The tactical focus is to maintain possession by providing effective off-the-ball support. The games below are in a progression but can be independent activities. We have adopted a less complex game-practice-game sequence of the Tactical Games Approach for our lesson examples to provide greater clarity on how we layer on and facilitate the learning of JEDI while students learn to play games. Since the modified games often include some GBA pedagogical principles (i.e., exaggeration, representation, sampling, and tactical complexity), it is important to ensure that the lesson ends with an opportunity for students to apply learned objectives in the game (e.g., a 3v3 game without the modified rules).

Throughout the lesson, teachers should remember that the intent is to help improve all students at their own pace, and modify the rules based on their improvements. It is also important to have students understand that the modification of games is designed to enhance learning of a particular tactic, skill, and life lesson (i.e., JEDI).

Table 16.2 Game 1: Keep away games in soccer (JEDI focus: Inclusion)

	Objective: / **Tactical Focus**	**Teacher's Intention**
Game 1: Keep away game Keep the ball away from the other team by passing the ball around. • Every 5 passes in a row, 1 point is rewarded. • Allow maximum of 3 touches. • Cold defense: no body contact (e.g., an arm-length away). • Possession change occurs: (1) intercept and (2) ball out of the bounce. • Include a 2-min time-out at the 5 min mark to allow teams to discuss their strategy.	**Objective:** Possession of the ball. **JEDI Goals:** Inclusion. **Tactical Focus:** Providing effective off-the-ball support.	**Teacher's Intention** ***GBA pedagogical strategy (GBAPS):* 1 Limiting touches emphasises "passing." 2 Make the space larger if students are having trouble possessing the ball. Or reduce the number of defenders. ++*JEDI strategy (JEDIS): Everyone is playing under the same rules first regardless of their skill levels.*
Question and discussion on Game 1: Question (Q): "What do we need to do in order to maintain better possession and play this game successfully?" **Expected Answer (EA):** "Moving to open space (i.e., offensive support)." "Talking to each other (i.e., communication)." "Controlling the ball and passing the ball with accuracy (i.e., skill execution)." "For everyone to enjoy the game and be successful as a team, it is important to include everyone on the team." Q: "What are additional rules that we could add while still focusing on maintaining possession?" EA: "You cannot pass back to the same teammate." If EA does not come up, the teacher may break down the questions, such as "Was everyone actively involved in the game?" If yes, "why is that important?" If no, "why not?" "What can we do to be more inclusive?"	Questions on tactical focus. Question on JEDI (Inclusion).	**Teacher's Intention** ***GBAPS: To address tactical focuses stated above.* ++*JEDIS:* *Good game players need to learn to become good problem solvers* (Mitchell et al., 2021).
Game 1 with additional rule Play the same game with the additional rule (i.e., no passing back to the same teammate).		**Teacher's Intention** ***GBAPS: The additional rule helps students to look up and find other passing options. Tactically, this rule teaches students to support and provide cover for the ball carrier. Additionally, this rule promotes the inclusion of everyone.*

(Continued)

Table 16.2 (Continued)

Critical reflection on inclusion **Q:** "With the additional rule, was everyone more involved in the game?" **EA:** "Yes, but the game is breaking down as we are passing the ball to our teammates who are not as skilful." **Teacher:** "I am glad to hear that everyone is more involved. Learning takes time and we all have to be patient. Your friends are making mistakes and that is part and parcel of learning. I want you to think about how you can support their learning, and what other rules we can include to make the game more playable for them."		*Important to acknowledge that in a real game, there is a need to pass back to the same teammate who passed to you, but stress to students that the modification aims to meet the above objectives which are key components of the game.* **Teacher's Intention** **GBAPS: Note that we have omitted the skills practice component in this plan as mentioned above.*
Final questioning and critical reflection **Q:** "What are some of the important things to maintain the possession as a team?" **EA:** Providing effective off-the-ball support. **Possible follow up Q:** Did you include and listen to all teammates in the discussion? What is consensus building? Why is the concept of inclusion important in our society? Who took the most power in making these decisions? Who benefited? Who did not?	Formative assessment on tactical focuses Formative assessment on inclusion. **This follow up process could be journal reflection.	**Teacher's Intention** ** GBAPS: Teach students that they need to provide support for the ball carrier by moving into space. Students also need to learn how to communicate.* *++JEDIS: Ask students' experiences during timeout. The final question is important as students see the relevance of JEDI and their importance in their everyday lives. Facilitate this at the start of the next lesson.*

** Game-Based Approach pedagogical strategy (GBAPS).
++ JEDI strategy (JEDIS).

Table 16.3 Game 2: Keep away games in soccer (JEDI focus: Equity vs. Equality + Social Justice)

Game 2: A keep away game Start with the same game as Game 1.	Objective and tactical focuses are the same as above. **JEDI Goals:** Equity vs. equality.	**Teacher's Intention (s)** **GBAPS:*Playing a familiar game allows students to get into the game quickly. Remind students of the tactical focuses from previous game about maintaining possession.*
Questioning & Group discussion on Game 2 **Q:** "How can we have an additional rule to provide individual support they need, and ALL players can play this game more effectively?" "Discuss as a group or as a team" **EA:** "Self-identified lower skilled players can take more than 3 touches." (Each team can decide 1–2 players who can touch unlimited touches.) If needed, ask students to reflect on the following question: What do I need to be successful? Providing options such as: More time during touches (negotiated amount) More touches (negotiated number) **EA:** "Creating a safe space where players can enter and have unlimited touches with no defender entering"	Question on equality vs. equity.	**Teacher's Intention (s)** **GBAPS:*Making the game playable to all is an important design principle. Not all students may agree and that creates a debate and an entry point for teachers to address the JEDI principles of equity and equality.* ++*JEDIS: Look for democracy in the selection process of the individuals who have greater touches – or what makes it work for an individual as some need time and some need touches.*
Potential Social Justice Discussion and Reflection If EA such as "girls can take more than 3 touches and boys stay with max of 3 touches" comes up, a teacher can include the discussion around social justice (i.e., gender bias) and lead to critical reflection. **Possible follow-up Q:** "Are all girls less skilled than boys?" "In our society, do boys tend to have more access to the opportunities to	Addressing JEDI: Social justice component around gender and unconscious bias.	**Teacher's Intention(s)** ++*JEDIS: Possible facilitation options: (1) take the discussion into depth and push back the following activities (i.e., playing games) or (2) have discussion to raise "awareness" of the social injustice around this issue and then*

(Continued)

Table 16.3 (Continued)

play sports and be involved in physical activities than girls? And why?"		return to game play followed by journal reflection or research project around this social issue to address the social justice matter in depth.
Game with additional rule (i.e., unlimited touch for certain players or safe space) Playing the same rule with adding a new rule for "equity." "Lower skilled players can take more than 3 touches" (Each team can decide 1–2 players who can touch unlimited touches). ***If the team decides they need more/less than 2 players for the adjustment, that is fine.*	Important to continue addressing the lesson objectives (i.e., maintain possession) with the tactical focus.	**Teacher's Intention(s)** ***GBAPS: The game may still break down even with the additional rule. Be ready to go through a few iterations with students to discuss the need to add more rules/modifications (i.e., increasing playing area, overloading).*
Final questioning and critical reflection Revisit the discussion and EA's from previous lesson about maintaining possession.		**Teacher's Intention(s)** *++JEDIS: Important to clearly define differences between equity and equality in game situations.*
Possible follow up Q: "Is it fair when everyone plays with the same rule? Is it fair when some players are given more touches?" and why? **Potential EA:** "It is not fair if everyone does not play under the same rules." "Same rules allow everyone to play and be judged the same way." "Allowing different touches allows for people who need extra to be successfully included."		*Explain that modifications are not the real game rules but promote segments of the game.*

** Game-Based Approach pedagogical strategy (GBAPS).

++ JEDI strategy (JEDIS).

Conclusion

Teachers need to see PE beyond just addressing the psychomotor and cognitive domains, prepare students to be able to cope with the challenges and trauma they may face in society, and to be able to work collaboratively and respectfully with others. By integrating JEDI into the learning focus when using a GBA, PE teachers can provide students with a more holistic learning experience which helps students to become not just a physically literate person, but also individuals who can contribute to the betterment of our society. While time may be required to design and layer on the JEDI learnings and address them during lessons (which may lead to a reduction in game/practice time), 21st century PE must have a more intentional holistic view. Grappling with and learning about JEDI concepts through games cannot, and should not, be left to chance.

References

Block, B., Haneishi, K., Zarco, E. & Megías, E. P. (2021). Thirdspace movement concepts in physical education teacher education. *Quest*, *73*(4), 323–341.

Bunker, D. & Thorpe, R. (1982). A model for the teaching of games in secondary schools. *Bulletin of Physical Education*, *18*(1), 5–8.

Butler, J. (2016). *Playing Fair: Using student-invented games to prevent bullying, teach democracy, and promote social justice*. Human Kinetics.

Center for Story Based Strategy. (n.d.). *#the4thBox*. https://www.storybasedstrategy.org/the4thbox

Evans, J. & Davies, B. (2015). Neoliberal freedoms, privatisation and the future of physical education. *Sport, Education and Society*, *20*(1), 10–26.

Hackman, H. W. (2005). Five essential components for social justice education. *Equity & Excellence in Education*, *38*(2), 103–109.

Light, R. L. & Harvey, S. (2017). Positive pedagogy for sport coaching. *Sport, Education and Society*, *22*(2), 271–287.

Lynch, S., Walton-Fisette, J. L. & Luguetti, C. (2022). *Pedagogies of social justice in physical education and youth sport*. Routledge.

McLennan, N. & Thompson, J. (2015). *Quality physical education (QPE): Guidelines for policy makers*. UNESCO Publishing.

Mitchell, S. A. & Walton-Fisette, J. L. (2022). *The essentials of teaching physical education: Curriculum, instruction, and assessment*. Human Kinetics.

Mitchell, S. A., Oslin, J. & Griffin, L. L. (2021). *Teaching sport concepts and skills: A tactical games approach* (4th ed.). Human Kinetics.

Race, R., Gill, D., Kaitell, E., Mahmud, A., Thorpe, A. & Wolfe, K. (2022). Proclamations and provocations: Decolonising curriculum in education research and professional practice. *Equity in Education & Society*, *1*(1), 82–96.

Williams, J. & Pill, S. (2019). Using a game sense approach to teach Buroinjin as an Aboriginal game to address social justice in physical education. *Journal of Teaching in Physical Education*, *39*(2), 176–185.

17 Decolonialising PE Using a GBA

Michael J. Davies, Shane Pill and John R. Evans

If colonised education systems intend to 'close the gap' (a political campaign in Australia aimed to achieve equality for Aboriginal and Torres Strait Islander peoples; Gardiner-Garden, 2012), it requires the 'coming together' of Aboriginal and Western knowledge systems. Intersections of pedagogy and epistemologies call out for physical education (PE) educators to move away from Eurocentric PE that fails to acknowledge Indigenous perspectives (Williams, 2018) and bridge this knowledge gap (Bishop et al., 2021). However, this can only be achieved through purposeful design finding synergy in ways of learning for engagement in reconciliation, respect, and recognition of continuous living Aboriginal cultures across Australia (Australian Curriculum and Assessment Authority [ACARA], 2020a).

In this chapter, we further a proposed opportunity to move PE from its colonised limitations using a cultural interface for PE (Pill et al., 2021). Nakata (2002) described a cultural interface as the intersection of the Western and Aboriginal domains of teaching, learning processes, and epistemologies. The specific cultural interface we put forward, for games and sport, is the synergy between using a Game Sense Approach (GSA) (Australian Sports Commission [ASC], 1996) and Yunkaporta's (2009) 8 Ways (Figure 17.1), in how they may act as a 'coming together' between Aboriginal and non-Aboriginal knowledge systems, with the potential for creating 'common ground' to decolonising games and sport teaching in PE (Burgess & Evans, 2017). Represented by the 'apex' of Yunkaporta's (2009) Boomerang Matrix of Cultural Interface Knowledge (Figure 17.2), our cultural interface to 'close the gap' between Western and Aboriginal knowledge is by a 'non versus' view to find the synergy between the 8 Ways and the GSA (Burgess & Evans, 2017; Pill et al., 2021).

We adopt use of the term 'Aboriginal', to mean Aboriginal and Torres Strait Islander people, cultures, and perspectives, instead of 'Indigenous' because we reside, teach, and research on the lands of Aboriginal Australians (Burgess & Evans, 2017). Authors 1 and 2 are non-Aboriginal researchers. Their positions are not intended to represent the views or perspectives of First Nations Peoples. Instead, their intention is to critically consider decolonisation of PE curricula and the opportunity to advocate how

DOI: 10.4324/9781003298298-21

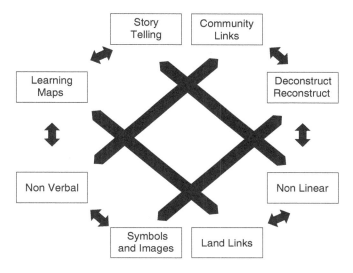

Figure 17.1 Yunkaporta's (2009) 8 Ways pedagogy framework.

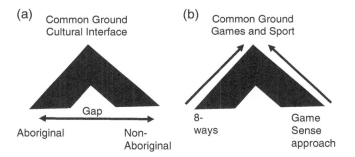

Figure 17.2 (a) Yunkaporta's (2009) boomerang matrix of cultural interface knowledge. (b) Our proposal to 'close the gap' between Aboriginal and Western knowledge systems in PE.

Aboriginal ways of knowing, being, and doing are delivered in PE. In doing so, they aim to offer scope for purposeful design of teaching in ways that challenge hegemonic conventions of PE (Evans et al., 2020). Author 3 is an Aboriginal academic who has a background in sport pedagogy and PE. His focus on sport pedagogy and PE and nascent work (Burgess & Evans, 2017; Evans et al., 2017), enabled our proposal and interpretation of a cultural interface for sport teaching in PE (Pill et al., 2021).

Evans et al. (2017) proposed teaching Aboriginal games alongside the sports that commonly comprise the PE curriculum, might help create a greater sense of community with and for Aboriginal people. They posited Yunkaporta's (2009) 8 Ways pedagogy as epistemological consistent with the 'Western' constructivist orientation of the Australian curriculum, where inquiry and problem-solving are positioned as a Key Idea informing educatively purposeful Health and PE curriculum decision-making (ACARA, 2020b) and teacher pedagogy, like the GSA (ASC, 1996; Evans et al., 2017). Thus, offering the potential for a 'dynamic space between ancestral and western realities' (Yunkaporta & McGinty, 2009, p. 58). We also acknowledge the extensive work of Edwards (1999, 2017) and the ASC collaborating with Edwards (2009) that produced a collection of Aboriginal games in the Yulunga resource (Edwards, 2008; Sport Australia, 2022) translated from Kamilaroi language to mean 'playing' (Sport Australia, 2022).

A cultural interface for games and sport teaching in physical education: An Australian context

The pedagogies put forward are a starting point for culturally safe entry into dialogue that engages with Aboriginal and non-Aboriginal knowledges (Yunkaporta's [2009] 8 Ways). However, we are conscious it is one of many perspectives or central ethics towards understanding Aboriginal knowledge systems in Australia. It is 'a way' but not 'the way' to embedding Aboriginal pedagogy into the curriculum (Pill et al., 2021). The approach interfacing the 8 Ways with the GSA is therefore offered as an example of a cultural interface, with the pedagogies, and the intersection explained in the following sections.

Story sharing

A GSA invites students into a narrative with a game through inquiry-based learning, while Yunkaporta's (2009) 8 Ways demonstrates why narrative is critical to Aboriginal epistemology. Stories connect us. In the context of PE, a pivotal reason people play games and sport is because of their narrative, their continuation of culture, and where individuals feel they belong to its story (Pill & Hyndman, 2018). The sport of Australian Football (AFL) is one such example. A colonised sport rich in Australian culture, said to offer modern ways for continuing culture in sport for Aboriginal people in the absence of traditional avenues (Williams et al., 2022). Although widely disputed (Hay, 2017; Whimpress, 2008), it has been asserted, Marn-Grook, a Western Victorian Djab-wurung game meaning 'ball-foot' using a possum hair ball, influenced the development into what is now the national game of AFL (Sutton, 2017). We need to teach the story to develop game sense in its broadest meaning. We are connected when we know story, just as we are connected to the game by our story of experience with the game as a player. Consistent with a GSA, in this kind of dialogue, the teacher acts as a facilitator of student knowledge, demonstration, and creation (Pill & Hyndman, 2018).

Central to the GSA is reflection and purposeful social interaction through play, and the process of inquiry to make learning visible. Meanwhile story as pedagogy is fundamental to Aboriginal processes of learning (Yunkaporta & McGinty, 2009). The importance of storytelling is also emphasised in the Ngunnawal draft guidelines where 'all students are told about the Indigenous background to activities or games prior to playing them, in order to understand their correct cultural context/nuance' (Ngunnawal Draft, n.d., p. 1). Understanding correct cultural context/nuance means when using a GSA in synergy with Aboriginal pedagogy, it is not about embedding 'ways' within a Western curriculum, or pedagogical approach. It is about broadening and deepening the existing curriculum to embrace ways of Aboriginal knowing, being, and doing (Arrows & Narvaez, 2016; Pill et al., 2021). This may be achieved through inquiry strategies, such as 'yarning modalities, narrative as pedagogy, narrative as process, narrative as ethics or values, storied experience, cultural meaning-making' (8ways, 2020). For example, these stories might include a local Kabi Kabi person from south Queensland, the lands in which Buroinjin was traditionally played. This might be achieved by speaking about Country within a Buroinjin unit of work or teacher/student-led yarning circles facilitating discussion around shared experiences of connection to the game, and to local lands through the game (Sport Australia, 2022).

Learning maps

Here, pathways of knowledge are valued through a communal approach to knowledge, ownership, and production (Yunkaporta & McGinty, 2009). We believe this kind of enaction extends Light and Harvey's (2017) work on the GSA as a positive pedagogy by its central focus on reflection and purposeful social interaction through play (Pill et al., 2021).

Games and sport have an inherent 'logic' created by their rules (Pill & Hyndman, 2018). However, similar games can also be seen to have a complimentary logic enabling them to be grouped into game categories. These categories are Invasion, Net/Court, Striking-Fielding, and Target, each acting as a Learning Map inherent in game-based teaching models through shared principles of play (Metzler, 2011). We draw on Yunkaporta (2009) to describe this element of learning as making game understanding explicit through symbolic representation. Synergy at the cultural interface for game-based approaches occurs when principles of play (e.g., game concepts and associated strategies and tactics) are seen as pathways of knowledge to be mapped from the game (ASC, 1996). Thus, contextualising learning, where students make sense of the performance narrative which may 'become the focus and starting point of practical sessions' (ASC, 1996, p. 1). However, it is necessary the interface be more than interpreting the tactical learning focus stemming from use of a GSA using the element of Learning Maps. To illustrate this point, consider how using the cultural interface might be used to assess students journey over a unit of work. Here, we will use the game called Keentan (Sport Australia, 2022), meaning 'play' in the Wik-Mungkan language from northern Queensland, as an example. Students could be tasked to design their own Learning Map from their experience in Keentan with the intention to share back to the class, where the PE teacher outlines the Learning Map must include illustrations such as:

- *Non-verbal.* How did students 'picture the game' of Keentan to make their learning visible?
- *Symbols and images.* What symbols and/or images have been learnt to understand Keentan?
- *Non-linear ways of playing Keentan.* What modifications to the rules of Keentan were implemented to enhance success, how were they implemented and why?
- *Community links.* How will students transfer their learning to effect students' future and their 'mob' (their community)?

Land links

Place-based learning links content to local land and nature, with local land referred to by Aboriginal Australians as 'Country'. Country is more than people and place, 'all entities that make up Country are alive with spirit; they are all sentient. Each local Indigenous group in Australia was, and is, responsible for their Country' (Karulkiyalu Country et al., 2021, p. 215). Country must therefore be at the heart of the cultural interface in game-based sport teaching in PE if we are to enable Aboriginal and non-Aboriginal knowledge systems to co-exist authentically in PE (Pill et al., 2021). In an Australian context, Yulunga (Sport Australia, 2022) offers an entry point to such an approach where background information about connection to land for traditional games is available for teachers. Information in Yulunga is advanced through the purposeful design of Land Links (Yunkaporta, 2009), which offers an ecological concept non-evident in the current format of the GSA that currently connects students to the game environment (e.g., the playing area). Instead, we advocate learning occurs with connection with Country, to enhance coming to know and care for the places we live and inhabit (Karulkiyalu Country et al., 2021).

By positioning the GSA as place-based we connect with Kirk and MacPhail (2002), who suggested 'a situated perspective assumes that learning involves the active engagement of individuals with their environment' (p. 183). These linkages could be made through both teachers and students researching and documenting stories about the Country, its people and where a traditional Aboriginal game was historically played, if known (Pill et al., 2021). Further, place-based significance and developing students' ongoing relationship with Country, stories for Country, and care for Country, through learning in Country can further advance the GSA as teaching games for understanding. An example could be the PE teacher, students, and local Aboriginal people working together to create a 'story' of song and dance about their shared experience of playing a traditional game in, with, and through the local Country (Pill et al., 2021). Establishing respectful relationships with Aboriginal people, Country, and self goes beyond the game, enabling broader socio-ecological well-being, with potential cross-community benefits (Arrows & Narvaez, 2016).

Non-verbal

Learning in a GSA is 'hands-on', involves critical reflection, and minimal teacher intrusive strategies. It involves applying intra-personal (i.e., internal thinking dialogue) with kinaesthetic skills (i.e., moving to learn) (8ways, 2020). In a GSA, learning the game is the starting point and focus. Critical reflection through the GSA may be fostered through player inquiry facilitated by well-considered teacher questioning in preference to more intrusive 'telling', creating 'hands-on with minds-on' learning contexts with the aim of developing 'thinking players' (ASC, 1996). Here, our cultural interface encourages PE teachers to facilitate student reflection to 'see' and understand shapes and patterns in play and resist the hegemonic conformity to PE as largely practice style pedagogy for the reproduction of teacher demonstrations (Evans et al., 2020). A GSA is a reciprocal process between the teacher constructing the movement challenge(s) and the students individually and collaboratively solving them. This way of learning is intertwined with several 8 Ways elements inviting students to express learning non-verbally through visual story, mapping, reflection, and a guided questioning process helping to uncover hidden meaning, value, and impact (Low et al., 2020). For example, in Meetcha Boma, played by the Noongar people in the south of Western Australia (Sport Australia, 2022), students could be tasked with using available resources and their imagination to bring individual or team tactics and strategies to life through visual story, symbols, and images. Thus, creating episodic Learning Maps within the lesson and illustrating the synergistic interface of the non-linear framework of Yunkaporta's (2009) 8 Ways of learning and the GSA.

Symbols and images

'Australian Aboriginal symbols are visual forms of knowledge that express cultural intellect within a sense of place and spiritual space' (Cameron, 2015, p. 69). Similarly, learning through the GSA, symbols and images foster the building blocks for memory and the making of meaning, which may be cross-cultural and dynamic (Pill et al., 2021). Symbols allow people to go beyond what is known or seen by creating linkages between otherwise very different concepts and experience (Cameron, 2015). The interface we propose requires use of a GSA in way that provides students with multiple learning representations to suit individual learning needs and combine those with their peers through storied experience, that is visual, pictorial meta-language relevant to the skill, game, task, or challenge (Yunkaporta & McGinty, 2009). For example, students exploring Parndo, a ball game played on Kaurna Country in the vicinity of Adelaide, South Australia, an initial starting point would have students explore what defines the Parndo as a 'ball to play with' (Sport Australia, 2022), and to investigate if inter-generational drawings, markings, or signs of Parndo exist. Through cultural sensitivity, the teacher could facilitate students to generate symbols and images to represent the mental representations and relationships of the principles of play of Parndo concepts to 'picture the game' and make their learning visible (Low et al., 2020). Thus, generating meaning-making through Parndo itself. These 'concepts' represented as symbols might later be used as non-verbal teaching cues, connecting with non-verbal representations of learning, or learning expectations in future lessons (Hattie, 2012).

Non-linear

Here, we understand students each create their own journey from the ideas they put together to create new knowledge (Yunkaporta & McGinty, 2009), and it is the acknowledgement that learning occurs across different periods of time. In Aboriginal cultures, learning, like time, is cyclical, rather than sequential. Past, present, and future are all connected (Yunkaporta & McGinty, 2009). From a Western sequential sense of learning, the time it takes certain concepts, patterns, and understandings to be attained is often linear in nature. However, for Aboriginal and non-Aboriginal pedagogy and epistemology to co-exist 'we should think more rounded', instead of in 'steps, taxonomy' (Yunkaporta & McGinty, 2009, p. 65). We suggest, a GSA is adaptable to this thinking.

The GSA is described as flexible and non-linear in its approach to teaching and learning (Pill, 2014). Therefore, offering a non-Aboriginal pedagogical approach to meet Aboriginal pedagogy at the interface, the 'apex', as illustrated in Figure 17.2 (Pill et al., 2021). Take the target game of Gorri, a disc-bowling and throwing game played in central Australia (Sport Australia, 2022). After an initial game, a period of reflection occurs. Following this reflection, the ideas that emerge can be tested in a return to the game. Another option is a pause in Gorri to isolate a micro-component for practice or inquiry, before re-starting to assess if the action has improved the intended behaviour. Similarly, individuals, a group of students, or teams might pause for an isolated practice task depending on the need identified during the reflection. A third option, after reflection, is the progression to development of the initial game with a modification or condition to increase the challenge point or complexity (Pill et al., 2021). These multiple ways or variations are provided for teaching Gorri detailed in Yulunga (Sport Australia, 2022).

Deconstruct reconstruct

This element of learning forms a strong intersection with the GSA, where whole-part-whole learning is considered critical to the practice of timing and coordination of whole movement challenges (ASC, 1996), or for enabling dynamic frameworks for memory and cognition to emerge (Yunkaporta, 2009). Practically, this can occur when the teacher facilitates students to elaborate selected tactics or strategies used successfully in previous games they have played before, then applying the most appropriate ones to the traditional game through the learning episode (Pill et al., 2021). The game determines the areas of learning, progressed through modelling, questioning, experimentation, and practice where necessary (Evans et al., 2017). For example, having students draw on prior knowledge in familiar football codes such as soccer, AFL, or rugby, and how they might transfer that knowledge and find opportunities for new discoveries in traditional possum skin football games of Millim baeyeetch, Marn-Grook and Parndo (Sport Australia, 2022).

Community links

Learning through a GSA in PE is applied for community benefit in the sense of developing more competent 'thinking players' with a Playing for Life philosophy supported by physical literacy (Pill & Hyndman, 2018). Through the cultural interface we propose, learning occurs in and through the game and as an expression of culture (Light & Evans, 2018). An example is provided from Ngunnawal Country in the Australian Capital Territory, where knowledge of a traditional game does not exist, the consequence of colonisation 'washing out of knowledge and culture' (Bishop et al., 2021). To bring together community through games and sport a version of Buroinjin, endorsed by the Aboriginal Corporation for Sport and Recreational Activities, and developed by an ACT Aboriginal Education Officer, and other Aboriginal and non-Aboriginal members of the community was created (Williams & Pill, 2020). However, Bishop et al. (2021) reinforces access to Aboriginal knowledge through a cultural interface must be approached with being 'humble in what is known and yet to know' (p. 205). It is a reciprocal process that takes time, while appreciating certain aspects of Aboriginal 'Lore' may not be culturally appropriate to learn for non-Aboriginal Australians (Bishop et al., 2021).

Conclusion

The challenge as we see it, is what does or could a game-based approach for a cultural interface look like upon various First Nation lands? If PE teachers are to embrace a cultural interface, for the benefit of all students, then the initial step must be one of cultural self-reflexivity, whereby the notion of 'coming together' for a culturally appropriate interface, is the acknowledgement of the different culture, background, and knowledge we (educators) and our learners (students) bring to the classroom. In doing so, PE may deepen student's cultural competency and physical literacy through a GSA (Pill et al., 2021).

References

8ways. (2020). *Aboriginal pedagogy: Every place, every people, has its own unique pedagogies.* https://www.8ways.online/about

Arrows, F. & Narvaez, D. (2016). Reclaiming our indigenous worldview: A more authentic baseline for social/ecological justice work in education. In N. McCrary & W. Ross (Eds.), *Working for social justice inside and outside the classroom: A community of teachers, researchers, and activists* (pp. 91–112). Peter Lang.

Australian Curriculum and Assessment Authority (ACARA). (2020a). Australian curriculum.

Australian Curriculum and Assessment Authority (ACARA). (2020b). *Australian curriculum. Health and physical education.* https://www.australiancurriculum.edu.au/f-10-curriculum/health-and-physical-education/

Australian Sports Commission. (1996). *Game sense: Perceptions and actions research report.* Australian Sports Commission Publishing.

Bishop, M., Vass, G. & Thompson, K. (2021). Decolonising schooling practices through relationality and reciprocity: Embedding local Aboriginal perspectives in the classroom. *Pedagogy, Culture & Society, 29*(2), 193–211.

Burgess, C. & Evans, J. R. (2017). Culturally responsive relationships focussed pedagogies: The key to quality teaching and creating quality learning environments. In J. Keengwe (Ed.), *Handbook of research on promoting cross-cultural competence and social justice in teacher education* (pp. 1–31). IGI Global.

Cameron, E. (2015). Is it art or knowledge? Deconstructing Australian Aboriginal creative making. *Arts, 4*(2), 68–74.

Edwards, K. (1999). *Choopadoo: Games from the dreamtime.* QUT Publications.

Edwards, K. (2008). *Yulunga games.* Australian Sports Commission.

Edwards, K. (2009). Traditional games of a timeless land: Play cultures in Aboriginal and Torres Strait Islander communities. *Australian Aboriginal Studies,* (2), 32–43.

Edwards, K. (2017). *Indigenous traditional games-planning resource.* University of Southern Queensland.

Evans, J. R., Georgakis, S. & Wilson, R. (2017). Indigenous games and sports in the Australian national curriculum: Educational benefits and opportunities. *ab-Original, 1*(2), 195–213.

Evans, J. R., Light, R. & Downey, G. (2020). Skilfulness on country: Informal games and sports exposure. In S. Pill (Ed.), *Perspectives on game-based coaching* (pp. 57–66). Routledge.

Gardiner-Garden, J. (2012). Social policy: 'Close the gap'. *Council of Australian Governments.* https://www.aph.gov.au/About_Parliament/Parliamentary_Departments/Parliamentary_Library/pubs/BriefingBook44p/ClosingGap

Hattie, J. (2012). *Visible learning for teachers: Maximizing impact on learning.* Routledge.

Hay, R. (2017, May 25). Indigenous players didn't invent Australian rules but did make it their own. *The Conversation.* https://theconversation.com/indigenous-players-didntinvent-australian-rules-but-did-make-it-their-own-76606

Karulkiyalu Country, Gordon, P. & Spillman, D. (2021). Embracing country as teacher in outdoor and environmental education. In G. Thomas, J. Dyment & H. Prince (Eds.), *Outdoor environmental education in higher education* (pp. 215–224). Springer.

Kirk, D. & MacPhail, A. (2002). Teaching games for understanding and situated learning: Rethinking the Bunker–Thorpe model. *Journal of Teaching in Physical Education, 21*(2), 177–192.

Light, R. & Evans, J. R. (2018). *Indigenous stories of success in Australian sport: Journeys to the AFL and NRL*. Palgrave Macmillan.

Light, R. & Harvey, S. (2017). Positive pedagogy for sport coaching. *Sport, Education and Society, 22*(2), 271–287.

Low, N., Thompson, K. & McKay, A. (2020). Making learning visible in health and physical education: Teachers' stories. *SET: Research Information for Teachers, 1*, 3–11.

Metzler, M. (2011). *Instructional models for physical education* (3rd ed.). Holcombe Hathaway.

Nakata, M. (2002). Indigenous knowledge and the cultural interface: Underlying issues at the intersection of knowledge and information systems. *IFLA Journal, 5/6*(5-6), 281–291.

Ngunnawal Draft. (n.d.). *Local guidelines for teaching Indigenous content in PE*. Canberra.

Pill, S. (2014). An appreciative inquiry exploring game sense teaching in physical education. *Sport, Education and Society, 21*(2), 279–297.

Pill, S., Evans, J. R., Williams, J., Davies, M. J. & Kirk, M. A. (2021). Conceptualising games and sport teaching in physical education as a culturally responsive curriculum and pedagogy. *Sport, Education and Society, 27*(9), 1005–1019.

Pill, S. & Hyndman, B. (2018). Gestalt psychological principles in developing meaningful understanding of games and sport in physical education. *Journal of Teaching in Physical Education, 37*(4), 322–329.

Sport Australia. (2022). *Yulunga*. https://www.sportaus.gov.au/yulunga

Sutton, M. (2017). Indigenous influence on AFL creation confirmed by historical transcripts, historian says. *Australian Broadcasting Corporation News*. https://www.abc.net.au/news/2017-04-13/historian-reveals-marngrook-influence-on-afl/8439748

Whimpress, B. (2008). Australian football. In W. Vamplew & B. Stoddart (Eds.), *Sport in Australia: A social history* (pp. 19–39). Cambridge University Press.

Williams, J. (2018). 'I didn't even know that there was such a thing as aboriginal games': A figurational account of how Indigenous students experience physical education. *Sport, Education and Society, 23*(5), 462–474.

Williams, J. & Pill, S. (2020). Using a game sense approach to teach Buroinjin as an Aboriginal game to address social justice in physical education. *Journal of Teaching in Physical Education, 39*(2), 176–185.

Williams, J., Pill, S., Evans, J. & Davies, M. (2022). ' … if my family didn't play football … we would literally have pretty much nothing': how high school Aboriginal students continue culture through rugby league and Australian football. *Sport, Education and Society, 27*(1), 57–71.

Yunkaporta, T. (2009). *Aboriginal pedagogies at the cultural interface*. Unpublished thesis. James Cook University.

Yunkaporta, T. & McGinty, S. (2009). Reclaiming Aboriginal knowledge at the cultural interface. *The Australian Educational Researcher, 36*(2), 55–72.

18 Moving from TGfU to 'Game-Based Approach' as the Collective

David Gutiérrez and Jeroen Koekoek

In this chapter, we explore the varieties that exist in the most central games teaching and coaching approaches and models incorporated in different countries. The underlying reason for this initiative is the increasing segmentation of game teaching models that often serve individual or institutional goals and priorities in the field of physical education (PE) and sports. We discuss this tendency and the necessity to move towards a global shift through alignment of elements in these concepts to overcome labels and definitions. To this end, this chapter is divided into three sections. In the first section, we describe the emergence of specific approaches on games teaching with respect to its primary goals and assumptions and how this further developed towards the global idea of game-based approach (GBA). The second section consists of an analysis of the perspectives of GBA in different countries in which the stage of development often differs with respect to the expansion of a particular pedagogical concept. In the third section prospects for future directions for research, pedagogical and dissemination development are considered.

GBA as a wealth of ideas born from a common and old concern

The construction of what we understand today as a GBA has an interesting and rich process behind it, that has promoted a great wealth of thought and well-established research-based pedagogy. From this process, that goes back beyond the publication of Bunker and Thorpe (1982), several stages of successive diversification and convergency can be recognised.

First stage: Identification of the problem

The identification of deficiencies in the traditional and technique-oriented way of teaching and coaching games, and proposals that addressed this issue partially (in contrast to a full approach or model) from a perspective that can be catalogued within the GBA spectrum of approaches and models, are significantly earlier to the publication of the Teaching Games for Understanding (TGfU) model. Furthermore, due to the lack of both regular use of

DOI: 10.4324/9781003298298-22

bibliographical references and translations in the first three quarters on the 20th century, the origin of the approach can hardly be attributed to a single and progressive line of reasoning or tradition. Of special relevance are the German, French and English traditions. For example, the works of Döbler and Döbler (1961) and Mahlo (1969) in Germany, Listello et al. (1965), Gratereau (1967) and Gallant (1970) in France, all referred to the existence of general technical-tactical principles to various sports games and the use of game forms for teaching team sports (Devis & Sánchez, 1996). Some of these proposals, mainly within the English tradition, were later identified with essential elements that were incorporated into the TGfU model, such as Wade's (1967) proposal of the use of small-sided games as a way of working together on both tactics and technique, or the classification of Mauldon and Redfern (1969) assisting the player development of game appreciation and knowledge transfer between games (Stolz & Pill, 2014).

Second stage: Convergence of ideas in the TGfU model

According to Hopper et al. (2009), the TGfU model was presented as the organisation of good practices rather than proposing it as an innovation. The TGfU model and subsequent development in the 1980s by Bunker, Thorpe and Almond (e.g., Thorpe et al., 1986) integrated the partial solutions mentioned in the first stage with contributions from various disciplines and knowledge domains. For example, Bruner's notion of spiral curriculum reinforces the idea of simplification and modification of games, Schmidt's schema theory demonstrated the importance of using variability in practice, the resolution of tasks through research based on the concern for less abled students of Morrison's educational gymnastics, or the professional development of Stenhouse (Sánchez et al., 2014).

Third stage: Wealth of ideas

Different variations and extensions of the TGfU model have been developed for games teaching starting from the 1990s to the present day (Oslin & Mitchell, 2006). Although it is not the purpose of this chapter to provide a complete picture of the different GBAs, examples of proposals developed in this period are the tactical games model (TGM; Griffin et al., 1997; Mitchell et al., 2003), game sense (GS; den Duyn, 1997), play practice (PP; Launder, 2001), tactical decision learning model (TDLM; Grehaigne et al., 2005), games concept approach (GConA; Light & Tan, 2006), invasion games competency model (IGCM; Tallir et al., 2005), ballschool (Kröger & Roth, 1999), step game approach (SGA; Mesquita et al., 2005), play with purpose (Pill, 2007), teamball (TB; Halling et al., 2008) and the inventing games model (IGM; Butler, 2016). In addition to the above-mentioned proposals of full approaches or GBAs, several partial theoretical and practical developments have led to an evolution, expansion and deepening of many GBA facets that stimulate student learning, motivation, creativity and/or equity.

In Almond's (2015) last work as first author, titled *Rethinking Teaching Games for Understanding* and published in a monograph dedicated to GBA (Gutiérrez & García-López, 2015), he describes this situation (referring to this third stage) as a 'wealth of ideas', although expressing concern when he stressed that in a number of quarters the diversity of thinking 'has begun to divide the community of practitioners and researchers within the games field into silos or camps that harm the emergence of new thinking' (Almond, 2015, p. 15). Based on the premise of Gutiérrez (2016), we challenge this concern through the analysis and categorisation of proposals developed during this stage and that match with the goals and concerns proposed initially by TGfU. Specifically:

- *GBA for early years.* Some proposals have been able to adapt GBA to early ages. These appear not as complete approaches, but as initial stages. Ballschool proposes an initial stage called playful situation-orientated, and Slade (2010) one with the title of Fundamental Movements and Tactics. The same contribution can be found in Play with purpose (Pill, 2015).
- *Structuring TGfU for teachers.* TGM successfully structured and simplified the TGfU model to facilitate professional development and programming by teachers. Other examples are SGA or IGCM.
- *Expanding learning-game designing.* PP simplification and game-shaping principles provided nuances of the TGfU pedagogical principles of design by representation and exaggeration. By contrast, GS provided indications for the design of rather open learning environments. Furthermore, the inclusion of students within the designing games approach was aimed to promote understanding (Hastie, 2010) and democratic behaviours (IGM).
- *Teaching in the game improvements.* Some proposals achieved the promotion of key aspects of teaching during the game, such as attention to diversity through principles of focusing (PP) and adaptation (Hopper, 2011), or the development of motivation (fantasy games by PP or animal cards by Butler & Hopper, 2016), and creativity (Memmert, 2015). Others have expanded the outcomes of questioning, including the social component (e.g., debate of ideas, TDLM) or affective issues (e.g., affective questioning by Sheppard, 2014).
- *GBA for coaching.* Some proposals solved the question of how to adapt TGfU ideas, initially designed for PE teachers, to coaches, both for coaches with deep content knowledge (GS) and instructors with little experience in games teaching (*PlaySport, TopPlay* and *Game Sense Cards*).
- *Widespread use.* Some approaches have successfully expanded the model, in either tailoring and institutionalising a GBA in a specific country (Singapore, GConA), or globally, by creating comprehensive easy to follow materials (TGM).

- *Authentic assessment for understanding.* TGM and TDLM developed and popularised the use of instruments to evaluate the most relevant aspects of the game. GPAI (TGM: Game Performance Assessment Instrument) ease of use also allows it to be used as a peer learning and assessment tool.
- *A more authentic sport experience in PE.* Some approaches pursue a more comprehensive sport experience and promote social learning by integrating some fundamental sport elements, as formal competition and affiliation (TB) or feeding TGfU into sport education model (SEM), such as Clinic-Game Day (Alexander & Penney, 2005).

Fourth stage: Moving to 'game-based approach' as the collective

Since the identification of different approaches with common purposes and similar pedagogical principles, there have been several attempts to bring them together under the same umbrella, in terminology, but also on an institutional level. TGfU SIG is leading the institutional attempt to move globally. Since its foundation in 2002 as a task force of the AIESEP, it has the purpose of harnessing the energy of those that have affinity with GBA underpinning educational principles through publications (Web, blogs, books and social media) and conferences (Ovens et al., 2021). The last concrete action has been precisely to seek a terminological agreement. To this end, and with the intention of ensuring the most global representation possible, this action was channelled through the TGfU SIG International Advisory Board, which at that time had representatives from 23 countries of the five continents. More information on the rationality and the process followed can be found at the TGfU SIG website.[1] The rationality and statement arising from this process of agreement are exposed as follows:

> In order to promote terminological consistency among researchers and practitioners, the TGfU SIG suggests the use of Game-Based Approach (GBA) to refer to the learner-centered teaching and coaching practice in which the modified games set the base and framework for developing thoughtful, creative, intelligent, and skillful players. The TGfU SIG also encourages the use of Game-Based Approaches (GBAs) to refer to several well-established approaches that follow a GBA like TGfU, Game Sense, Play Practice, Tactical Games Model, Ballschool, Invasion Games Competence Model and other similar proposals. (TGfU SIG, 2021)

From the situation that has been achieved regarding the agreement on GBA in a consensus statement, it is valuable to further explore what following steps can be made for expanding the terminology within the global community. Possible purposes regarding the shift towards GBA and what is needed to achieve as a collective understanding with respect to the teaching practice, scholarly activities as well as curricular developments in PETE faculties, will be discussed in the last section of this chapter.

Perspectives on GBA from different countries: A brief summary

The following sources have been used in order to perform a multi-analysis method of different perspectives on using a GBA in several countries: (a) TGfU IAB[2] 'What's happening' TGfU SIG web section; (b) an ad hoc exploratory questionnaire with topics regarding the adoption of GBA for each country; and (c) presentations made by scholars and teacher educators from 11 countries about the particular GBA variant they use in their country, displayed during the symposium 'Game-Based Approaches Globally'. This symposium was organised by the Network Teaching Games in Eindhoven, The Netherlands, as part of the events for the TGfU 40th anniversary (Figure 18.1).

The questionnaire consisted of 12 main questions exploring the status of a GBA for each country, whether or not a specific concept has been incorporated, and, if so, how this has been operationalised. We asked current and former International Advisory Board members, Executive Board members and significant individual persons who advocate game-based teaching (authors, developers, educators) to reflect on the questions. We finally received responses from 15 countries: Australia, Hong Kong, Singapore, Malaysia, Germany, England, Greece, Italy, Spain, the Netherlands, Iran, Japan, Australia, United States and Portugal. The information collected through the different sources has been organised into four topics that are set out below.

Figure 18.1 Overview of several international contributions to the 40th anniversary symposium 'Game-Based Approaches Globally', Eindhoven, the Netherlands.

Intranational acceptance and expansion of GBA

The information available from the different data sources allows us to categorise countries with regard to the tradition on GBA and if there is a predominant approach or not, into the following four groups:

1   Countries that hardly use a GBA, or have not implemented any specific games teaching approach in practice.

   GBA in these countries (e.g., Italy, Iran, Argentina, Brasil) is often not part of either an educational setting or a national sport organisation with respect to teaching team sports. In general, these countries use traditional games teaching approaches (e.g., drilling techniques, teacher-centred).

2   Countries that have expanded GBA and use a specific and strongly developed approach.

   In these countries (e.g., Australia, Canada, Malaysia, New Zealand, United States) there is a strong tradition in using a specific GBA in educational settings. Several academics and teacher educators in the country play a prominent role in developing specific knowledge in GBA and have shared this within the international community.

3   Countries that use a general approach that is often influenced by multi perspectives of GBAs.

   These countries (e.g., England, the Netherlands, Spain) specifically use a general approach (still also including technique centred) that is derived from a variety of approaches and elements of a GBA. Pedagogical principles are used in practice and integrated within the educational curriculum. Mostly, a GBA is not exclusively adopted on a national level although specific GBA characteristics are recognisable (e.g., using small-sided games, game-based and learner-centred perspectives, guided discovery).

4   Countries that have developed a specific approach.

A few countries (e.g., Singapore, Japan, Germany) have developed a particular and unique approach that largely fits with the national educational goals. The specific and clear existing PE objectives and corresponding curriculum content are mostly aligned with a GBA that specifically has been developed.

The way a GBA has influenced the practice in different contexts

The introduction of a GBA and the extent to which it is implemented in a particular country is often dependent upon whether a games teaching approach is already implemented in an educational setting (primary, secondary, PETE). When a GBA is part of the educational curriculum it is often easier to expand and further develop the approach. Countries from group two and three have indicated that a GBA or GBA-principles are part of the PE practice.

Perceived barriers to incorporate a GBA

Several countries experienced resistance when implementing a GBA. Specifically, this is due to the gap that is perceived between the knowledge of GBA scholars working at universities and the practice of PE teachers in schools. Barriers were found in the way PE teachers are informed and feel whether they are skilled enough to work with the approach. It is recognised that teachers still face in practice the difficulty of their changing role, that is, from instructor of teaching technique skills to 'teacher as facilitator'. Besides the limitations of this kind of 'teaching beliefs' about a GBA, time issues, lack of space and large class sizes were also mentioned as perceived barriers. Furthermore, the responses of countries specifically in group one (but also from group two and three) reflected the perceived lack of good resources and knowledge about a GBA. In addition, teachers face heavy workloads and therefore wanted to keep what they are doing (in the traditional practice), which indicates that they perceive that the incorporation of new approaches entails stressful additional efforts.

An important notion that also derived from the answers of countries in group one is the lack of significant resources that are written in native languages. Several non-English speaking countries therefore must rely on English written resources which, on the one hand, are mainly only accessible to scholars and, on the other hand, can result in translation issues that lead to misconceptions.

Prospects and wishes for developing GBA on both national and global level

With respect to future directions and prospects for the development of a GBA, almost all countries from the four groups have stressed that organising national and international seminars, workshops and conferences can lead to expanding the global ideas. Also, in countries in which a GBA is already well-established (group two), there is still a call for data and valuable resources that becomes available for academics, and in particular for practitioners. This indicates that the next generation of researchers should also be mentored and learn from past developments and good practices in different countries, to contribute to successfully developing a GBA. This may result in teachers who experience in practice the success of the GBA approach which necessitates that they reflect on their teaching beliefs and how they can be aligned to the philosophy of a GBA. Countries without a specific implementation of GBA (group one and three) have stated that the first important initiative for developing a GBA in practice is by developing in-service professional development and pre-service teachers' training.

Concluding thoughts and future directions for developing GBA as a collective

We propose that the direction of thinking towards a global idea of GBA can be structured by expanding research activities, developing the approach from a pedagogical viewpoint, and providing suggestions to disseminate the approach on a global level.

Research

It would be pertinent to organise scientific collaboration, both nationally and internationally, to conduct review studies and inventory studies on the degree of implementation of GBA in specific countries, as mentioned in the second part of this chapter. This means that academics, educators and policy makers can learn and benefit from the expertise and stadia of countries in which a GBA has been expanded and incorporated. Such information may contribute to global knowledge and understanding of the several stages of developing an approach. Besides investigating the pedagogical principles of a GBA (i.e., making appropriate teaching decisions during game play), research set ups should also be made that can inform how a GBA addresses global issues, such as social justice and equity (see Chapter 16). In addition, studies that focus on the integration of a GBA with other scientific disciplines and theoretical frameworks (e.g., complex learning theory, ecological dynamics) should be included in future research.

Pedagogical development

A second aspect that may contribute to the development of GBA as a collective is seeking new avenues of thought by: (a) exploring the existence and development of new types of knowledge through, for example, the use of new technologies and students as game designers; (b) designing new games and game categories that allow the creation of new tactical problems with which to expand the tactical repertoire of the apprentices; (c) export the proven potential of the application of GBA and SEM in an integrated way, to youth grassroots sports and to the training of teachers and coaches. Also explore the integration of specific strategies (not the complete model) from other pedagogical models; (d) use the GBA pedagogical principles to inspire methodological changes in other areas of PE and sports outside of teaching games. For example, in those that include a high decision-making component, such as fighting sports, or those that would benefit from modification strategies that allows for the design of developmentally appropriate real-like practice in educational setting, such as outdoor or adventure activities.

Dissemination

A third and essential aspect is the dissemination of GBA at different stages of development as well as on different national levels. Countries from the first group (neither knowledge nor GBA implementation) that want to expand a GBA, must first start networking at an educational level. This means that teacher educators and academics start networks to share knowledge for pre-service and in-service teacher professional development. If this stage has been reached, then this situation may create the opportunity to slightly change the national curriculum by including GBA as part of a model-based PE, or as part of pedagogical renovations and quality PE.

To achieve this stage, the promotion of a national network or community of GBA would be helpful, together with being members of the international community (i.e., TGfU SIG). The Dutch 'Network Teaching Games' may serve as an interesting example of how faculties for PE teacher education with similar (but also their particular own) ideas on GBA, can collaborate, benefit from each other's pedagogical ideas, and share knowledge regarding GBA on a national level. The stage of creating networks and communities of practice could be elaborated as soon as the promotion and knowledge from the national networks shift from educational contexts and universities towards collaboration with other networks such as sport federations and associations. For this stage of disseminating the collective understanding of GBA, we would encourage developing strong ties with national sport federations and organisations to promote GBA materials for youth grassroot sports.

Notes

1 http://www.tgfu.info/game-based-consensus-statement.html
2 Currently, 23 countries are involved in the International Advisory Board and take part in IAB meetings hosted by an Executive Board member of the TGfU SIG. Institutional information can be consulted on http://www.tgfu.info/iab.html

References

Alexander, K. & Penney, D. (2005). Teaching under the influence: Feeding games for understanding into the sport education development-refinement cycle. *Physical Education and Sport Pedagogy*, *10*(3), 287–301.

Almond, L. (2015). Rethinking teaching games for understanding. *Agora for Physical Education and Sport*, *17*, 15–25.

Bunker, D. & Thorpe, R. (1982). A model for the teaching of games in secondary schools. *Bulletin of Physical Education*, *18*(1), 5–8.

Butler, J. (2016). *Playing fair*. Human Kinetics.

Butler, J. & Hopper, T. (2016). Inventing net and wall games. In J. Butler (Ed.), *Playing fair* (pp. 157–178). Human Kinetics.

den Duyn, N. (1997). *Game sense – developing thinking players workbook*. Australian Sports Commission.

Devís, J. & Sánchez, R. (1996). La enseñanza alternativa de los juegos deportivos: antecedentes, modelos actuales de iniciación y reflexiones finales [Alternative games teaching: background, current models and final reflections]. In J. A. Moreno & P. L. Rodríguez (Eds.), *Aprendizaje deportivo* (pp. 159–181). Universidad de Murcia.

Döbler, H. & Döbler, E. (1961). *Manual de Juegos Menores [Minor games manual]*. Ed. Stadium.

Gallant, M. (1970). *Juegos deportivos [Sport games]*. Ed. Vilamala (segunda edición).

Gratereau, G. (1967). *Iniciation aux sports collectifs [Initiation to collective sports]*. Bourrelier.

Grehaigne, J. F., Wallian, N. & Godbout, P. (2005). Tactical-decision learning model and students' practices. *Physical Education and Sport Pedagogy, 10*(3), 255–269.

Griffin, L., Mitchell, S. & Oslin, J. (1997). *Teaching sport concepts and skills: A tactical games approach.* Human Kinetics.

Gutiérrez, D. (2016). Game-centered approaches: Different perspectives, same goals-working together for learning. *Research Quarterly for Exercise and Sport, 87*(S1), S23–S24.

Gutiérrez, D. & García-López, L. M. (2015). Theory and practice of game–based approaches in school context (II). Foreword. *Agora for Physical Education and Sport, 17*(1), 3–14.

Halling, A., Engell, C. & Hansen, T. (2008). Ballgame teaching-the Scandinavian way. *International Journal of Eastern Sports & Physical Education, 6*(1), 231–254.

Hastie, P. (2010). *Student-designed games: Strategies for promoting creativity, cooperation, and skill development.* Human Kinetics.

Hopper, T. (2011). Game-as-teacher: Modification by adaptation in learning through game-play. *Asia-Pacific Journal of Health, Sport and Physical Education, 2*, 3–21.

Hopper, T., Butler, J. & Storey, B. (2009). *TGfU … simply good pedagogy: Understanding a complex challenge.* PHE Canada.

Kröger, C. & Roth, K. (1999). *Ball school: An ABC game for beginners.* Hofmann Schorndorf.

Launder, A. (2001). *Play Practice: The games approach to teaching and coaching sport.* Human Kinetics.

Light, R. & Tan, S. (2006). Culture, embodied understandings and primary school teachers' development of TGfU in Singapore and Australia. *European Physical Education Review, 12*(1), 100–117.

Listello, A., Clerc, P., Crenn, R. & Schoebel, E. (1965). *Recreación y educación físico-deportiva [Recreation and physical-sport education].* Ed. Kapelusz.

Mahlo, F. (1969). *El acto táctico en el juego [Tactical action in play].* Pueblo y Educación.

Mauldon, E. & Redfern, H. (1969). *Games teaching: A new approach for the primary school.* MacDonald and Evans.

Memmert, D. (2015). *Teaching tactical creativity in sport: Research and practice.* Routledge.

Mesquita, I., Graca, A., Gomes, A. R. & Cruz, C. (2005). Examining the impact of a step game approach to teaching volleyball on student tactical decision making and skill execution during game play. *Journal of Human Movement Studies, 48*, 469–492.

Mitchell, S., Oslin, J. & Griffin, L. (2003). *Sport foundations for elementary physical education: A tactical games approach.* Human Kinetics.

Oslin, J. & Mitchell, S. (2006). Game-centred approaches to teaching physical education. In D. Kirk, D. MacDonald and M. O'Sullivan (Eds.), *The handbook of physical education* (pp. 627–651). SAGE Publications.

Ovens, A., Gutierrez, D. & Butler, J. (2021). Teaching games for understanding: From conception to special interest group. In S. Mitchell & L. Griffin (Eds.), *Lifetime contributions in physical education: Celebrating the lives & work of Len Almond (1938–2017) & Joy Butler (1957–2019)* (pp. 104–119). Scholary.

Pill, S. (2007). *Play with purpose: A resource to support teachers in the implementation of the game-centred approach to physical education.* Australian Council for Health, Physical Education and Recreation.

Pill, S. (2015). *Play with purpose: For fundamental movement skills teaching.* Achper.

Sánchez, R., Devís, J. & Navarro, V. (2014). El modelo Teaching Games for Understanding en el contexto internacional y español: una perspectiva histórica [The Teaching Games for Understanding model in the international and Spanish context: A historical perspective]. *Agora for Physical Education and Sport, 16*(3), 197–213.

Sheppard, J. (2014). *Personal and social responsibility through game play: Utilizing the teaching games for understanding instructional model.* University of Toronto.

Slade, D. (2010). *Transforming play: Teaching tactics and game.* Human Kinetics.

Stolz, S. & Pill, S. (2014). Teaching games and sport for understanding: Exploring and reconsidering its relevance in physical education. *European Physical Education Review, 20*(1), 36–71.

Tallir, I. B., Musch, E. & Valcke, M. (2005). Effects of two instructional approaches for basketball on decision making and recognition ability. *International Journal of Sport Psychology, 36,* 107–126.

TGfU SIG. (2021). *Game-based consensus statement.* http://www.tgfu.info/game-based-consensus-statement.html

Thorpe, R., Bunker, D. & Almond, L. (1986). *Rethinking games teaching.* Loughborough University of Technology.

Wade, A. (1967). *The F.A. guide to training and coaching.* Heinemann.

Index